MY SKY BLUE TRADES

Sven Birkerts is the author of *The Gutenberg Elegies, Readings, American Energies,* and other books. He teaches at Mount Holyoke College, is a member of the core faculty of the Bennington Writing Seminars, and is the editor of the journal *Agni*. He lives in Arlington, Massachusetts.

Praise for *My Sky Blue Trades*

"Birkerts uses the skills he has honed as a literary critic with calm efficiency, probing his past in the same purposeful way he might take on the latest novel by Anne Tyler or a new collection of poems by Seamus Heaney." —*The New York Times Book Review*

"In fresh, sometimes even startling prose, Birkerts records the epiphanies and the stupidities of his long and messy coming of age. Birkerts deftly manages—sometimes within the space of a sentence—to navigate back and forth between his current adult awareness and his juvenile perceptions. *My Sky Blue Trades* is a vivid child-of-immigrants/child-of-the-sixties memoir; it's also, inherently, a moving testimony to the power and place of a genre—literary journalism—that's frequently dismissed as a simple-minded handmaiden to the Higher Arts." —*The Washington Post*

"[A] graceful and ultimately melancholy memoir." —*San Francisco Chronicle*

"With *My Sky Blue Trades,* Birkerts turns his critical skills . . . onto his own life. That Birkerts succeeds without resorting to the tawdry or spectacular is a measure of his skill." —*Los Angeles Times*

"Birkerts's refreshing coming-of-age memoir weaves near-mythical episodes from the lives of his Latvian grandparents with his own tale of self-discovery . . . with poignant humor and grace."
—*The Oregonian* (Portland)

"Very appealing . . . free of pretentiousness, artifice and grandstanding. The strength of Birkerts's memoir is its lack of the standard memoir appeals: It is neither hilarious, uproarious, heart-tugging, inspirational nor edifying. He neither claims too much nor rides any one horse too hard. His words are quietly heart-tugging, hilarious and highly edifying, but only in the most roundabout way could this work be the model for becoming a leading literary critic. Peter, as Sven called himself then . . . is an agreeable, brief-winded, unassuming narrator, and his story of differences and reconciliations . . . is told from a critic's perspective and is as much about the process itself as his own special version of it."
—*Milwaukee Journal Sentinel*

"Birkerts has been instrumental in defining literature's role in an evermore fanatically technological society. He now brings his considerable writing skills to a memoir . . . Birkerts excels at documenting the intensity of childhood impressions and the baffling hat trick of growing up speaking one language at home . . . and another at school, and close scrutiny of his family yields emotionally complex portraits, including those of his moody architect father and book-loving mother."
—*Booklist*

"A splendidly crafted set of essays interweaving his youth as the son of immigrant parents during the sixties with tales of his ancestors in Latvia. [His] gifts are evident here, as Birkerts takes us on a journey at once deeply reflective of American culture and touchingly his own."
—*Library Journal*

"[A] keen, affecting, suspicious, evocative, subtly cool memoir of Birkerts's first thirty years. His complex narrative mimics the action of a mind . . . Birkerts paints the big picture through the slow accrual of vivid portraits and images anchoring all that is forgotten. His act of excavation here uncovers a man of analytic intelligence who also listens to the logic of his heart. A piece of hard work, dredged and sifted often to the dregs of misery—but it registers and holds." —*Kirkus Reviews* (starred review)

"The literary world isn't lacking for memoirs about growing up, especially lately, but it could certainly use more like Birkerts's. He infuses every topic with a sense of curiosity about his place in the world and in his family. Every riff about going barefoot or drinking wine has the kind of grace achieved only through the combination of hindsight and exceptional writing skill. The book gets its title from a line in Dylan Thomas's poem about childhood, 'Fern Hill.' It's appropriate, because Birkerts often adopts Thomas's dreamy tone and knack for crisp language. As his ruminations about being a kid gently give way to descriptions of adult excursions, there's a sense of maturation, both in the writing and the subject matter. Although the realm of early experience is overly trod terrain, Birkerts makes it fresh, compelling and well worth another trip." —*Publishers Weekly*

"Birkerts's voice is so genuine, his look back at youthful misapprehensions and lost love so honestly told, that the reader experiences the energy of the writer's life. It is quite wonderful to observe the mind of Birkerts, the brilliant critic, engaged in the moving performance of self-discovery." —Maureen Howard

MY SKY BLUE TRADES

GROWING UP COUNTER
IN A CONTRARY TIME

SVEN BIRKERTS

PENGUIN BOOKS

PENGUIN BOOKS

Published by the Penguin Group

Penguin Group (USA) Inc., 375 Hudson Street, New York, New York 10014, U.S.A.

Penguin Books Ltd, 80 Strand, London WC2R 0RL, England

Penguin Books Australia Ltd, 250 Camberwell Road, Camberwell, Victoria 3124, Australia

Penguin Books Canada Ltd, 10 Alcorn Avenue, Toronto, Ontario, Canada M4V 3B2

Penguin Books India (P) Ltd, 11 Community Centre,
Panchsheel Park, New Delhi – 110 017, India

Penguin Books (N.Z.) Ltd, Cnr Rosedale and Airborne Roads,
Albany, Auckland, New Zealand

Penguin Books (South Africa) (Pty) Ltd, 24 Sturdee Avenue,
Rosebank, Johannesburg 2196, South Africa

Penguin Books Ltd, Registered Offices: 80 Strand, London WC2R 0RL, England

First published in the United States of America by Viking Penguin,
a member of Penguin Putnam Inc. 2002
Published in Penguin Books 2003

1   3   5   7   9   10   8   6   4   2

Grateful acknowledgment is made for permission to reprint an excerpt from "Fern Hill" by
Dylan Thomas, from *The Poems of Dylan Thomas,* copyright © 1945 by The Trustees for the
Copyrights of Dylan Thomas. Reprinted by permission of New Directions Publishing Corp.

Portions of chapter 4 were originally published in *Dissent* in different form.

THE LIBRARY OF CONGRESS HAS CATALOGED THE HARDCOVER EDITION AS FOLLOWS:
Birkerts, Sven.
My sky blue trades : growing up counter in a contrary time
p.   cm.
ISBN 0-670-03109-7 (hc.)
ISBN 0 14 20.0309 3 (pbk.)
1. Birkerts, Sven.   2. English teachers—United States—Biography.
3. Critics—United States—Biography.   4. Latvian Americans—Biography.   I. Title.
PE64.B57 A3 2002
[B]   2001046907

Printed in the United States of America
Designed by Nancy Resnick

To all of those who appear in these pages,
who taught me everything—
in gratitude, or with a plea for forgiveness,
as the case may be,
To Lynn for her wise counsel and strength.

And honoured among foxes and pheasants by the gay house
Under the new made clouds and happy as the heart was long,
        In the sun born over and over,
            I ran my heedless ways,
            My wishes raced through the house high hay
And nothing I cared, at my sky blue trades, that time allows
In all his tuneful turning so few and such morning songs
        Before the children green and golden
            Follow him out of grace

—DYLAN THOMAS, "FERN HILL"

PROLOGUE

THE BOOK OF THINGS THAT I HAVE FORGOTTEN CONTAINS MOST OF my life. But then, what would we do without forgetfulness? I feel like there is hardly room for everything I do recall. How do these things work? Why Susie-Q?

I mean: Given all the charged vital moments that have slipped away, probably never to be recovered, how is it that I remember so clearly sitting in the Walnut Lake School cafeteria and volunteering to whomever I was sitting beside: "Oh yeah, we went out to Susie-Q last night"? This would have been in the second grade. Certainly it's not the first outright lie I ever told. But it's the one that comes back to me right now, as vividly as anything else I preserve in the jumbled archive of my experience.

I can decode it easily enough. Susie-Q was a bright, aggressively middlebrow restaurant somewhere on Woodward Avenue near 8 Mile Road—between Birmingham and Detroit. Our family drove that stretch often, and I would have noticed it the same way I noticed Earl Scheib's auto body shop or Roy O'Brien's car lot, or the huge open space leading to Grand Circus Park. But my parents would no more have eaten at Susie-Q then than they would eat at McDonald's now. Still, I turned in my seat and lied to my lunchmate because probably more than anything on earth I wished that we *were* the kind of family who would eat there.

· · ·

Both sides of my family going all the way back are from Latvia, a place I used to find on the globe at school by looking first to Scandinavia, then to the Baltic Sea, and finally to the thumblike projection just across from Finland. That, I knew, was the country my parents had fled during the war, just a few years before I was born. In that short interval it had ceased to exist as an independent entity. The globe had it labeled "Latvian S.S.R." Now, on the globes made since the fall of the Berlin Wall and the dismantling of the Soviet state, it is again Latvia, though if that earlier designation did not seem right, this does not either—quite. I'm not sure why.

I know that to this day I cannot touch my finger to that irregular little puzzle-piece shape without experiencing an uneasy twinge. I have no simple explanation for this. Susie-Q is only a part of it. Indeed, in trying to figure out my confused feelings about my ancestral culture, I start to see that my relation to things American is no less fraught. The roots of my self-conception twist down through murky layers of guilt, regret, loathing, and desire, and who knows how I will ever sort it all out.

Sitting at my desk this morning, an adult, almost fully tranquilized by routine and responsibility, I find that last sentence somewhat extravagant. But I nevertheless resist putting a line through it. For I know that in other moods I will find truth in it. In the midst of a childhood I have preserved as basically happy—at once busy and pleasantly distracted—there was also a fierce interior struggle. It had to do with my deep-down refusal of my family's Latvian heritage and my great yearning to assimilate, to lose the telltale oddness of my name, the accents of my parents, and the language that was always there in the background, the mark of our essential difference.

This is a very common American story, as I eventually learned. Members of every assimilating culture struggle with shame and desire. The old ways, the revered traditions of the displaced parents, are tainted, feel in some basic way "wrong," even as the images of American normalcy—the blond families with their solid, square-jawed fathers and perkily chittering mothers—exert tyrannical appeal. But for me it was all new. I may have been living an archetype, but I registered it as an anomaly, as my own distinctive experience. I looked around where I lived—the suburbs of Detroit—and I saw, no joke, rank upon rank of wholesome Americans, and then I looked at us, the family, oddball speakers of something routinely confused with Latin, a private little group of four separated out from the easy fraternity I imagined was shared by all of the other neighborhood families. This was hardly tragic, or even, in the big picture, unusual, but then, in the dark ages of formation, it was everything.

When I sometimes see photographs of my parents as they were then, I am shocked. Not only by their disconcerting youthfulness—in some pictures they look like they are just barely out of their teens—but also by how stylish and attractive they appear. My own children will find nothing comparable in our photo albums, at least where their father is concerned. It does make me wonder: What chimeras was I wrestling with? How can I explain the discrepancy between feeling and apparent fact?

Be assured that I am not writing this to blame my parents. They had self-possession and dignity—in most respects—and if they did not understand my discomfort, it was because I concealed it so well. I was a two-face, like most kids. My mother and father had no idea—I was not about to tell them—how I yearned in my heart for the most basic tokens of acceptance, though maybe they should have worked harder to guess, to figure out that all of this cultural difference meant a great deal to us, my sister and myself. Maybe they should have done something to ease our passage into American childhood.

But adulthood is, above all—I grasp this now—distance. We become adults by trading one scale of mattering for another. The parent has a very hard time getting back in behind the eyes of the child, seeing what the world is when it is not yet governed by hard-won perspectives and rationalizations, when every encounter is unprecedented and rawly consequential. Who can now remember what makes the kid at the bus stop with his crewcut and silver lunchbox the king of the universe, his casual sneer the measure of all things?

Still, how could my parents not have known? For most of the years of my childhood and adolescence I wanted nothing more than to be a happy freckled American kid named Rob or Tom, with a normal gregarious mom named Barbara (though my mother's name, Sylvia, was tolerable) and a dad named Jim (Gunnar was *not*) who did something in the automotive profession. I wanted us to ride around in a big Detroit-looking car, not some odd-looking import, with the AM radio blaring bouncy popular music as we headed for a ball game. It sounds like a cliché, but a child's desires are seldom very original. At the game we would sit in the bleachers with everyone else and cheer sincerely for the home team. Afterward maybe there would be a neighborhood cookout, my dad drinking a beer—a *can* of beer—with dads from down the street, my mom chipping distractedly at her nail polish while she gossiped with Betty and Fran.

Instead, we lived buried in our isolated privacy, speaking the language that cemented our division from everything around us. Nor did it help when we were all together in public—at a restaurant or in a store—that we shifted into English. That was almost worse. It made us seem like spies trying to pass. But in a hundred telltale ways—my father's odd inflections, my mother's saying *s* instead of *th*, so that "think" came out "sink" and "thank you" was "sank you"—we announced ourselves as outsiders, ill-rehearsed players in the great game of pretending to be American. In public I hung back whenever I could, dreading the moment when my father would call out, *"Nāc pie mums!"*—"Come be with us!"—but dreading even more that some classmate might appear and take in the whole charade.

What vexed me, I think, was that my parents didn't seem to get it. They were fine with their distance, did not *want* to be drinking beer with the neighborhood adults or following the fortunes of the Tigers in some hot ball park. They took pride in what they called their "Europeanness." My father wore good suits and classy shirts; he refused in every way the crewcut look favored by the dads all around us. Worse, he joked all the time about what he called the "average Joe"—the gum-chewing, T-shirted, ball-game-obsessed character we seemed to see everywhere in our part of the world. I flinched whenever we pulled into a gas station or went to the hardware store—anywhere there was some risk of encounter—as if my father might suddenly decide to speak his mind.

I had no real understanding back then of what he did, or wanted, or believed. I didn't yet know the story of my father's war years, his displacements, how he had arrived in this country a few years before with just his suitcase. I did know that he worked for a man named Eero—adult conversation in our house was "Eero" this and "Eero" that—that he was an architect who sat up nights working at his drafting table. I had no idea then of the religion of modernism, or that Eero and the others who worked at his office—Kevin Roche, Cesar Pelli, Bob Venturi, Chuck Bassett, Charlie Eames—were trying to mount a revolution in American design. I saw only the disdain my father had for the trappings of our suburban American life—the bulb-and-pennant extravaganzas of the car lots, the neon exuberance of the fast-food joints springing up everywhere. I read into his quips and pronouncements a rejection of everything that thrilled me.

Our own house, the inside of the cave in which we so quietly carried on our lives, was, I thought, bare and cold. No clutter, no soft, padded places. Everything was open and angled—books neatly filed, magazines stacked. Dishes appeared only so long as they were needed, then disappeared. The radio and record player produced only classical music. How strange it felt to set foot inside some other kid's house—fluffy carpets, comfortable chairs, friendly chaos. I decided that when I grew up, I, too, would have a warm, rackety nest packed to the rafters with things.

In the meantime, circumstance was against me. I was not Rob or Tom. I was, at least on the first day of school every year, before I instructed my teacher to call me "Pete," Sven, which always came out either "Seven" or "Swen," or else there was just a long pause while the teacher squinted down at her roll book. Nor did I ever come home at day's end to a comfy family kitchen where I had cookies and milk. When I pushed open the front door, I stepped into that coolly modern interior, with its elegant European furniture and hard, flat carpeting. I did not hear, "How was school today?" but *"Kā gāja šodien skolā?"* Which was the same thing, but of course it was not the same thing at all. I was stepping, always, from one world—a world in which I played and joked and tried to make myself just like the guys around me—into a world where completely different sounds made sense and other rules applied. And then, as I got older and learned to read and involve myself in private imaginings, I moved increasingly into a third world, which was not that of school or neighborhood or family, but my very own place.

My relation to Latvia—the culture, the language—remains complicated. For so long it was what I hated—because I felt it barred me from being an American, because it was always being touted as some kind of ideal place by my parents, and because the language seemed to belong to the invariably formal older people who sometimes came to visit, who would ask me questions and then correct my grammar when I answered. Latvian was the holy language, presided over in some symbolic way by my grandmother Mērija, my father's mother, who still lived in Riga, and who I did not meet until I was in my early teens, but who had taught the language to generations at the girls' gymnasium in Riga, and who sent grammar books and wholesome-looking "readers" in her annual Christmas packages. To speak Latvian properly, one had to enunciate certain consonants and to trill one's *r*'s in a way I found intolerable to listen to. How I wished to be native to American idioms and speech patterns, to the loose midwestern drawl that I heard all around me. American speech seemed right and natural. Latvian was hard work—it was all cod-liver oil and stern-faced ancestors and my grandmother vigilant with upraised finger.

A few years later I would give it all back, discharge all my discomfort and shame as I tried to explode those silences, muss up the careful, tasteful orderings. The era of transformation and liberation had arrived. Everything was up for grabs, and those of us who were angry had a heyday. The image I have of myself then—disheveled and wolflike—still burns through everything I have since laid over it. I think, politely, to ask, "Who was I?" But in fact I know very well.

One scene in particular comes to mind. It is the fall of 1969, my first semester at the University of Michigan. Finally released from what I have come to see, increasingly, as the tyranny of family life—my father and I have been in a standoff for years—I have flung myself into full rebellion. I have been gone for only two months, but already my hair is long and matted, worn in a quasi-Rasta style. I don't shower. Underwear is a bourgeois conspiracy. I move about in a haze of Marlboro smoke, feral, provocative.

And now I have hitchhiked home from Ann Arbor for the weekend. I have put in my time on the windy exit ramps, made small talk with strangers and fellow hippies, hiked on foot the last long stretch into our neighborhood, getting myself ready. It is to be an occasion. My grandmother Mērija has arrived for a several months' visit from Latvia. This will be the first dinner with the whole family.

As soon as I push open the front door, I catch what I think of as the old country smell. I will learn later that it is the smell of the valerian drops that my grandmother takes for her heart. Instead of calling out to announce my arrival, I pause on the landing. I hear voices and music upstairs, and I feel myself tighten. I have a sense, suddenly, of how I look. Should I make a quick stop in the hall bathroom to clean myself up, comb my hair, soap off the smoke smell? But no, this is not my season of compromises. Dropping my backpack by the front door, I take a deep breath and clomp my way up the steps.

It will be a minute before my grandmother registers me. She has cataracts; her eyesight is very bad. She is sitting on the black leather couch right next to my father, who is holding her hands as they talk. My mother, sitting slightly apart, gets up and moves toward me.

"Pete—"

"Hi, Mom—" I know I should go right to my grandmother and hug her. But already, making my way around the coffee table, giving my mother a quick kiss on the cheek, I see the flash of my father's look. He takes in my jeans, my leather jacket, my hair, the stubble on my face, and I can see—physically, as if he were literally swallowing some vile medicine—how he makes the decision. He will be civil. He will do it, this once, for his mother. And I understand that I have a momentary edge.

"*Vecmāmin—*" Grandmother. My father is helping her to her feet. She is blinking in my direction, her eyes swimming behind her thick, ancient-looking glasses. I take everything in—her neat blue jumper, her ruffled blouse, the amber pendant she wears.

"*Mans Pēterīts!*"

We stand for a moment, embracing. I catch my father giving my mother a sharp, narrowed look, almost as if she were to blame for what I have become.

After a long moment, my grandmother pushes me back to look at me. She has not seen me since I was thirteen, when our family traveled to Riga together for the first time. I have changed. I can see her puzzling behind her smile; she, too, is holding back. She sits down slowly and pats the place beside her. I am to sit with her.

. . .

Before dinner there are negotiations. My father comes into my room while I am perusing some of my old books. He waits for me to look over. When I do I see that he is clenched; only the prospect of this welcoming dinner keeps him from lashing out at me. "Here." He hands me one of his shirts, freshly banded. Blue-and-white striped. Brooks Brothers. "Try to clean up a bit before dinner. This is your grandmother. She has been waiting for years to see you."

I nod. I know not to push it.

When I come to the table my father gets up to appraise me. He steps forward, gives the shirt collar a sharp tug, makes a sniffing noise. "You have BO," he mutters. "Aren't you ashamed to be going around like that?"

"Not especially." I put an edge of challenge on my smile.

It is not our most successful family dinner. My grandmother cannot quite leave my appearance alone; neither can my father.

"Your hair is very long and tangled," she says.

"He's something they call a *hippie,* Mother." My father's tone is bemused, but I'm not taken in.

"It's the style, *Vecmāmin*—"

"*Hippie . . .*" My grandmother pronounces it slowly. "*Hip-pie.* What is that?"

"*Vandervogel,*" says my father. "Hippies are young people who want to be *free.*" He laughs the last word.

"Free . . ." My grandmother searches across the table for our faces. I suddenly see how this is the perfect setup for my father.

"Ya, free." He sighs, as much for my benefit as hers. "They don't know how it is in Russia or China or anywhere, but they want—"

"What do these *hippies* do?" My grandmother looks genuinely perplexed.

I glance over at my mother. She smiles nervously. She feels something coming.

"Do?" My father snorts. "They do *nothing!* They don't bathe, they listen to insulting music, they smoke marijuana—"

"*Kaņepes.*" My mother quickly supplies the Latvian word, and my grandmother nods gravely.

"Gunnar—" My mother now intrudes the mildest cautionary note.

"Sure, they smoke their little weed and they live together in little nests. They have no idea about what life is, or who is paying their way—"

I can feel my father heating up. He refills his wineglass with a quick dipping gesture. I know these moments. I should pull back, say nothing. But I am getting inflamed, too. Turning to my grandmother, I say, "They do that, *Vecmāmin,* because they hate the mess that the adults have made—"

"Mess—" My father sets his glass down.

"Yes, mess. They smoke marijuana—*kaņepes*—because that's the only way they can stand things."

This talk of *kaņepes* clearly disconcerts my grandmother. She draws up into a prim posture, and I can feel her formulating judgments for later. Still, I push on.

"People smoke it everywhere. It's common, like drinking." I pause and turn away from my father. And then the words just come out: "I smoke it, too. It's nothing. I smoke it all the time."

The last phrase floats on the new silence. I have gone too far, way too far. In my peripheral vision I see my mother touch my father lightly on the forearm. But I know my father. He won't say or do anything; he will not make a scene right now. He will do something worse. He will blink and dab his eyes, and it will twist my heart. The scene will become part of how we are with each other.

I am suddenly emptied out. I try to think of something I might still say to my grandmother, some act of salvage, but I find nothing. She is now looking to my father, trying to draw him back. My mother glances at me as if to say, "Couldn't you guess what would happen?" I excuse myself and go to my room, where I crack the window and smoke a cigarette.

I have thought of this scene many times over the years, my righteousness each time yielding more ground to shame. How could I have done that? How would I feel if one of my children acted that way toward me? But I still remember how my words tumbled out, how they had to, how there was no question at that moment of acting differently, of being someone else.

CHAPTER 1

I HAVE ON MY DESK A CLUMP OF PHOTOCOPIED SHEETS, THE RESIDUE of a project I was at one point very keen on but which I then quite abruptly abandoned.

I'd had the idea that I would write a family history of sorts, only not a history proceeding on the premise of impartial objectivity, but a history projected as a fate. The modest assumption was to be that my own arrival into the world had all along been the point, the concealed reason-for-being of all those generations toiling in oblivious proximity in a faraway country. You might be guessing that I was twelve, or fourteen, but no—the notion was one that compelled me in my late thirties. In my defense I can only offer that I thought of it as a clever conceit, an interesting way to arrange material—I did not *really* think of myself as the monarch of the family genealogy.

But, too, don't we all at times fancy this, or regard ourselves as if we did; don't we act as if merely by coming *after* what was, we are somehow superior? It is the job of education eventually to convince us otherwise, to make us understand, as T. S. Eliot knew, that we are so much smarter than our forebears because they are what we know.

In any event, I was caught up in my imagining, my romantic—narcissistic—conceit that after long generations of backward branching isolation, only son had, in exile in Germany, met only daughter, and that in their second exile, in America, they had married and begotten me, their eventual chronicler. That it had fallen to me to shape the millennial meanderings into a figure bright with purpose.

With this scheme in mind, I gathered and arranged a large number of photographs that I had culled from various family albums. Suddenly they were of interest to me—the stern, suited figures I had gazed past contemptuously in younger years. All of those vague, incidental backgrounds—street corners, parks, farmsteads—now served the purpose of my narrative; I studied them hungrily. Looking, I suppose, for premonitions of myself and wondering how certain people had dared to look so pleased or self-possessed when their mission was nowhere near to being fulfilled yet.

These photographs in their various old albums were for years stored in my mother's old brown trunk—the trunk she had brought from Latvia—so that the very act of reaching down to find them took on a symbolic, ritualistic cast. I used to search them out with a compulsive interest. And while I felt a fairly strong sense of oppression about things connected with our Latvian origins, and professed scorn for those block-faced old-timers in their studied poses, I loved to stare at photographs of my mother and father in their younger years, looking from face to face, from setting to setting, as if there were some kind of code that could be cracked. Feeling, too—if I can say this without sounding too heavy-handed—that mystery of time that we first apprehend as children and never get any closer to solving as we age. I'm talking about the obvious—but still staggering—insight, driven home over and over as the pages are turned, that that was once and is no longer; and that *this,* so immediate, so full, will someday be as unreal as that.

When I went back to those old albums with my project in mind, it was precisely those elders I was after. And I saw that, yes, these were indeed glimpses back. I stared again at the faces of my grandparents, faces I knew but very nearly didn't, so different did they look; and then I found a few photos of gatherings where they, as children, posed among their elders, some of whom were surely born before Daguerre had made the mind-boggling discovery that one could trap grades of light on a chemically treated surface and produce an image that more or less conformed to what we saw with the naked eye.

It took some work, but I did gather from these albums a collection of photographs that I thought were somehow significant, and I tried to arrange them in an alternating pattern that would suggest forward-moving events on one side of the family, then the other, the strands finally twining together when my mother and father stood side by side in the Princeton Chapel on Christmas Day 1950. I tried different sequences, but I could not achieve anything that approached the sense of staggered simultaneity I wanted. I arranged the pictures as best I was able, and then, anticipating failure, still hoping that the Xerox process would function alchemically, I took my cache to the public library, where I spent a long afternoon laying clusters of images on the glass of the photocopier and printing them out on legal-size sheets of paper.

When I took my photo history home and studied it, I was deeply disappointed. I sat at the downstairs table of my parents' home, poring over sheet after sheet, and I got the same deflated feeling I sometimes get when I read over what I've just written and realize that I did not begin to capture the thought or sensation I was after. On those pages I confronted a bleached set of images, a static arrangement of faces and bodies, a jumble of instants excerpted from various lives. There was nothing of the dynamic or suggestive narrative I had fantasized about. The Xerox process may have preserved the essential contour of the images, the basic likenesses, but by stripping from the photographs their sheen, their shadowy subtlety, it had further depleted artifacts that were already but the merest counters of actuality. The images on the sheets refused my projections; they just lay there. And after I had paged through my would-be narrative once or twice, I rolled everything together into a newspaper-size bundle and put a thick rubber band around it.

Then, years later, cleaning and sorting to get ready for an attic renovation, I brought a box of miscellaneous papers into the light. There—I recognized it with an anxious pang—was the bundle. I felt compelled to unroll and inspect it immediately.

Now, as I sat in a different place—my own house—distanced somewhat from parental entanglements, caught up more in the toils of my own daily business, I was, for whatever reason, suddenly vulnerable to the images. I leaned forward on my knees and the room grew silent around me as I turned the pages. I still did not find the narrative movement I had originally hoped to suggest, and the images—faded, even more granular—were less than ever of some world I could recognize, but here and there I felt the flash of a terrible poignancy. It was the poignancy of genetic distance. These whorls of light and dark, these face images that looked to be made up of pixels, were all that remained. They were the barest husk of the human moment, yet they still conjured it.

Now—it is another now—the sheets of photographs are stacked near me on the desk. On top, there to be taken in at a glance, is a sheet holding four images of my grandmother—my father's mother, Mērija. Two of the images are small and have been cropped by the copy machine. The third, which reproduced poorly, shows an illuminated profile of Mērija as a young woman sitting before what looks to be an open window. She looks pretty and of pensive disposition. The picture just above it is quite stunning and confirms my conjecture. Here is Mērija as a young woman—anywhere between fourteen and eighteen years old, I would guess—and she has been photographed, from the waist up, against a fleur-de-lis wallpaper. She has a long braid pulled down over her right shoulder and across the front of her white blouse. She holds a sprig of wildflowers in her right hand, and her left has reached up to pinch a few stalks. The expression, however, is the arresting thing—the gaze detached from any local object, directed wholly inward. The pretty mouth is set resolutely, as if to insist on a young woman's prerogative to look elsewhere, away.

The image is compelling to me, and not only because it features such innocence or because so much time—the better part of a century—has passed. These things do reach me, of course, but I am affected even more by what I know. I assume a godlike perspective—outside the frame of the photo and also largely outside the frame of the life. Looking at Mērija's face, imagining her in that room, in that moment, I cannot, even by concentrating, purge myself of story. Simply: I know what happened in that life; she waits on the brink of it all and cannot begin to guess how things will fall out for her.

There is no innocent study of these photographs, not for me, anyway. Everything that happened—and continues to unfold in my own life—is part of the peculiar figment that is the family narrative, the longer story that has grown up out of all the stories told, of which these pictures are the flimsiest, but most evocative, tokens.

When I study that image of Mērija, I cannot see just a girl holding a sprig of flowers. I see her face as if through a whole array of transparencies—older versions of those features known from other photographs and, from what I remember from the few times I saw her in my life, when she was already an old woman. I see her face as it was the very last time I was with her, sitting by her bedside in her apartment in Riga, asking her questions about her life while she clumsily manipulated a tinfoil shield she had devised as a protection from the "rays" that were being transmitted by the Communists in the apartment opposite. I don't mean to suggest by this one detail that my grandmother had lost her senses—she was, in all other ways, as lucid as a person could be. But she was, after all, a woman in her late eighties who had spent most of her life living under a regime that wanted its citizens to believe that they were being watched.

What an extraordinary leap that last paragraph charts. But the mind makes such leaps incessantly, juxtaposing past and present, suddenly extracting from beneath some ordinary moment a gleaming root of memory. What is no less striking is how readily we project upon simple images the complex narratives we carry around with us. As I look at Mērija as a young girl, it would seem that I'm taking in everything but what was really there in the aperture. True enough—I cannot see her simply for what she may have once been. I cannot view her apart from the stories, the ones I heard from my parents, and the ones she herself told.

Mērija's is a classic account of thwarted love. Like all such accounts, it bears the shape conferred upon it by the imagination of the times. I cannot conceive of it taking place in our day, even though many of the components are familiar. But few people are still proud in this manner, so in thrall to ideas of greatness or so repressed. This is a story from a time of war, when distances were very different from what they are today and when time passed at a pace we can no longer even imagine.

During the First World War, Latvia is still under the czar's regime. Mērija, then a schoolteacher in her early twenties, is working as a volunteer for a refugee organization in Riga. There she meets two brothers, Anton and Peter Birkerts. Both are writers and intellectuals, and both pay court to her. Anton, the elder, is the gentler spirit, and for a time Mērija is more drawn to him. But then her feelings change. Peter, volatile and moody, wins her heart. He is the more serious one, the real intellectual. Though still in his thirties, he has traveled far; he already has a romantic past. As a Social Democrat, he had sympathized with the anticzarist uprisings in 1905, writing articles and polemics. For this, he had been arrested, consigned to a prison. Later, freed, he had found his way to Switzerland, where he befriended the great Latvian poet Janis Rainis. Then, America: law studies at Valparaiso and Columbia, a period of working as an attorney (I have taped up over my desk a photocopy of his business card, his office on LaSalle Street in Chicago). Now he is back in Latvia, about to be conscripted into the Russian army.

I have only the bare-bones facts and a few hints of atmosphere, most of these gleaned from Mērija's various tellings of the story, but also from my mother, who is the real narrative archivist of the family and who has always had the knack for conferring dramatic shape on past events, making them seem interesting. From both I have built up a picture of what Mērija herself called the turning point of her life.

In Mērija's account, everything happened over the course of a single long night. Peter had just received his call-up notice, and while her heart inclined her to Peter, Mērija and the brothers still made up a friendly trio. They decided to spend Peter's last night in Riga together.

These are the wartime moments, recast in imagination by the romantic dramaturgy of cinema. I can't compose the scene except in black and white. I see troop trains, railway platforms, a landscape smoky with fatalism. Anton, Peter, and Mērija pass the night walking the streets of the city, talking. Old Riga is a perfect setting—a medieval stage set with narrow, cobblestoned streets giving on to a waterfront. They walk. At some point toward morning, all three have linked arms—three comrades. As they walk, Mērija feels what she will later describe as a questioning squeeze of the hand from Peter. She hesitates—as she hesitates when she tells the story—then returns it. It is her moment of truth. That slight muscular contraction of the fingers became, over the long years devoted to retrospection, the crossroads. She has signaled to Peter that he is the one, and from that signal, from the decisive impulse in the heart, everything else follows.

Mērija's story belongs more to the era of Hardy or James than to our own time. The drama is not manifest; it is to be inferred. I remember when, in my thirties, I paid her what was to be my very last visit. I was in Riga, alone, walking every afternoon from my room in the Riga Hotel to Mērija's apartment, where I would take my seat by her bedside and listen while she told me the story of her life. I was amazed. The events of that night, over sixty-five years ago, were absolutely vivid to her—or else she had created them into vividness. I stared at her as she lay in her bed—her eyes were entirely occluded by cataracts, and she could not see me. She was shrunken, mottled, cut down by time. But when she talked, suddenly taking me by the wrist every now and then with a startlingly powerful grip, the emotion rose in her voice. And then, for moments at a stretch, it was as if those intervening years were nothing at all. I fell—with her—into that place of storytelling, where, as in dreams, things agelessly just *are*. And what a story it was, or became. She had made the choice for love, and love had betrayed her. But she never—not to my father, not to me—allowed that she had been done wrong. Her whole life was shaped around that denial. *Viņs bija ļoti liels gars.* She said it over and over. He was a very great spirit. And when I look at that photograph and see the set of her mouth—then her pretty girl's mouth—I can hardly avoid the thought that character is destiny.

Of course—and now I speak as one who has seen thousands of montage and time-lapse sequences and double exposures of every sort—I also cannot look at that image of Mērija without glimpsing in ghostly overlay certain images of Peter, her husband-to-be.

Peter was older, and he wore his seriousness, his sternness, like a reproach to the rest of the world. I see it in each of the dozen or so photographs of him that survive. There is never a smile. Nor is he ever not wearing a suit, even when he has been captured out in nature, propped against a tree with a book or leaning against some sort of outdoor shed, again reading. I cannot imagine how he would have presented himself in our era of triumphant informality.

When I study photographs of Peter—and I do—I am sometimes seized by a kind of genetic awe. For his is the face that did not used to be, but is, ever more distinctly, my father's. Not feature by feature, though there are strong similarities, but in terms of something underlying the features, some archaic template of identity. Then it strikes me, the inevitable ironic afterthought: that seeing himself in the mirror is as close as my father will ever come to seeing his father. For Peter left when my father was born.

But I am getting ahead of myself. In this narrative, he has just squeezed Mērija's hand somewhere in the streets of Riga, and she has returned the pressure. And with that exchange some profound understanding has been ratified. By night's end, Anton has grasped that Mērija prefers his brother (though I did hear her interject, almost as a kind of conditioned reflex, "He was such a *good* man"). Mērija, for her part, understands that as soon as the war ends, or Peter is released from his service, they will be together.

There follow many blanks and gaps. If my grandmother filled these in once, I have forgotten. I did not think to take notes during that last visit—I just wanted to listen. A few parts of the story can, however, be reconstructed.

Though Russia and Germany are at war—it is 1916, the Revolution has not yet erupted—Peter is not at the front. For a time, I learn, he is billeted in a town in Estonia, and Mērija goes to visit him there. Later, in 1918, Peter is in Moscow, and Mērija—this is another story shaped through many tellings—violates all sorts of wartime restrictions to get to him. She travels across the front by train, passes out bribes to get through checkpoints; at one point she even treks through the forest to get around the guards. Then they are together.

What does Peter do during the Revolution? Is there a role to play for an old activist? I don't know.

In Moscow, in 1918, Peter and Mērija are married in a civil ceremony. After the war they live for a time in Smolensk. Mērija—and this detail surprises me—studies singing. Peter works at his writing. His output over the next few years will be prodigious. He will publish various books, as follows: *Psychology* (1921), *The Psychology of Creativity, Part I* (1922), *Pedagogical Psychology* (1923),

The Psychology of Creativity, Part II (1925), and *The Psychology of Love* (1926). The second *Psychology of Creativity* would have been published the year my father was born. *The Psychology of Love*—well, that would have come out the year after he left Mērija and their baby.

The Smolensk period was given over to work and to private life. I have no reason to dwell on this time—and little information, in any case—except that a certain photograph has survived, one that compels my imagination. It is a group scene. Outdoors, under a tree, people are standing around a long table. There are glasses—for tea, kvass—and a samovar and, in Russian style, a large vase of cut flowers.

Who are these people? Teachers, scholars, and members of the local intelligentsia. They are all neatly dressed, and while some flash smiles, others look pensive, ill at ease before a camera. Peter and Mērija stand together in the back. Seldom have I confronted a family photograph that so tangibly evokes *history* for me. That is, I cannot look at it without starting to think about the larger arrangement of events, what we call "the times." The two dozen people arrayed around this table are obviously intellectuals. They are intellectuals as Chekhov might have cast them—with beards, glasses, and that certain look of not being at home in their bodies. They would all have been liberals, anticzarists, and in these heady post-Revolution days they would have seen themselves as the victors, the vindicated. I note, on Mērija's face especially, an expression of righteousness and purity, and I imagine—alas, I never asked—that she, and those around her, saw themselves as standing on the brink of a new age, a new order.

After the Smolensk interlude, Peter and Mērija return to Riga to live. But marital peace will prove short-lived. Soon there are troubles, harbinger scenes. In one account, this from my mother, Peter and Mērija had a bitter argument about something, after which Mērija left to attend a wedding out in the country. When she returned, Peter had vacated the apartment. They lived apart for nearly a year after that, then they came back together. This would have been in the early 1920s. Mērija had begun teaching at the girls' gymnasium, a job she would keep for long decades. Peter was in the throes of his own production. They were deeply divided, it seems, over whether to have a child. The division became absolute when Mērija announced that she was pregnant. Peter moved out and never returned.

He did not, however, leave Riga. He moved out to the Jurmala, the Baltic shore on the outskirts of the city—for many years a popular Russian resort area—and there he set up housekeeping with Anton. Riga was a big enough city so that Peter and Mērija did not have to encounter each other at every turn—indeed, they arranged not to. I have heard the story, though, that in the years that followed, Peter would come into the city and time his walks so that he could pass by the neighborhood park where my father—his son—might be playing after school. The story could be apocryphal, a detail required for the artistic elaboration of the situation. My mother, who told it to me, cannot vouch for its accuracy.

Every such narrative is the sum not just of its events, but of its associations as well. When I think about Peter writing his books, sacrificing marriage and family to his vocation, I have to picture the glass case that my father had built in his studio some years ago. It is there that he keeps his most precious mementos—special photographs, medals, and citations, and, yes, the collection of his father's books. When I visit home I sometimes stand there and survey that row of thin, unmarked spines. Browning paper, fading print—the achievements of another place and time. What a distance—chasm—between the urgency of composition as I imagine it and the survival into the present of the printed relics, among them *The Psychology of Love*.

But the strangest thing of all in this tale of Peter and Mērija has to be that she never, not to my father or anyone else, railed against the man who left her. In the family mythology, Peter still wears his hero's cloak. "He was a great spirit. He left so that he could do his work." I can see why she wanted to believe that, and why she raised my father to believe it, too. In her world—and now his—genius excuses; it writes the exceptions. To genius everything is permitted.

And there Peter sat, year after year, in the seaside cottage that he shared with Anton and their housekeeper, a woman Anton married late in life, after Peter died, so that she would have some legacy when his time came. I visited that cottage the last time I was in Riga. Anton's widow was still living there—a talkative older woman with a dash of henna in her hair—and she showed me around. It was a small place, surrounded by towering pine trees, just a short walk from the seashore. Everything was immaculate, carefully preserved, a kind of museum shrine to the brothers' quiet industry. Peter's books were neatly shelved in his study; his desk was arranged so that he could return at any moment and resume where he had left off. The silence was deep, but it felt brittle.

Ironies continue to proliferate around father and son. Some years ago, when the Soviet empire was dismantled, properties were returned to their rightful owners and heirs. As Anton's widow had herself passed away, my father inherited the Jurmala cottage. He made plans to donate it to the city of Riga for preservation, as both Peter and Anton have entered the Latvian history books as leading literary figures of their day.

Mērija, then, raised my father by herself, and she did so with vigor and resolve. My father never suggests that his life was hard or that the arrangement was in any way wanting. In fact, he tells with some pride how well he and his mother managed, how orderly things were. Mērija was strict in matters of child rearing—my father often talks about the routines and chores he grew up with—but he seems to have flourished. He became a most orderly adult. To this day there are always checklists on his desk, each task with a small box beside it.

Was my father lonesome? He will not admit it, but I can hear it in his stories, the ones he tells to illustrate his devotion: how he would let himself into the apartment after school, get himself a snack, and then settle into his spot by the window to watch for his mother. He once pointed out that apartment building during a family visit to Riga. We all stood together in the street, craning up at a set of windows on the fifth or sixth floor. "I sat there," said my father, a note of proud disbelief in his voice, "with my eyes glued to a patch of sidewalk on the corner. I knew almost to the minute when my mother would be coming home from the tram." He also told how he had a friend, a little girl, in the apartment opposite and how they would each light candles for the other at night. Then there are the photographs. Like father, like son: I do not recall a childhood picture in which my father is smiling. He is always so serious and alert—posing with his mother, holding her hand; working intently on a model airplane; standing with others in a field during a summer of working in the country ... The truth is, I cannot imagine him horsing around, letting go entirely the way some kids will. Somehow Mērija is always in the background, watching.

I don't know if Mērija was strict by nature or became that way because she was a teacher and a single mother. Certainly her photographs show her to be a young woman without much nonsense in her. She was never one for chattering and making nice. When I met her for the first time—when our family traveled to Latvia in the mid-1960s, after my father had been away for nearly twenty-five years—she allowed herself a long choked-up moment, but then she got down to business. Our conversations—certainly hers and mine—always had an agenda. She had set aside times when we would meet by ourselves. I would go into her room and she would indicate the place on the couch beside her. Books and papers would be neatly stacked on a nearby chair. The questions she had for me had all been prepared, as had the accounts from her life that she wanted me to know about. Passages in various books had been marked for my edification, and these she read aloud to me.

I was dutiful and played my part. But the simple fact was that I was thirteen, a teenager, interested in clothes, rock and roll, and friends. I was shocked that she either could not guess that about me or chose to ignore it entirely. She was, as my other grandmother said in later years—after they had met and established an uneasy cordiality—a "great pedagogue."

I do not have a sustained narrative to present, only a cluster of episodes and characterizations. I want to understand my relation to the family past, to figure out why the contemplation of it should unsettle me so. Why am I such a bad Latvian? Why do I feel such a ready impulse to refuse any commemoration of bygone glories? It must be that my feelings are all wrapped up with these stories, with the sad events that somehow echo through me.

As a child who wanted above all to be a white-bread American, I professed an absolute aversion to all things Latvian. I cringed when I heard the language spoken in English-speaking contexts—if my parents lapsed into the home idiom at the beach, say, or at a restaurant. I imagined people glancing over with chilly Yankee condescension, though we were not within miles of a genuine Yankee. I winced at the brown-paper parcels that arrived several times a year from Riga and always contained some books that I had to feign interest in. Yet such was my feeling of obligation and guilt that I could not throw away any of the brown wrapping sheets with their garish Soviet stamps and my grandmother's carefully inked lettering. I wanted to be rid of that hump of pastness that I carried and other kids did not. I wanted the very "lightness of being" that Milan Kundera disparages in his novel—and I did not even come close.

The outer symbol of all this emotional turmoil was the city of Riga, which, until I finally went there some years later with my parents and saw it for myself, was for me a stern medieval presence, a northern Prague, all narrow cobblestoned alleys and darkly ceremonial buildings. I even imagined squatting gargoyles. I discovered, eventually, that the city was not quite as I had imagined it, that the streets were wider, the buildings more modern, and the mood not nearly so somber. My impression had derived, apart from the projections of fantasy, from seeing endless photographs and postcards of the same few sites in the Old City, which really *was* narrow and cobbled. But the recognition came too late. I had already animated our whole family history, what I knew of it, against just such a background. The mise-en-scène could not be changed, even as my understanding of the ancestral narrative shifted with every new piece of information. I somehow needed that impression of an older, more picturesque world, and the moody backdrop survives despite all the impressions gleaned from my adult visits to that city.

The truth is, I have two very different versions of the city present to my imagination. There is the Riga that my father grew up in, physically of course the same, but taking on the coloration of my reconstructions of his life with Mērija. It is a quieter, less populous city—a city seen from the vantage of a gray Sunday afternoon. My mother's Riga, though still that antique place, has a very different "feel" to it. It is more prosperous, and warmer, though the story of her side of the family is no less problematic psychologically. Maybe the difference is just that my mother was able to hold certain illusions about family life longer than my father, was, indeed, able to hold them at all.

My mother's girlhood is, for me, encoded in the words "Elizabeth Street," invoked so often in family conversation that it has taken on its own mass and solidity. Elizabeth Street was not, for me, a street at all; it was the bright, prosperous-looking residence where my mother, her parents, and her beloved *tante* Aija lived for some years before the war. There, in addition to the large apartment, were my grandmother's millinery shop and my grandfather's photo studio. Nearby—and my mother pointed everything out the first time we all traveled to Riga together—was the French lycée—the "litz"—where she went to school; near, too, at least in anecdotal proximity, were the shops my grandmother frequented with her fashionable friends and the theater where she and my grandfather went at least once a week.

A different city and a different life, certainly, from what Mērija and my father knew. Tokens of this other existence survive in a large number of photographs, many more than what we have to document my father's younger years. For while Mike, my grandfather, was by training and passion a landscape painter, he made his living running a photo studio. Most of the photographs from my mother's—the Zvirbulis—side of the family bear the embossed logo *Fot. A. Zvirbulis.* There are hundreds of pictures of my mother in her girlhood years—alone, with Aija, with one or both of her parents, on the streets of Riga, on a carousel, at the seashore . . . With their two businesses, Mike and Emilia were even well-off enough to afford a beautiful summer house at the Jurmala.

If the images of my father project a lonely seriousness, those of my mother declare a bourgeois privilege. She is always immaculately styled and dressed—very pretty. But even in these child photographs—we see her holding a kitten or standing in her bathing suit by the sea—my mother looks posed. She has interrupted her moment, her activity, to present an expression. She shows the world what she wants the world to see. And she is like that to this day. The family joke is that my mother cannot be captured by a camera lens in her natural, candid, state. This she gets from Emilia, who took it even further, who sought for every photographic event some dramatic definition, who is always gazing out at the world with a look of great emotional intensity.

But posing is, by definition, deception—it is putting a face on things. A casual comparison of the photographs of my mother and father as children would suggest that my mother was the more pampered and quite the happier of the two. And in some ways this is probably true. She was less constrained by the demon of discipline, freer to indulge her whims and fancies. But despite all the posed photographs, the coddled smiles, is the likelihood that her home life, with two parents and her aunt, was no happier than my father's. The rooms of their spacious Elizabeth Street apartment held distances, evasions, and unspoken recriminations. Emilia and Mike, though they stayed together—in Latvia, in Germany, and finally for a good many years in America—were not especially suited to one another and were not, maybe ever, happy as a couple. Even in their earliest photo portraits—and I study them, as I study everything, with hindsight—one can see, from Mike's air of detachment and in Emilia's obvious beseeching of the lens, that these are two people with very different characters.

Emilia—Ūm (pronounced "Ooom")—was, no question, the family "character." Charming and vivacious to those who knew her casually—and "charming" was the word everyone always used—she was often exasperating to those who had to deal with her more regularly. In later years—this is what I remember from childhood and my teens—she was at every moment complaining, wheedling attention, or looking to foment discord within the family. Nothing was ever right or enough. She plagued my mother with telephone calls, especially after Mike died and she was living by herself; she was forever muttering about "him"—my father—what he had done or failed to do, what he had said or omitted to say. My most insistent recollection from those later years is of hearing my mother on the upstairs phone, sighing, saying over and over in the most plaintive tone, "Jā, Mamin"—until she could take it no more and had to vent herself, releasing with a ferocity that always surprised me the words that would force her to slam the receiver down. Whereupon she would generally collect herself, sigh, and pick up the phone again. The slow retracting whir of the rotary dial signaled the start of the next round.

My sister and I will now tell anyone who will listen the stories of what it was like to be left in Ūm's care for weeks at a time while my parents took their annual trips to Europe. How when we upset her, or simply when she grew bored—we could feel her fidgety exasperation growing by the minute—she would with a great show pack up her suitcase, put on her hat, and pretend to call the taxi company, saying ominously as she put her hand over the receiver, "I don't know what you two will do, but I can't stand it anymore. I'm going back to my house." Other times she might grab at her chest and turn suddenly like some figure out of Greek tragedy, Medea or Clytemnestra, and, her voice shaking with imprecation, cry out that she would be dead soon, and that after she was buried *then* we would understand how good she had been; *then* we would come clawing at her coffin with our fingernails and begging her forgiveness. Or maybe she would sit on the edge of the couch, gasping and pressing at her heart, asking me with my strong hands to help her get the top off her bottle of heart medicine because she could feel a heart attack coming.

Outsiders went into raptures over her accent, her sweetness, that special "old world" quality she exuded. They found her to be original, memorable—"charming"—and listened with interest as she bragged about her long-ago successes as milliner to the most elegant ladies in Riga. Even in her eighties, Emilia moved with dramatic flourish—sudden overt gestures, vivid grimaces—and when she confided herself in anyone (she was always confiding herself), she generated a kind of supplicatory moistness about the eyes. She sucked people in.

My grandmother came by her neediness naturally. Both of her parents had died before she was ten years old, leaving her to grow up in the care of her two older brothers. One, Fritz, became a successful attorney; Robert, the other, was later a master brewer—also successful. But they were busy young men and could not supply much of a home life. So Emilia was sent away to a boarding school and later to what was then called a "commerce school," where she learned bookkeeping. This was in Jelgava, a sizable city not far from Riga.

Emilia was still in school when she met Mike, then a young art student getting ready to attend the Moscow Academy. The two had been seated together at a dinner given by a mutual friend. Mike, as the story goes, had later commented favorably on Emilia, had found her "pretty." ("Don't laugh," my mother would always say, "they had different standards back then. She was buxom and had those big eyes. She was considered *quite* good-looking.") Emilia's surname was Kringelis, which was also the name of a kind of braided sweet bread; Mike's was Zvirbulis, or "sparrow." There were jokes going around that the sparrow was going to take a nibble at the sweet bread.

Mike and Emilia had a seven-year courtship. Mike attended the Moscow Academy and wrote to her. Emilia took a job as a bookkeeper in a lumber mill and acted in the local theater company, specializing in scenes of romantic melodrama. But when the First World War broke out, Mike abandoned his studies and returned to Jelgava. Then, with the German army advancing from the south, Emilia and Mike (together with Mike's mother) fled to Riga. There, in 1916, they were married, in part so that Mike would not be conscripted.

The end of the war brought independence to Latvia. For Mike and Emilia things fell out advantageously. Mike, who had dabbled with photography and had even run a small concession taking pictures of soldiers and their girlfriends, was suddenly offered the chance to buy out the studio of a well-known Riga photographer named Hebensberger. He took the risk and, happily, it paid off. The studio prospered.

Then, just a few years later, the millinery shop next door was poised for bankruptcy. The owner, hurrying to leave town, offered to sell out very cheaply. Emilia, who had no training whatsoever in fashion, announced that she was interested. A deal was struck, and before long, Mike and Emilia had shops side by side on Elizabeth Street. Later, when the upstairs apartments were vacated, they decided to move in.

Emilia was, finally, a good deal more successful at her business dealings than Mike was at his. At some level, or so my mother hypothesizes, his dreams and energies were still wrapped up in becoming a painter. On days when the studio was closed, he took his easel and canvas outdoors and painted landscapes. Emilia, meanwhile, had the vigor, the love for detail, and the instinct for flattery to put the millinery shop back on a sure footing. In a few years her hats were the most fashionable in the city. "All of the most elegant ladies—the grandes dames and ambassadors' wives—came to me." Indeed, for a number of years in the 1930s, she traveled by train twice a year to Paris to attend the big seasonal fashion shows. She would study the styles carefully, sketching them from memory as soon as she returned to her hotel room. Back in Riga she would have her "girls" produce what she had drawn.

All of this was narrated to us many times while we were growing up. Our grandmother had us—my sister and me—as her captive audience for weeks at a time, and the possibility that she might be repeating herself never deterred her in the slightest. We heard all of the stories—how she had starred on the Jelgava stage; how her hat shop was the toast of Riga; how she would sit with the finest society ladies in Rumpelmayer's Café . . .

The one story she never told, though in her last years she would make occasional allusions to it, was the most important one. But telling it would have meant exposing Mike and the hollowness of the marriage; it would also have undercut the posture of the sorrowing widow that she used to such advantage. Emilia, like Mērija, faced her sorrow privately. She, too, in public honored the man who had so betrayed her trust.

Mike had been, by all accounts, an indulged child. He had a talent for drawing and an interest in nature, and when he was old enough he pursued his formal training as a landscape painter. Mike had a gift—many teachers and dealers testified to that—but he never achieved the kind of success he wanted. His early paintings did not find many takers. But Mike—and this is part of his mythology in our family—was lucky; good things fell into his lap. For while the paintings languished unsold, the photo studio that he had opened just as a backup prospered. Very early on, during the late war years, he had picked up the art of tinting studio portraits with light washes of color. Suddenly people were lining up to have their pictures "done."

In later years there were other surprises. A good friend of Mike's, a Mr. Rupners, a banker, who figured in Ūm's stories as a kind of guardian angel, once got him a post as a broker for real estate transactions. Mike knew nothing of the business. He had only to preside in a notary capacity over the sale of a property, and for this he received a fixed—and generous—percentage. There is a story that after one such piece of business, Mike impulsively bought a Steinway piano and had it delivered to the apartment on Elizabeth Street—where they already *had* a piano. For the few years that Mike and Emilia were moderately rich, they flaunted it.

Along with being temperamental and impulsive—"artistic"— Mike was also known to be a bit of a dandy and ladies' man. "More than anything else," my mother has told me, "he liked to be pleasing to people, to women especially. He couldn't say no." This is hard for me to credit from my perspective—when I knew Mike he was a slow-moving figure in his sixties and early seventies— but some early photographs show a very intense, even passionate-looking, young man. Staring at these, I can begin to imagine a different life for him.

The core event—the scandal—in my grandparents' marriage, an event that remains somewhat mysterious to this day, owing in part to the long-term reticence of all concerned and in part because it was a situation carried on *as a secret,* was the fact that Mike had a second family. This was not just an affair, a liaison with a mistress. Mike spent long hours, unbeknownst to Emilia or my mother, at another house, with a woman who loved him and their child.

The whole business is mind-boggling. The secrecy and logistics, sure, but more perplexing, to me, is the fact that this state of affairs was not only discovered, but was, after discovery, somehow survived by all concerned. So that my grandparents could drive to our house for Christmas or Thanksgiving, a benignly rancorous old couple, and things just continued. This, along with other details that will emerge in the telling of the story, reveals a good deal about the psychological dynamics of our family. On both sides.

Mike had first met this woman—Olga was her name—when she was still a student in Riga. She and some friends had come to his studio to have their pictures taken. Mike was, doubtless, charming and flirtatious. Enough so, apparently, that Olga later came back by herself to ask Mike if he would teach her to operate a camera. They began a relationship, and by my mother's account, it was intense enough that Olga begged Mike to leave his wife. Emilia was then pregnant with my mother, and Mike refused to break up the marriage. With that, the relationship ended. Olga disappeared, and Mike later heard that she had married a soldier.

But then, several years later, Olga resurfaced in his life. Her marriage had ended. She claimed that she was still in love with Mike. It was at this point—my mother does not know under what arrangement—that Mike began his double life. The long periods away from home and studio were attributed to a renewal of his interest in landscape painting.

The deception must have lasted for some years. I once asked my mother if she had had inklings of any sort. She then told me a story of how she and Mike had been riding together somewhere in the tram, when a girl, a few years younger than my mother, had made her way over to him and said: "Come over—Mommy's up front." Mike had shaken his head, made some excuse, and the girl had returned to her seat. My mother was old enough to be curious, but Mike had brushed off her questions. Later, though, walking home through the park, he had stopped for a moment on the walkway. "It would be better if you said nothing about that meeting to Mother." That had been all. He had not explained himself.

Who knows how things would have fallen out if the war had not come? Once again, Latvia was beset from both directions, by Soviet armies from the east and by German forces from the south. The Soviets prevailed first, shipping many thousands of Latvians to Siberian camps, methodically breaking up families, inflicting terrible brutalities. The oncoming Germans, who then pushed back the Soviets, were seen not so much as invaders as liberators. They did not deport Latvians, but they gave permission, selectively, for families to emigrate to certain zones in Bavaria. But notice was short, in some cases merely hours. Families packed essentials, buried their precious goods when they could, and hurried to the ships docked in Riga's harbor. This was in August of 1944.

Mike, Emilia, my mother, and Aija were given papers to leave. Insisting that he had to close things up and promising to join them as soon as he could, Mike sent the others off on a ship called the *Montrosa*. Here follows a significant blank. No one knows exactly what happened, what Mike did or tried to do. Was he agonizing over a choice? My mother thinks not. She reports that he wrote to Emilia daily—passionate letters such as he had never written before. Guilt? A ruse? In late September he arrived to join his family in the Bavarian town of Nördlingen. There, exhausted, depressed, he took to his bed for a month, talking little, scarcely eating.

Did Emilia understand, seeing him thus, what was happening? Could she have guessed that he was in mourning for his other life? She did know, it appears, that Mike was involved with another woman, but it is not clear that she suspected the extent of the involvement. She seemed to be able to live behind a buffer, never alluding directly to Mike's infidelity—indeed, appearing in a sentimental way to cherish him at times, referring to him with fond diminutives—but when she was very old, long after Mike had died, she would sometimes make cryptic observations, unspecified, about certain people who did not know how to mind their own business, who did not understand what they were talking about.

My mother offers some clarification. What Emilia may have been alluding to was the fact that one of her "friends," one of the fine ladies in her social circle, had one day called her on the telephone—in Riga—to give her some news. "Did you know that your husband has a lady friend?" she asked, her refinement scarcely masking her cattiness. To this Emilia had replied, in less genteel tones: "And might *you* be that 'friend'?" The woman hung up and the matter was not aired again, though of course no one ever knows what goes on behind the closed doors of a marriage.

The thread of the story then disappears—the outward thread, that is—for a half century. It reappeared again, most strangely, quite recently. Since the collapse of the Soviet regime and the reemergence of an independent Latvia, my parents visit the home country fairly often. My father has several architectural projects in Riga, including the design for the new national library. His arrivals and departures get noted in the papers. One day, shortly before they were scheduled to leave for another visit, my mother received a letter from a woman named Ieva, who wrote that she had important reasons for wanting to meet with my mother during their stay.

Upon their arrival in Riga, my mother contacted Ieva and a lunch was arranged. "I went to the restaurant," my mother tells me, "and suddenly I saw a woman coming toward me who looked just like Mike's mother. It was spooky." Ieva was, of course, her half sister, the same person who had come up to them so many years before on the tram. The lunch was awkward at times, but also revealing. There were stories to tell, versions to compare. Enough years had passed so that the facts could be brought forward. Ieva had with her photographs of her mother and Mike—windows onto her father's other life.

From Ieva my mother learned what had happened during those weeks when she and her mother and Aija traveled to Nördlingen. Staying behind, Mike had moved Olga and Ieva into the family's summer home at Jurmala. There they lived out the remainder of the war. Only when he had done what he could to secure their comfort and safety had Mike made his own travel arrangements to Germany. As for those letters to Emilia, what prompted them— we will never know.

In Nördlingen, after taking to his bed to nurse who knows what doubts and regrets, Mike rallied. He took up his new life, which was to be, at long last, that of a painter. Now there was time. All of the clutter and distraction, not to mention the enormous expenditure of deceit, was gone. Mike took his easel and canvas and began painting scenes from the local countryside—one of these paintings, of a wooded lane and a German-style house, now hangs in our bedroom. His work found favor among Germans as well as among fellow Latvian exiles. This was, however, wartime, and cash patrons were few and far between. Often, instead of getting cash payment, he would trade his work for food and staple goods—and he was glad to be able to do so. It was another instance of his "luck."

With Mike's taking up his vocation again in Nördlingen, the main drama of his married life ends. He and Emilia will live together for quite a few more years, in Germany, in America, but the onlooker's focus naturally slips to the next generation. My mother, now a young woman not yet twenty, is introduced to a young Latvian who has left home to study architecture in Stuttgart. A courtship begins. But I am not going to unfold that story here.

What draws me so compulsively to these fragments of family lore is the feeling that there is a burden, something difficult and heavy, in our past, and that this has in various ways directed the currents of family life. For one thing, each of my parents has had to wrestle with an unhappy legacy, with the fact that their fathers did not want to be with their mothers. Moreover, on both sides of the family there emerged a powerful ethic of concealment. This is no great mystery—we find a similar drawing of the veil of privacy in most families. But here unhappy things were not named or discussed even among intimates. Instead, we had—and have—our myths. Mērija's strength and self-sacrifice, her legendary discipline; Peter's solitary need, the claims of his genius; Emilia's cleverness and cosmopolitanism and dramatic flair; Mike's luck . . .

I knew three of my grandparents. Emilia and Mike moved from Princeton, where they first lived after coming to America, to Michigan after I was born. They wanted to be near their daughter and grandson. Mike was able to find a job at the Cranbrook Art Academy, helping to curate exhibitions, and they were given the upper floor of a small house right on the Cranbrook estate, only a few minutes' walk from the academy, the three private schools, and the science museum. We lived a few miles away and saw them quite often. My sister and I even lived with our grandparents at Cranbrook for a part of one summer while my parents were selling one house and buying another.

Mike died many years before Emilia. I remember him fondly, as a gentle and soft-spoken, if somewhat withdrawn, man. I spent quite a few hours with him that one summer. He would carry his easel and canvas down to the lake at Cranbrook to paint, and I would accompany him. I don't remember that we spoke much. My memories have him stationed by the side of the lake, staring off, contemplating his subject, or else bending over to get the proper mix of oils on his palette. I would play nearby, or stand and watch, but I knew better than to interrupt his reflective trances.

After Mike's death, my grandmother moved to a small house in nearby Birmingham and for the next fifteen years burdened my mother with her emotional neediness and her elaborate psychological wiles. She would call several times a day, always when my father was out, trying to get my mother to visit her, either to bring her back to our house for dinner or take her out somewhere, to Machus, her favorite coffee shop. She became a source of great family friction, cause of more than a few snapping arguments between my parents, in which my father insisted that my mother set

limits and my mother protested that she couldn't. When Emilia—
Ūm—finally died in her late eighties, people remarked upon the
change in my mother, how much freer she seemed.

Mērija, too, lived on into her late eighties. She died in the same
apartment that she had moved to when my father was still a boy. I
remember how, when we first visited there, my father paced
around, showing me things, saying, "This is where I used to sit and
do my homework," and, "This was my favorite spot on the floor."
He could not get over the fact that the Russians had requisitioned
the space, putting up walls to create another apartment, leaving
kitchen and bathroom communal. He called me into the bathroom
at one point and said, with tears in his eyes, "Look—" There was a
narrow, ancient-looking toilet, with neatly torn squares of newspaper piled on the floor beside it.

Mērija's health was in decline for her last few years. She lost
nearly all of her sight to cataracts, and her heart was weak. Her
good luck was the lifelong devotion she had inspired in a group of
former students—her "girls," never mind that some were in their
sixties, with grandchildren. These women, three in particular,
took charge of everything. They set up a calendar rotation, coming
in to clean, shop, cook, visit, help with medicines and doctors, and
do whatever was necessary for their old teacher's well-being.
When we visited, they followed Mērija's every command, preparing and arranging dishes of food, setting out flowers. She was for
them a cause, a mission. At some point each of these women confided to me how important my grandmother had been to her, how
her teaching had given inspiration. After her death they continued
to meet on her birthday to share a meal and reminisce.

The generation of grandparents now fades. They have all been
dead for more than a decade, some much longer than that. As their
passing on is accepted and absorbed, as their influence wanes and
their stories get smoothed into family lore, and—no less impor-

tant—as I move into my own American middle age, a husband and a father, I feel the power of the spell start to wear off. I am no longer oppressed by the Latvian past. It's hard for me to summon up the prickly sense of guilt and obligation that dogged me for so many years. I almost long for the clarity of that old dissent. Indeed, a kind of reversal seems to be taking place. If I turn against anything now, it's the craven desire for conformity that I succumbed to in younger years. How I despised the fear of being thought different, other. But isn't this the way things have always gone: we end up cherishing what we feared and hated, because the fear, the hatred—and whatever occasioned them—made us what we are. That past is suddenly distant enough to have become a story, not just for others, but for ourselves.

CHAPTER 2

FLANNERY O'CONNOR ONCE OBSERVED THAT FOR MOST WRITERS everything of importance happens before the end of adolescence. Provocative, almost preposterous, the insight begins to make more sense as we reflect upon it. O'Connor does not mean that these writers-in-the-making will have had by that time most of their life experiences. Certainly not. What she means is that the writer, almost by definition observant and questioning, will have extrapolated from whatever has befallen him a set of intuitions about the basic laws of human nature. He will have settled on his phenomenology. He will be far along in the formation of the chrysalis, the sheath, that most delicate binding structure of language and perception out of which the mature artist eventually emerges. And no matter what the writer later ventures and achieves, his work will always be imprinted with the strong trace of origins.

What O'Connor is affirming is that all human subject matter is likely to be there in those early experiences, provided the writer knows how to find it; that the path to all of our later discoveries—about love, betrayal, goodness, and evil—was set down for us even as we wandered in ostensible ignorance.

I believe in the truth of what O'Connor says, if not for all writers, then for many, certainly the ones in whom we sense the struggles of language to repossess the bygone—Joyce, Woolf, Proust, Nabokov . . . And in these writers we discern the other great truth about childhood, namely that everything about life comes at us then in the particular. Childhood is the seedbed of all later understanding and expression, and its content is the unrepeatable detail. Things happen, first—beautifully—just for themselves; later they warp, become instances of some discerned pattern, and are measured according to how they conform or diverge. Our original contacts with the world are in advance of all extrapolations. We live, if very briefly—though it does not *feel* brief, for we have not yet extrapolated the category of time—in the face of raw immediacies. Even our sulks and boredoms are raw and immediate. Which is why, partly, the boredoms of childhood are so profound. We are pushed right up against it, the unstructured persistence of things, and we have not yet figured out how to arm ourselves.

I have been wondering lately: What was for me the first thing, the memory that predates all others? I don't know, not for sure, but I like to think that if I *did*, if I could find the core fossil, I would be on to something important. If I had the shapes, colors, and sounds—the real feel—of the first preserved experience, I could discover all sorts of things about the person who now holds the pen. But so much doubt enters in, so much distortion. Nearly everything I can call up from my earliest years has been examined, doctored, and—worst—brought into line with the logic of what I believe to have been my later development. The mystery remains.

I have always been told how much I adored my *tante* Aija, who lived a few miles away in Detroit when my parents had their first apartment in Pontiac, where I was born, and who once a week took the city bus down Woodward Avenue to visit and to baby-sit me. I can't remember Aija herself, though when I look at the few photographs of her we have, I feel a sense of comfortable familiarity. These photos show a solidly built blond-haired woman with a wide, thin mouth. She looks to be keeping a joke to herself, though I may be saying this now only because my mother has so often told me how funny she was. Aija had been like a second mother to my mother, or a close older sister. She had been there, reliable and warm, while Mike and Emilia pursued their careers and negotiated the hazards of married life.

Aija figures into what I consider to be my earliest recollection, which is a strange compound picture/sensation. It is strange because I seem to be looking from above and at the same time seeing myself. I am sitting on a carpet in the center of a large room with someone I know to be Aija. The room is dim, with only a glow, as if from a shaded bulb off to one side. Aija and I are trying to build a house from playing cards. She is good at it, and we are getting somewhere. She lays a card like a roof upon the cards she has already propped together. I am entranced by the delicacy of the structural balance, by the idea that something like this can be raised up from little flat pieces of cardboard. The face cards—jack, queen, king—intrigue me with their diagonal mirroring, and I feel them to possess some magical valence.

And that's most of what I can recover. My first impression of the world? I can't say for sure. But these few details and feelings—detail and feeling here almost inseparable—are embedded in me, vivid, distinct from all that comes later. I have nothing else specific; the rest is second-order business, interpretation. But I do find power in this rude primacy; the flashes feel freighted, important. I am haunted by the almost cubistic perception that has me viewing the scene from an altitude even as the room stretches away around me in a diffusion of oversize shapes—a table (my father's drafting board?), various clumps of furniture. I have a feeling, too—I don't think I'm inventing it—of other rooms and spaces away from where we are crouching. I say "we," but I cannot even with the greatest pressure of focus coax forth anything that would make this person Aija and not my mother or grandmother. Yet I know with absolute certainty that it was she, that something of her patience and initiative—and her easy love—was there in the making of that structure and in my excited absorption in the whole operation.

"She had a way with people, especially children," my mother tells me. "She loved you very much."

There are adjacent moments—glimpses from the same period. I'm in the kitchen in that apartment, in a high chair, spooning porridge—*manna* in Latvian—from a bowl. The special thing about the bowl, which has all my attention, is the fact that it has a clear plastic bottom, inside of which, suspended in a transparent gel, are a number of little colored fish. It is a renewable miracle. I eat up all my porridge, delighting especially in the buttery rifts; I scrape the bowl clean so that I can once again study these wonderful little shapes.

Or else, I am pushing hard at the mesh of a screen door—from the outside—frantic, trying to get in to get away from a ladybug that has landed on my arm. I am not afraid because it is a bug, but because it has little black spots on its shell-like wings. I was terrified of spotted things. I especially feared dalmatians. I could not even bear to be left alone in a room with any of my little Golden Books because they had printed on their endpapers repeating cartoon images of dalmatians. I cried out in terror when my mother closed the door. I had no language to explain myself.

How far can I get pulling out these various strands, these fragmentary glimpses? Is there any significance to my remembering the construction of that teetering house of cards? I don't imagine that I was in any way symbolizing my primitive awareness of the nature of life—*he remembers, before anything else, building a house of cards.* Could it have some relation to the fact that my father was—is—an architect, a designer of homes and buildings? I think not. I probably didn't know what my father did, except that he sat long hours at a desk, though he does have a story of my sitting on one side of his drafting table while he worked and suddenly—how was I sans diaper?—peeing all over everything. As for those colored fishes or that panic about dots and spots—just further evidence of the ultimately wonderful impenetrability of personality.

My early childhood unfolded almost entirely in Latvian; my

own children now speak only English. Apart from whatever impact the language and its various associations and resonances may have had, there was also the fact that I knew it was not the language spoken by most of the people around me—the neighbors, the mailman, the people I saw in stores. I must have known very early that my family was in some peculiar way turned in on itself.

The implications of difference are as elusive as they are important. I don't just mean the fact of starting out in one language and growing into another. I also mean the sense, more obscure, that once a person, a child, has been expelled from his first enclosure, there is no going back. With the learning of a new language, the original closed circuit is broken open: there are other words for everything. Now that I have English, even though my Latvian is still intact, I cannot return fully to the place, the feeling world, I then occupied. For that world was saturated by the sounds, constructions, meanings—the totality—of Latvian.

Sometimes, especially when I am feeling vulnerable or unmoored, I find myself testing the difference for myself. Lying in bed in the dark, I will think—or mouth—some primary word like "river" or "tree." I will try to focus on the sound-shape to see if I can get some purchase on the thing it names. It hardly ever works. There is some very subtle but undeniable distance there. But when I then say the Latvian words—*upe* and *koks*—I am fully connected, embedded, even though they are words I may not have spoken out loud for years. In spite of this, I inhabit the world, even in my thoughts, as an English speaker.

For most two- and three-year-olds, home is the center of the universe and everything else is the unknown other. Those who live in their native culture move into that larger other place by degrees, experiencing, learning, and annexing. But where that other is at the same time the other of a different language, the situation changes. The child does not just go into the surrounding world, he *translates* himself into it, and the process is fraught with difficulties.

I wish I had more memories to check against. I can only imagine the first collisions—Latvian-speaking child trying to play with American child. When did I realize—and in what way—that the other language was the language of everybody else and that my words for things were the anomalies? I don't ask this idly: much of my life has been shaped by this most basic feeling—the intense awareness of being outside of something that most others were on the inside of. It has never been enough for me to be like an American or even to pass for one in the eyes of most people. I wanted the mystery of *being* American, and I could never have it. And even though I've pushed my way close to the threshold—I married an American woman; we are raising our kids as American kids—I will never be able to cross over.

This is the child's view, and I am at some level still swayed by it, even though on many other levels—and increasingly—I exult in my difference. To be among Americans but not *of* them, this seems best. I feel myself as something recalcitrant inserted into a host tissue, a grain of resistance. I will do what I am asked, I will play all the required roles, but I will not come over. I couldn't if I wanted.

Early family life. I have so few impressions, and even some of the ones I have are, I suspect, after-the-fact interpolations from photographs and, in one bright instance, some eight-millimeter film footage. The fact of these artifacts—and my intense interest in studying them—has much to do, I'm sure, with my always relating to my earliest self from an outside vantage, as if the adult were a god, watching. I can *see* myself—in my powder blue snowsuit, or behind the wheel of my wonderful push-pedal car, or (and this is the film) being thrown up into the air and caught, over and over, at a mechanically accelerated rate, by my father. But I cannot, in memory, see much *as* myself. What do I recall?

The birth of my sister, Andra, when I was two and a half must have been a vivid marker. And I do have what feels like an authentic memory of standing on the grass outside a huge redbrick building—St. Joseph's Hospital, in Pontiac, where I, too, had been born—waving up at a high window. Do I remember seeing my mother, or my mother holding up my sister for view? I think not, though I am assured this happened. But the feeling of standing there, the indescribable sense of deepness that has somehow to do with the afternoon softness of the light—this I feel quite certain about.

Surrounding—and possibly undermining—this moment is a family story. When my mother was very pregnant, she asked me to carry a wastebasket down to the basement for her. I slipped on the way down, fell so hard that I suffered a concussion, and had to be rushed to Beaumont Hospital. "Your eye . . ." My mother always tells it the same way. "Your eye was black, as big as a grapefruit. I was horrified." The trauma was enough to send my mother into labor, and she was taken to nearby St. Joseph's. My father remembers spending days just driving back and forth between hospitals. It must have been right after I was released that we went to see my mother and sister.

But these few image clips of the hospital window are like partial reconstructions at an archaeological dig. Should there be more? Is there some expectation, some norm, about how much a child ought to remember? What do the great remembrancers have that I don't? Am I repressing my origins? I ask this for myself, as one who is always hoping to crack the code, solve the mystery. But I also ask as a parent, wondering what my children will end up retaining of the things that strike me, the adult, as being so important. And what becomes of these deep strata, the traces of our first encounters with the world, if they are lost to active memory? Do they become part of the stuff of personality itself?

My mother, my father—I hold no early images of their faces, no discernible memories of their bodies, none that I can bring back, at any rate. Have they disappeared to become part of how I am with my body—shy, reluctant? My mother breast-fed me for a while—so I'm told. Both parents must have held me tight in those deep butterfly chairs we always had. But I don't remember.

There is at the center of everything a terrible scorch hole. When I was not yet three, Tante Aija was killed right before my eyes by a hit-and-run driver. I was there, I saw it happen, yet I keep the story as something told to me. The images are gone.

Tante Aija was on her way to see us for her weekly visit. We were standing on one side of Woodward Avenue, waiting for her to cross from the bus stop. She had just stepped around the front of the bus, into the street, when a car swerved over from another lane and knocked her down.

My mother was holding Andra in her arms. She hurried us quickly to a neighbor's and went back. I don't know what happened next, and I have been reluctant to press my mother for details. Aija had been the dearest person of her childhood, close as any sister. There is no way to measure the effects of trauma.

I retain only the faintest wash of sensation from the afternoon. Aija had been carrying a shopping bag with groceries (had this blocked her view?), and these were scattered all over the northbound side of Woodward. That sprawl of things is vivid. Sorrow, mourning, the jolt of our great loss—I don't remember. I was not even three. But I know that for a very long time after, whenever we drove past the spot, I would look from the car window for signs of those groceries. Curious, detached, I thought of death as a mark on the road.

Soon after Aija's death, we moved from the Pontiac apartment—called, always, "Terraces"—to a small house in Birmingham that we would from that time on call "Henrietta," after the street. Some years ago there was a long-running TV show called *The Wonder Years,* which used for its opening some jumpy Super 8–looking footage of young kids mugging and posing on a street in a 1950s suburban development. Henrietta—not exactly, of course, but close, in feeling anyway.

When we moved there, to a small one-story house on a street packed with small one-story houses, I finally entered the social world. Before Henrietta I have no memories at all of playing with other kids. Now the street—the stage set of the world—comes into view. There are neighboring houses on either side. I have a strong feeling about the wide expanse of sidewalk in front of our house. My first turf. Recollection—which is almost always the recollection of perception—makes this area disproportionately wide. I see myself there, running back and forth between the sidewalk and the front steps of the house. I am possessed, building what I think will be a grand airplane. I have cardboard and crayons strewn all about. The air feels rich and lemony; the future tense extends only as far as the next task to be accomplished.

Our house was the second from the corner. From that corner it was only a short walk to Pierce School, where I attended kindergarten. These were my first real distances, and my primary sense of the size of the world derives in large part from what I absorbed from my first unaccompanied rambles between our front door and the schoolyard. Child's space, which seems in memory to be such a magnification of the known, is in many ways truer than what we later experience, richer. It is space known down to its most particular dents and striations. Playing with my own children brought this all back to me. When we are young—and small—we not only possess what feels to be endless time, but we are also physically present with an astonishing vigilance. We are true scientists. We lie on our stomachs on the carpet, crawl under tables, get behind couches. Pushed right up against things, we study them. Not for any reason, necessarily, just because they are there in front of our interrogating gazes. We lie in bed and stare at the screws on the wall-socket fixture; from the floor we contemplate the cord of the window shade, its frayed pull ring. Doorknobs, mattress stains, the accordion pleats of the little hallway radiator, the kitchen tile coming loose in the corner and revealing its tarry underside, the enchanting dial of the black rotary phone, its little portholes giving on to clusters of capital letters, all of which I am just learning to identify in school.

Outside, too, the prominence of texture. I knew so fully the minuscule patch of grass in front of our house, the walkway with its nubbled slabs of concrete, the wide, smooth curb, the pavement of the street with its faded yellow paint lines, so warm in the midday sun.

The best shade was in the backyard of a house catty-corner across the street. I had a friend with the wonderful name of Johnny Foreacre, and he and I and some of the neighborhood kids used to gather in the cool spot where the grass had long ago been worn away. One afternoon, I remember, some of us were playing with empty bottles we had found; somehow we decided that we should try to melt the glass and do something with the molten liquid. I volunteered to get some matches. My mother had a collection of matchbooks strung on horizontal threads across their bedroom wall. I was very aware of doing something forbidden as I made my way with deliberate casualness into my parents' bedroom and lifted one of the matchbooks from a spot where its absence might not be noticed. I knew I was doing something wrong, but I was also very keen that our experiment should proceed. I don't think I was ever found out. In any case, the initiative fizzled minutes later after we lit one or two matches and sent the whole book up in a quick *whoosh* of flame.

Only a few other fragments remain. My father helping me pull a very loose tooth with a string he has tied to a doorknob. Kneeling in our small living room, my ear pressed to the rough speaker cloth of our radio, listening to a western—*Gunsmoke,* I believe—entranced by the sound effects: the creaking doors, the receding footsteps, the sudden percussion of hooves. Lying on my stomach, a dollar bill positioned in front of me, determined to copy it perfectly. Why, I wonder, has no one ever thought of such a clever thing before?

. . .

Somewhere in the background, or up in the adult altitudes where important things happened, there was talk from my parents about moving again. They sat in the kitchen after dinner with the newspaper spread open on the table. We drove places on Sunday, my sister and I forced to squirm and fidget in the backseat of the car while my parents paced up and down in front of some house or disappeared inside with some person they met. Then, out of the blue—the usual way of things back then—came the surprising news that my sister and I would spend a few weeks living with my grandparents at Cranbrook.

Mike and Emilia—Ūm—had been living for several years now on the top floor of a small Bavarian-looking house up near the greenhouses and flower garden. They lived on the estate because Mike had a job at the art academy, helping to mount exhibits.

My grandparents' apartment, reached by loud wooden stairs that twisted up a narrow stairwell, was dark and dense with smells, nothing at all like the unmysteriously bright house at Henrietta. Enormous pine trees leaned over the road that passed right to the side of the house, and only my grandparents' bedroom, in the back overlooking the garage roof and the gardens, got any sun. But sun was not important here. This was an old people's place. It had that quality of silence—silence that has gone unbroken for a long time, which held the quiet movements and separate thoughts of two people who no longer had much to say to each other, but who were now bound by their own strange history.

My grandparents were, I think, glad to have the two of us there. My grandmother suddenly had some tasks to give point to her day and an audience for the clucking that Mike had long ago learned to parry with a simple *"Jā, mīcīt"*—*mīcīt* being one of those private endearments I never understood. Ūm fussed over us with great energy, rousing us and getting us dressed for the day, herding us to our places in the cool, roomy kitchen, where she prepared the one food I associate exclusively with this short period in our lives: hard-boiled eggs that were peeled and cut lengthwise and served with a dab of butter melting on the yolk. Sometimes now I will think of those eggs and feel a burst of secure happiness, a sensation that over and above its particular pleasure conveys a deeper message about the essential rightness of things. Why these eggs? I don't know. Nor do I know—remember—how it felt being away from our parents for so long.

They did, of course, come to see us from time to time—they were still at Henrietta—and I have a very clear image of my mother on one of her visits standing in that kitchen singing the Doris Day song "Que Será, Será," which was so popular then. I thought she looked very pretty and happy, even though the song, as I listened, seemed to me the saddest thing I had ever heard. I didn't otherwise think much about the future, but here was a jolt—whatever will be, will be—made irresistible by the lilt of the melody.

But a child cannot think for long about any time but the time of the moment. I was six, my sister was not yet four, and we were fully immersed in the time of childhood, that sticky awareness that marks the things but not the space between them, and that is the closest we ever come to creature life. We stayed in that little house, billeted on the living room couch, for only two weeks. But it survives in my memory as an epoch, a long dream embedded in a daily life that was itself in the throes of some great transformation.

Our Cranbrook stay was a procession of long summer days, days that began with the sound of running water in the bathroom across the hall. Other noises were added on in layers: the back-and-forth creaking of that bathroom door, the bursts of muffled conversation, the steady thudding of my grandmother's passage through the adjacent room as she made her way to the kitchen to begin a whole new set of disturbances. I have always loved waking up to the clatter of other people's purposeful activity. Back then I would lie with the sheet pulled tightly under my chin and take in the signs of the morning—the slow lancing of pine-branch shadows across the blind, the little puffs and fidgets of the curtain, the pretend irritation of my sister once I began to coax her with my foot.

I was being mildly sadistic. Andra was still very much under my grandmother's watch. She did not have the freedom I did—to go anywhere within calling radius of the kitchen window. I would remind her of this and a good many other things besides with a few well-placed elbow digs followed by an expression of hammily feigned innocence that would reduce her to furious pouting.

The Cranbrook estate, conceived by the Booth family—Detroit's early newspaper barons—had been designed and landscaped by the great Finnish architect Eliel Saarinen (the father of Eero Saarinen, whom my father had, in a sense, come to America to work with), with an appropriately baronial manse on a hill overlooking a serene man-made lake, with private schools conjured in the British mode, museums, an outdoor Greek theater, and extensive gardens to which flower enthusiasts made pilgrimages every Sunday in the summer—it was a dream of aristocratic Europe set down in southeastern Michigan. But of all this I knew nothing. To me it was where my grandparents lived, and my encounters and discoveries were firsts, small glinting details added to the picture of the world I had begun more earnestly to assemble. This as much as anything else created the feeling of magic—I was finally pushing out beyond the apron of sidewalk in front of our house on Henrietta.

Mike and Ūm lived above an Italian family, the Morantes. Wally, the father, was one of the large staff of Italian caretakers, most of whom lived on a road of little houses on the far side of the estate. He was a handsome man, with thick black hair and a strong, expressive face. On Sundays he put on a policeman's uniform and presided over the main visitors gate—he seemed to be a person of enormous consequence. Dorothy, his wife, was fat in the way of the "mamma mia" and wore baggy print housedresses. She called my grandmother "Millie" and would often yell to her up the stairwell that she was going shopping and did we need anything. The yelling was the main thing about the Morante family. Wally and Dorothy did nothing but yell—in anger, in good spirits, I was never sure which. I had never heard such noises between grown people before and was sometimes scared. Especially of Wally. He was the loudest—the whole street would be ringing with his commands, his curses, and then his unexpected cannonings of laughter. I would not go near the man unless I was with Artie, the younger of his two sons, my friend.

Artie was more or less my age. He played with me some days and took me around, both of us making it a point to stay out of arm's reach of his big brother, Vince, called "Vincy." Vincy, moody and handsome like some teen idol, though I don't think he was even yet a teen, had charge of Artie—a task he clearly resented. Vincy and Artie were always at it, gibes leading to prods, prods to slaps, slaps suddenly breaking into such caterwauling fights that both would be called in for punishment—more slaps and yells— and I would be left to play alone.

Vincy and Artie were the lords of that whole kingdom. They knew their way around everything; they knew the workers and the kids who lived down in the row houses. They had access to the greenhouses and storage areas. Most thrillingly, they came and went as they pleased in the great garage that was down in the yard below their own place and was reached by a separate road.

The garage was where Wally had his office—an open cubicle on one side of the cavernous space where all the trucks and buses were brought in for repair. In the mornings he raised up the great green sectioned doors—a string of harsh wooden explosions—and the rest of the day vehicles of all sorts drove in and out and men stood in the shadowy entrance, talking and flipping onto the sunny pavement their cigarette butts, which Wally would sweep up every so often with a long-handled broom. It was a man's place, saturated with the sweet smell of exhaust and oil, and my pulse would quicken whenever Artie took me there with him.

Once, I remember, I followed my friend, both of us creeping along the side walls, playing at something, heading toward the far back. Artie wanted me to see something. "For real," he kept saying. "For real." At one point I peered through the space between two parked grounds trucks and saw Wally. He was wearing a white T-shirt, sitting fully reclined in his swivel chair, smoking a cigarette, lord of all he surveyed. "Look!" Artie was nudging me. There, on the back wall, somehow hanging from a nail, was an enormous furry thing. An animal. "It's a coon," announced Artie. "My dad shot it last night. It was in the garbage can." I could not stop looking. Now I picked out the little paws hanging down, the pointy nose, the soft tail with rings that looked like they had been carefully painted on.

I played with Artie when I could, but mostly I was by myself. Not allowed to go down to the lake, and afraid of venturing too near the garages, I often wandered up and down the curving road in front of the house or else hiked up my courage and explored the dark pine woods that began right across the street.

I was entering, naively of course, the landscaper's mind. I followed the needle-strewn paths as they wound around to sudden exposed clearings; I found old stone benches and fountains; in the distance, across a small, gracefully arched footbridge that spanned part of the entry road, were the eerily echoing spaces of the deserted Greek theater. I would stand there, strangely conscious of myself, listening as my shouts turned hollow and died away.

One hot afternoon, I remember, I was wandering by myself on the lower part of the road, across from a small soccer field, heading in the direction of the greenhouses and garage. The heat had softened a seam of new tar in the road, and I suddenly found myself on my knees, occupied with prying bits of the stuff loose with a chip of stone. The rich, oily smell and the perfect viscousness of the black taffy were a revelation. I collected enough to fashion for myself a golf-ball-size ball, and then I had an inspiration. After running across to the greenhouses, to the outdoor spigot, I plunged the ball into a sputtering column of ice-cold water and felt it immediately harden up. This oversize marble I then rolled back and forth across the paved area in front of the garage, feeling very pleased with myself.

The vitality of that memory for me is in the sensations. The heat of the afternoon, the air of desertion everywhere around me, as if this were siesta time in some remote Mediterranean backwater, as if I were the only person still awake in a world enchanted into sleep. Then, too, the increments of my immersion, the feeling of my knees digging into the pebbly road surface, the stretchy pulls of the warm tar, the deep, sweet smell of it on my fingers. I am flush, replete. There is no measuring the moment and no setting it alongside other moments for comparison. It is a scene, like only a few others, that juts out of my childhood.

Other details from that time are distinct, if somewhat less charged: the stems and leaves of the giant rubber plants my grandparents kept in their living room; the smooth, dense stone of an Eskimo carving on a low table nearby; and the strange thrill I shared with my sister, of watching television for the first time.

How things change. Now the object of our patronizing nostalgias, black-and-white television in the mid-1950s flashed with the power of its newness. We would all sit together in those late summer evenings—Ūm, Mike, Andra, and I—watching what was to me the incomprehensible chaos of *Amos 'n' Andy* or the stark matter-of-factness of shows like *Cheyenne* and *The Rifleman*. Later—sometimes I was still awake—came the air force segment, the serious voice intoning, "We have broken the surly bonds of earth," as jet fighters went streaking toward the horizon.

Of all the dark corners and crannies in my grandparents' apartment, by far the most compelling was my grandfather's closet directly by the upstairs entryway. Coming up the steps from the outside, enclosed in that hot, ringing stairwell, I could always make out the first trace of that broth of smells that became almost overpowering when Mike opened that little closet door. This was where he kept his things—the dozens and dozens of tubes of oil paints, their colors banded across the middle; the myriad little jars of tacks, coils of hanging wire, and scraping blades; the various solvents, including the turpentine in which he soaked his brushes and which I would have happily stood around inhaling if Mike had not warned me away.

Here were stacked canvases on frames, some blank, others with lines sketched in charcoal. The closet was too narrow for two people, so while Mike stood under the hanging bulb making his preparations—selecting the paints he might need for that day's palette—I waited in the doorway, staring up as often as not at the horseshoe he had hung on a nail high on the wall. He had told me once that he had found it on a street in a city in Europe and that he kept it for good luck. I did not know this superstition and thought it was wonderful that we had such a guarantee of good fortune in our keeping.

I waited at the closet door on those special mornings when Mike had decided to paint by the lake. It would be my job to help him carry his equipment and keep him company, though even at my age I understood that I did not have much company to offer. But he seemed glad enough to have me come along.

I went because I liked carrying Mike's paint box and liked playing down by the lake while he worked. But mainly I hoped that Mr. Vishnevsky, my grandfather's Russian friend, would decide that it was a good day to come fishing.

The preparations for departure seemed to take forever. Mike was a slow-moving and methodical man. He dried his brushes carefully, running the bristles back and forth along a special rag; he hovered over his arsenal of tubes with the same deliberation with which he would later ponder the canvas before applying even the slightest dab of color. The tubes were then arranged in the box, the brushes arrayed alongside. Then, when he finally began fussing with his easel and canvas, Mike would send me out into the kitchen, where Ūm was getting our lunch ready.

Seeing my sister sitting there at the breakfast table, her braids fixed for the day, the prospect of endless indoor errands with Ūm before her, made me feel mature and capable. Ūm, however, did not understand just how mature and capable. For she would start in promptly on her list of cautions and bewares. I would nod, listening to Mike getting everything ready at the top of the stairs. "Don't get too close to the water. Always be where Mike can see you. Don't drink cold water if you get too hot, and don't be running in the sun all day." She would lean over to make sure she had my attention, and then she would call, "Addie—"

"Addie" was short for Adolph, Mike's middle name, and Ūm used it when she wanted him to listen. She would wait for Mike to show himself in the kitchen doorway and then renew her instructions, adding a few new flourishes. Sit in the shade, rest after you eat . . . He greeted her words with a compliant expression, nodded when she finished. And then we were ready. With easel and canvas wedged under his arm and the bag of lunches in his other hand, Mike started making his way down the stairs. The paint box, with its shiny brass clasp, leaned against the wall. For me.

The walk down to the lake could seem very long, depending on the day and whom we encountered. To reach the path leading through the trees, we first had to go down a steep flight of stairs and then down the center aisle of one part of the flower gardens. There was every chance that Mike might meet up with one of the gardeners and start to talk. For though he was taciturn at home, and with me, he genuinely loved plants and flowers and all kinds of gardening talk. When we did meet one of his friends, we would stop for a time, Mike setting down his load so that he could wander about the flowers to have a look. I would wait patiently with my own load, staring at the enormous watering cans and the serious-looking tools that were laid out along the edge of the pebble path.

Eventually, though, we would make it through the stone archway at the garden's end and start down the path between the great pines. Sudden coolness and silence—the long, tawny needles underfoot and the first premonition of the lake in the near distance. Mike seemed happy at these times. The closed-off air he had indoors blew off.

At last, after crossing a wide, grassy field, we would arrive at my grandfather's painting spot, an open patch right on the shore of the lake, with a view of the boathouse to the left and of a flat little bridge with a wrought-iron rail on the right, beyond which a small waterfall delivered water to the first of a series of what were for some reason called "Japanese" ponds. As soon as I had set down the paint box, I was free to roam, Mike's only restriction being that I never get entirely out of earshot—though now, recalling this, I realize that I never even heard the man raise his voice. This allowed me considerable latitude, for I could play almost anywhere along the shore, or in the boathouse, or even back in the woods we had just emerged from. Mike didn't need to signal when it was time to eat—I knew.

I don't remember much of what I did—I was a six-year-old boy—but I do recall spying on Mike from different vantages and occasionally trying to sneak up on him without being spotted. Sad to say, he was a disappointing quarry. When I studied him from whatever hidden spot I had found, he was usually standing motionless. I watched him stare out over the lake for long periods and then slowly tilt his gaze back to the canvas. Back and forth, back and forth, as if he were moving things in one direction and then the other with just his eyes. He hardly ever painted—painted, that is, the way I imagined real painters painted. The brush was in his hand, but it was as if he had forgotten it was there.

When it was time for lunch, we moved to a shady area not far from the boathouse. In memory, the hill where we sit, and the path that followed the shore—indeed, the whole estate—is deserted. My grandfather and I unpack the sandwiches neatly wrapped in waxed paper and secured with rubber bands. Do we talk? I honestly don't recall that we ever exchanged more than a few comments. Instead, comfortable silence, his benign distractedness.

Only now, forty years later, knowing parts of his story, do I find his inwardness mysterious and compelling.

I did not wander off much after lunch. I knew that if Mr. Vishnevsky were to come, it would be soon, so I would park myself in the grass near Mike's easel and study the far shore down by the other bridge, which was where he usually appeared.

And then, suddenly, there he was, moving toward us along the fringe of the lake. With his legs hidden behind the tall shore grasses, he seemed to be not so much walking as slowly inflating—a figure with a fishing pole, tackle box, and a wicker creel. I knew he had seen us and was coming to be near my grandfather.

Mr. Vishnevsky's arrival was Mike's signal to change momentum. He would start to hatch out from his meditative silence then, and though he would still be painting—looking outward, slowly mixing a color on his palette, and then examining it studiously before leaning forward to touch just the tip of his brush to the canvas—he would also be able to talk. In Russian.

This may have been the basis of their friendship, I don't know. My grandfather knew Russian from the years when he had studied art at the Moscow Academy. Mr. Vishnevsky *was* Russian. I thought it was as simple as that, but of course it wasn't. Things between Latvians and Russians can never be simple. This friendship was probably an exception. I never found out what Mr. Vishnevsky's (my grandparents both called him "Vishnefsks") story was, but I could tell from the looks and gestures and the quality of their low chuckling laughter that there was goodwill between them. I know that my grandfather was always pleased when I pointed out Mr. Vishnevsky in the distance. *"Labi,"* he would say. Good. "Maybe he will let you try to catch a fish."

When Mr. Vishnevsky reached our spot, he would set his things on the grass and then step over to have a look at what my grandfather was doing. "Pyotr . . . ," he would say, patting me on the head. Then off would come his cap—folded neatly and put with his things—so that I could contemplate the shiny dome of his head. If he saw me looking up at him, he might jokingly give it a rap with his knuckle.

Mr. Vishnevsky would stand behind Mike's canvas, bunching and flexing his massive brows. After a time he might make some comment, to which Mike would mutter back, also in Russian, or else he might point out something with the end of his brush. With that they would be off, filling the air with their incomprehensible syllables.

I loved listening to the language, hearing that fluid dip at the back of the throat. Mike suddenly seemed so different. He had only to speak a few sentences in Russian and I was able to imagine him inside a completely different life—a life that had nothing to do with Ūm and her instructions and the weary accepting tone with which he replied to her.

They talked and talked, and though I understood nothing, I was not bored. I watched everything attentively. I knew that Mr. Vishnevsky would soon seat himself on the grass near my grandfather and, extracting a few slices of soft bread from his pocket, start making bread balls. These were bait for the fish. Carp. He would pinch the bread until it was completely firm, adding bits of spit with his thumb, and then, at long last—after what felt like an almost intolerable interval—he would rouse himself and move over to where I waited, next to his tackle box and fishing pole.

And then, once, it happened. Mr. Vishnevsky saw me watching him and he winked. With a single gruff gesture he extended the butt end of his pole toward me. "Fish?" I was at his side in a flash. Not only did I get to slip the bread ball onto the hook as I had seen Mr. Vishnevsky do, but I was allowed to cast the line with its bobber, sinker, and hook out over the still, murky water. And there I sat, alone, triumphant, waiting for the bobber to stir while Mr. Vishnevsky went back to talk to my grandfather.

I can summon up the sensation, just how it happened. I am sitting Indian style in the grass, staring intently at the red-and-white bobber, but staring past it, too, out over the lake. I am exultant. I hold the smooth cork end of the pole and the line plunges into the water and connects me with the whole world. Everything gathers around that stillness. I don't know how long the feeling lasts, but at some point reverie takes over, because when the bobber suddenly vanishes—*plonk*—I am entirely unprepared.

In an instant—so it seems—I am on my feet, calling out, clutching the grip with all the strength I possess. Even so, I feel myself being pulled steadily forward, toward the muddy edge. I feel giddy, sick. The pole is slowly slipping from my hands and I don't know how much longer I can keep my balance. I am about to cry out when, like a dream of rescue, I feel Mr. Vishnevsky's arms come around me from behind and his two big hands close over my own.

Together we got the fish to shore. To my astonished eyes it was enormous, fearsome, punching its tail against the grass, opening and closing its bloody-looking gills. *"Ya,"* said Mr. Vishnevsky. He moved quickly, which surprised me, for he was a short and stocky man. Holding the fish to the ground with one hand, he produced from somewhere a flat stone; this he knocked a few times against the fish's head. Then, when the thing was still, he pulled a sheet of newspaper—Russian—from his creel. After bending over to dip part of the paper in the water, he wrapped it around the fish. "He sleeps," said Mr. Vishnevsky, finally looking at me. He was puffing slightly from the exertion. With the same gruff gesture with which he had handed me the pole earlier, he now passed the bundle to me. I stared at it, alarmed, then slowly put out my arms. "For *Oma* when you go home," he said. If he winked at my grandfather, I didn't see. I was too awed by my achievement and my sense of mission. It did not occur to me to wonder what my grandmother would do with the fish.

When we started back later that afternoon, my grandfather carried all of his equipment—easel, canvas, and paint box—and I followed, gripping the stunned fish with both hands. But even though I had the lighter load, I fell behind on the path going up through the woods. It was growing dusky. I kept stopping to make sure that the wrapping was secure. I tried not to look at the head protruding from one end—the enormous, still eye and the fleshy lips, which, with a mounting sense of panic, I thought would start moving at any moment. I tried to call to my grandfather, but he was already making the turn into the gardens. I closed my eyes and ran panting after him.

"Ach," said my grandmother when I came bursting into the kitchen with the fish. I held it toward her in the standard posture of a man making an offering, but she didn't take it at first. She paced back and forth in front of the sink. She said it again— "Ach"—and then, in a tone of unaccountable exasperation, she spat out: "Vishnefsks!"

After taking the bundle, Ūm hurried down the hallway to the bathroom. I was right at her heels, and my sister was at mine. In the bathroom, standing tall on four clawed feet, was their old bath-tub. Pressing the bundle firmly to her chest, Ūm bent over and inserted the rubber stopper. Then she turned on the faucet. When there were a few inches of water in the tub, she held one corner of the paper and let the fish slide in. It was enormous, like something from an earlier era. We stood side by side, the three of us, watching. Slowly, fin twitch by fin twitch, the fish revived. In a few minutes it was steadily following the circumference of the tub.

I went to sleep that night feeling that there was some kind of magic in the house.

The next morning, standing in the same spot, I watched as my grandmother let the water out of the tub. Then, drawing a deep sighing breath—for she always told us that she could not bear to hurt even a moth—she grasped the fish in the middle and clubbed it hard against the rim of the tub. Wrapping it in another sheet of wetted newspaper, she suddenly fixed all of her attention on me. "Do not tell Vishnefsks," she said. I nodded solemnly.

Later, again carrying the fish, I accompanied my grandfather back to the lake, my job now being to return my prize to its proper home.

A day or two later, my parents came to collect us. They had found us a new house, they said, and in the early fall we would be moving.

CHAPTER 3

THE MAIN THING ABOUT CHILDHOOD, MY CHILDHOOD, ANYWAY, WAS that it felt permanent. Not that I ever thought about notions like permanence back then. When you have permanence as your assumption, you experience things as just being—that's all. It's only later, when you suddenly get that you were wrong, that every aspect of that world looks different. You see that there's a border, a limit, beyond which what you thought would go on in the same way forever changes, turns into something else. When you understand that and feel the true sadness of it, then you have stopped being a child.

1830 East Tahquamenon. When I was just starting first grade at Pierce School in Birmingham, we moved. To Bloomfield Hills, which most people now think of as being rich and suburban, like Shaker Heights, but to me—then—it felt like we had landed on the very edge of the known world. Lone Pine Road was still unpaved and rutted, and our street, some ways in, was dustier and even more rutted. Around us there were three or four houses set apart on big lots, with open or wooded areas everywhere you looked. The world was new—people had just gotten to it a few years ago. Right nearby, down another dirt road, Indian Trail, was the fence that marked off Cousins Farm, which ran as far as the eye could see, with cornfields, grazing land for cows, extended pine woods, and a large weedy pond down in the central valley. The rural feel was everything.

Mine was, in those early days, a world of thickets and paths, and it began beckoningly with a cleft in the bushes right behind our house, which itself looked forlornly modern in the midst of so much greenery. If I worked it right, I could follow one path up the hill in our backyard, push through a scrubby area of sumac—those little weedy trees we liked to break and peel—and with a very short interruption across a corner of the back neighbor's yard re-enter woods, following trails down alongside Breedlove's yard, behind Dwelley's unfinished house, staying hidden all the way to the top of another hill, where Indian Trail ended. There, just opposite, was the preferred entry to Cousins Farm, and once over the barbed-wire fence it was possible to be out of sight of all houses and markings of civilization for hours on end, utterly unsupervised, safe from all adult intrusions so long as we kept one eye open for the farmer on his tractor.

Though things were changing all the time, with houses going up here and there, each construction the occasion for new hauls of scrap lumber for new forts that we built on the far side of our wooded hill, the sense of wild spaces—Cousins Farm, the big swamp down by Cindy Bette's house, other extended pockets that seemed immune to the bulldozer—lasted out my grade-school years. Now, of course, it's all gone. When I go back to visit my parents, once a year or so, I can scarcely even remember how things were then. The roads are all paved, and the lots are all built over. And Cousins Farm, the place where I spent my best hours, was years ago sold off and subdivided into a posh community of half-million-dollar homes built around a golf course. The pond where we fished for bluegills is now landscaped and—this baffles me—glittery blue; the open stretches where cows often grazed are fairways. But this is by now such a familiar American story.

In the house next door to us lived the Malones—Sherry, who was a year older and with whom I actually played doctor for a short but very exciting period not long after we moved in; and Jimmy, who was Andra's age. We hardly ever saw their mother,

Fran, but their father, Dick, whom my father for some obscure reason insisted on calling "Richard"—maybe because he called my father "Gunner" instead of "Gunnar"—was very much in evidence, tinkering, mowing, or fussing with the army relics he kept in his garage. Dick—to us always "Jimmy's dad"—had seen action in the war, had been a GI, and he had helmets and pistols and a webbed belt and all sorts of other paraphernalia that he would on certain occasions set out for us to look at. He looked like my then ideal of an American dad, with a bristly crewcut and an eagle tattoo that we could see whenever he took off his shirt. Which was often. Dick Malone mowed his lawn religiously, at least once a week, using one of the early sit-down tractor mowers, almost never without an open can of beer propped between his legs and a lit cigarette between his lips, and I loved to watch him move in and out of view as he rode circular patterns around their sizable property.

Across the street, in a surprisingly small bungalow house, lived Chris Chrysler, who had two much older sisters and lived the neglected easeful life of a kid whose parents always worked. His mother, Ethel, had bright red hair. She worked in some department at Northland, a huge store that I've heard described as America's first mall, and whenever I saw her at home she was sitting at their kitchen table with her shoes off and her feet propped up, smoking cigarettes that she extracted one after the next from a special clasped little purse.

Opposite the Chryslers lived Billy Wilbur, whose father was a TV repairman who came to our house a few times when we finally got a set. He was a fat, friendly man, nothing at all like Billy, who was skinny, wore glasses, and made himself known to the world only on those few summer evenings when he stood on the little hill by the side of his house and flew a motorized airplane on a long lead wire. The Kirkpatricks, two neat and coddled boys, lived only a few houses away, but they might as well have lived in Texas for all that we ever saw them. Otherwise, I remember mainly houses staffed with reclusive adults, all those older people we never saw or thought about until Halloween, when we would ring their door-bells and discover, shocked, that they knew who we were and where we lived.

Then, separate from all the others, were the Hendersons—Neil, Mark, and Jack—the three brothers who pretty much ruled over our end of the world, and their pretty older sister, Rose. They had my attention. I admired and feared them and craved more than anything to be of their ilk. To be a Henderson. Their father, also Neil, had died of a massive heart attack a year or two after we moved in, a tragedy that in my mind conferred unlimited tragic permission on the kids. They were raised by their mother, Kate, a short, pepper-haired woman with a smoky voice—she taught school somewhere in the area—and Rose, who sometimes also baby-sat for us and whom I would terrorize with great hilarity by pretend-ing that I had just seen a mouse in the kitchen.

All three boys were rowdy and enterprising, and they seemed to roam at will through the world. I would hear them outside, yelling and playing, long after my sister and I were already in our paja-mas. Neil, the oldest, was already in the upper grades when I be-came aware of him. He was a muscular kid with a blond crewcut, taped-up glasses, and a reputation for fighting that went with him everywhere. He instigated trouble, and then when he fought it was with a murderous frenzy that brought teachers running across the playground. We all felt that there was something slightly off about Neil. This was confirmed years later when word came down the high school grapevine that he had almost died jumping out of a dormitory window while on a bad LSD trip. But kids sensed this edginess even then and walked wide circles around him. The lore at Walnut Lake School was that Neil had once gotten the "paddle," which hung on the wall behind the desk of the principal, Mr. Schumm, and which, as we all saw, had large holes drilled in it to allow for a faster downstroke. I don't know that Neil ever said a word to me—he was always up there, ahead, with the gangs of mighty elders, already gunning around in cars while we were still building tree forts.

Mark, his younger brother, a year or two older than me, was somewhat more approachable. He had all the protection and cachet of being Neil's brother but had an easy slangy manner. Like Neil, Mark was a crewcutted blond powerhouse, tall and built for feats of daring. Somewhere, somehow, he had lost his front tooth and wore a silver one in its place. I idealized him for years. I thought that my whole life would be different if I had but a bit of his magic. In the world as I dreamed it then, Mark was everywhere—in the big tree by the side of his house, hanging by his knees from one of the upper branches; swimming his breathtakingly fast crawl down at the lake (he became a champion swimmer in high school); or coming up from Cousins Farm in the late afternoon with a string of fish in his hand.

Alas, the only Henderson I got to know was Jack—"Jackie"—who was younger than me and who lacked in my eyes the mighty family aura. Though he was scrappy enough—willing to go after his brothers in a blind fury when teased—he was also in some way sneaky, the kind of kid who could very well turn on you in the middle of some schoolyard showdown. My clearest memory of Jackie is of being with him in the woods behind Breedlove's when he stepped into a nest of red ants. I stood by ineffectually as he flailed and screamed, stripping off his pants and underpants and plucking at the ants that were streaming over his bald little penis.

But these are impressions gathered over years of living on Tahquamenon. When we first moved there, I knew only that I was being hurled without much warning into the dark and perplexing world of Walnut Lake School. I have forgotten almost everything about those first years, but the sense of literal darkness has stayed, a kind of retinal afterimage. It was not a frightening darkness, but neither was it soothing. The simple fact is that for some reason the corridor that ran alongside all of the lower-grade classrooms was unlit. And the corridor dominated everything. I stood there waiting to get a drink from the fountain or hanging my jacket on the peg outside our room. Late in my first-grade year I fell off the playground merry-go-round and broke my leg. When my mother came to get me, I was carried down that dark passageway toward the far exit, where the sunlight suddenly flashed off the square of window glass. When school ended that year, we lined up there for final dismissal, all of us waiting anxiously for the bell to ring, someone then starting up the rhyming song "School's out, school's out, teacher let the monkeys out." So much else has drowned, but the feeling of that dark waxy corridor survives.

The next year I was in second grade, and while I could look at the class photo today and name off almost every kid, I have only one real memory that feels etched into place. Once again that corridor is present, only now as a backdrop. Our whole class—Miss Carpenter's—is lined up inside the room, waiting to go to lunch or recess, and I am standing right by the open doorway, talking to a girl named Jess Zachariah. She is bragging to me that she can already read, indeed that she has finished something called *The Wizard of Oz*. I don't know what kind of book that is, but I'm suitably impressed. Jess faces me, and the dark corridor is just behind her. I distinctly recall my pleasure in the brightness of the room and the consequentiality of our conversation.

From that moment on (so it seems now, anyway), Jess and I were always warily friendly with each other—and deeply competitive. With second grade began the various contests that were conducted a few times a year in all the grades, the spelling bees and "number downs," in which the teacher blazed through the times tables and whoever missed at their turn had to sit down. My father had drilled me in multiplication, and I usually won the number down. But from second grade on Jess never lost a spelling bee—the more prestigious of the events.

The memory of that short exchange by the door would take on great significance years later when Jess reappeared in my life. I know I tried very hard then to reconstruct that original moment, hoping to discover that there had been some special tremor of premonition in the air between us. But no, I think we simply faced each other then, as we would in class after class until junior high. We scuffed our shoes against the linoleum and waited for Miss Carpenter to dismiss us.

I didn't have any special friends during those first few years at Walnut Lake. Like most kids, I moved around as part of the great playground pack. At recess time we would gather into teams to play dodgeball or prison-ball, wall-ball or tetherball, or, if it was winter, we would throw snowballs at each other and slide around at the back ravine. I stayed near Bobo Spriggel, Mark Bergeron, Marc Crorey, Steve Chudik, and a few others. I love to say the names; each one releases a sharp flash impression, an essence. Dave Van Horn, Steve Driver, Steve Whitmer, Frank Vaclavic . . . I can recall exactly the flushed, close-to-tears look that Steve Driver would get, and feel, almost on my skin, the elbowy aggression of Bobo Spriggel. I see the neat checkered shirts that Clark Greenshields always wore, neat T-shirt underneath, or the strangely dressy pants that David Mariano had on most days and which marked him off as somehow belonging to a different tribe. Everything was so intimate and close range. How deeply we inhaled each other's smells and how well we knew each other's bodies, what impact and insult they were capable of.

There were two classes for every grade at Walnut Lake, and the groups were always being reshuffled. Kids moved in and out of focus over the years. Someone you had scarcely seen since third grade might suddenly be right beside you, borrowing your paste, asking to be on your team. It worked the other way, too, of course. If a friend was assigned—banished—to the other class, he was to most purposes lost for the year. Partnerships could still be struck up during recess time, of course, but in some deeper way that person had become part of a new system.

My friendship with Howard was different, had almost nothing to do with class assignments. Howard arrived at our school in the middle of the third grade. He was walked in, in time-honored fashion, by Mr. Schumm, the principal, and introduced with awkward formality to Miss Macklin, our teacher, and the rest of the class. Miss Macklin smiled and acted much more teacherish than she usually did. She made a big point of assigning the boy a seat and walking him over. Only when Mr. Schumm left did the class resume. Though, of course, nothing was the same and no one was concentrating. Everyone was now craning over toward the window where he sat. The new kid. He was more than a little bit odd, and everyone knew it. You could tell from the looks that were going around, by the way that some of the girls were cutting their eyes around to see what the boys were thinking. He—"Howard" was the unfortunate name—had a large head, with rabbity front teeth and high color in his cheeks. He wore his shirt buttoned all the way up—obviously his mother still dressed him—and his pants were hiked high.

Nowadays the word for Howard would be "nerd," but we didn't know that word. Still, the concept was there in everyone's mind. By the end of morning recess, Arquette, his last name, had mutated into "Egghead," a nickname that would stick for the rest of his time at Walnut Lake. By the end of the day he had already been in a fight—a few of the more venturesome, or cruel, boys had discovered that he could be baited into throwing tantrums, that his flashpoint was right under the skin.

Howard was seated in the row right next to mine, one desk ahead, so I found myself studying him at close range, memorizing the shape of the back of his head, taking in the vulnerable-looking lobe of his ear—it seemed to redden every so often of its own accord—the rigidity of his posture. There was, overall, something soft and undefended about him, the faintly embarrassed flush of his cheeks, and I think I knew before he ever spoke that he was not going to fit in, that there was going to be trouble.

Howard's strangeness gave rise to all sorts of taunts, and before I even knew him I felt somehow enlisted as his defender, not that I ever dared to come out for him publicly—my own standing was not that secure. I see him, very early on, alone, facing off against a whole group of kids. He was not heroic, but he was not cowardly, either. He was just a third-grade kid, but he stood his ground with a weary, practiced air. He had been teased before. He was trying to be good about taking it. But then, unexpectedly, thrillingly, he detonated. He went after one of the group, Larry Driver, I think, Steve's twin brother, with a red fury, his arms flailing, his face in a terrible grimace. Larry was hammering him back, shocked. I turned to see one of the fifth-grade teachers, Mr. Faust, hurrying toward us from the side door. I was rooted in place, electrified. Something was really happening here—there would be no going back. The girls had lined up, too, and were watching from a slight distance. The nearby jungle gym reared up stark and strange, no one on it. And then, faster than anyone would have thought, it was over. The grand inflated moment collapsed. Mr. Faust had Howard on one side, Larry on the other, and was marching them both at a serious pace down to Mr. Schumm's office.

Another time, still in the early days of his arrival, Howard exploded in class. I don't remember exactly how it happened. There was some triggering insult I missed. But then I looked over and saw Billy McKenzie rocking in his seat, faster and faster, as he did whenever he got the least bit excited. And some of the kids up front were turning around in their seats. I kept my gaze fixed on the back of Howard's head. He was sitting utterly immobile. I tilted forward to check his profile. Nothing.

Miss Macklin was somehow involved in this provocation. I saw kids looking back and forth between Howard and the teacher's desk. Then, in that ancient familiar way, everything grew absolutely still. Everyone was poised, holding a breath while Miss Macklin translated herself from behind her desk to the front of the room. She was staring intently at Howard. In a low, menacing voice I had never heard her use before—our pretty young teacher—she said: "Bring the pen-cil up to my desk. Now." Howard still did not move, but I could see his ears start to color. The silence between them held, and then, just when it had become excruciating for us to sit one instant longer in this way, Howard leapt to his feet. He had his pencil in his hand and he flung it, point first, like a spear, at Miss Macklin. And without waiting to see where it landed (on the floor right by her feet) or what her reaction would be, he ran in his high-elbowed way from his seat to the door, and with a shattering slam of that door he was gone.

This was more than any of us had dared to hope for—a royal blowout. We turned as one to Miss Macklin to see how we ought to be acting. What a shock! Miss Macklin was still standing by her desk. There was a moment before she caught herself—we all saw it—when she appeared almost happy. Her face shone. She looked at us as if we were all in league together, joined by our contempt for this misfit, this "queer." Then, promptly, she caught herself. Installing the ever-reliable Mark Bergeron in her seat to act as monitor, she picked up her purse and hurried out the door.

This was Howard's real debut, and it was promptly inscribed in the mythology. For the next few years, Howard was the guy who had gone crazy in Macklin's class; he was the oddball, the egghead. And though he was grudgingly allowed into playground games, he was never granted full status. Howard was a liability—all the kids understood that.

In spite of this powerful collective recognition—and probably in some ways because of it—Howard became my best friend. The bond was established quickly. One day after school he appeared at our front door. I could see him from the living room couch where I was sitting. Oddly, my heart did not sink. Rather, I felt a flash of expectancy, almost as if I already knew that we were marked out for each other. I asked him in and we went to my room. He looked over my things and then told me where he lived. His subdivision, we figured out, was only four or five backyards away, and a few minutes later we were making our way up the back path, pushing through the sumac grove to the connecting woods. His house, tidy and new, was perched on a small hill looking down on those woods. Cousins Farm—I pointed this out excitedly—was only a few hundred yards away.

If we took each other's measure—and of course we did—it was in the obliquely casual way of young boys. I didn't mention his tantrums, his fights. I didn't even allude to them, but they were there between us, something we both agreed to look past. For his part, Howard worked hard to accommodate me. We could do what I wanted, that was somehow made clear. I accepted this, then stepped back, let him show me his room and the magnificent electric train that was set up in his basement, a set complete with mountain tunnels, blinking lights at key crossings, and an elaborate station building with realistic figures arranged in front. I can't reconstruct now how our various understandings were arrived at or exactly how we expressed our interest in each other, but I know that as I made my way home for dinner, I was elated. I had made a friend, my first real friend, and somehow I was not especially worried about how I would deal with this at school.

I think now that Howard had a high degree of self-awareness, a perfect instinct about where the caste lines in our world were drawn and how he and I should conduct ourselves in public. At school he pressed no claims on me, did not presume that we would connect in any way at recess. He did not, ever, force me into the corner where I would be called upon to proclaim my loyalty to him. And for this I was very grateful. Because of course there were situations. Howard was teased and picked on and more than a few times provoked to some explosion. Once, most memorably, he got into a fight with somebody while the whole class was on a field trip at Greenfield Village, Detroit's great shrine to its automotive history. When the chaperone tried to intervene, Howard swore at her—called her an "old bitch," in fact—and then ran off in a fury, disappearing so effectively that the whole tour had to be suspended while mothers, teachers, and guides scoured the vast grounds for sight of him. He was found, at last, hiding in one of the cars of the visitor transport train. Another scene for us to replay and analyze.

My response when Howard and I were in public was to stand aside. I did not ignore him, but I did not seek him out, either. I never turned on him, never joined in any of the playground teasing, but neither did I intervene to help him when things got tense. Looking back now, I feel a prickling sense of shame—that my desire to be accepted as one of the group was strong enough to override my devotion to my friend. But back then that was just how things were. Howard accepted that our friendship belonged to after school. He never reproached me, and I never apologized or explained.

In the after-school world, though, we were almost inseparable. It was assumed that unless some unexpected family requirement got in the way, we would play together—at his house or mine, initially, and later, increasingly, at Cousins Farm. When I did get invited to join in some after-school touch-football game, I usually went, but never without a wince about leaving Howard in the lurch.

What did Howard and I do? Well, we wandered around a great deal. Weather permitting, we headed to Cousins Farm, slipping through the fence at a point up near his house. There, accompanied always by my German shepherd, Chipper, the great black dog that we had acquired as a puppy after I had broken my leg in the first grade, we stalked the cornfields with our bows and arrows, hoping to scare up some pheasant or grouse; or we poked among the high weeds that lined the edge of the pond, looking for turtles; or, most often, we headed to the far edge of the pond, where we crossed a low plank bridge and headed up into the pine woods, patrolling all of the trails we had come to know so intimately, dragging big branches and pine boughs to the hilltop where we always had one or another shelter in progress. But the doing—however strenuous or absorbing—was always secondary to whatever fantasy was being generated. *That* was Howard's gift to our friendship—the ability to enter fully into whatever narrative gave our rambles their point. That was the core of our friendship, the spark we set off in each other. Picking our way through those pine woods, alive with imaginings, we were merged in companionship. We stayed silent much of the time. We were not so much concocting stories as making ourselves absolutely susceptible to the suggestions triggered by our explorations. An empty cigarette pack in a clearing produced an atmospheric bowing of the strings—we would be hunting clues all afternoon, elaborating possibilities that grew so richly ominous that we would sometimes go hurtling back over the bridge and into the open field beyond. We kept our eyes open for the lairs of drifters and escapees, evolved complicated signal systems, fantasized about capturing poachers and turning them in for a big reward. All the while the sunlight powdered down from the rifts between the trees.

Our play was everything. I don't think that we talked about school or our classmates very much at all. To do so would have been to come brushing up against the unstated truth of things: that Howard was an outsider, that we made sense as friends only within our bubble. When we confronted each other in the context of school, as we did every day, it was almost as if we were embarrassed. We made no moves to acknowledge our other life.

There was, I'm now sure, another element to this great friendship. Apart from my intuitive sense of ascendancy—of being in charge—I somehow also knew that Howard was a person around whom I could create myself in the way I wanted. Though he had glimpsed what I saw as the debilitating otherness of our family life—the stark formality of our house, my parents' accents, the constant background presence of a strange language—he was in no position to judge me. Around him I felt none of the preemptive tension that hampered me in my interactions with other kids. If my father arrived home unexpectedly to veto some plan of ours, I could simply say, "My dad says I can't." That would be that. I did not have to wrestle with my shame.

With Howard I was sprung from that. As long as it was just us, things were simple. As soon as we got outside—as we did almost every day—I felt the spell of our quiet rooms quickly dissipate. I could push aside the tightness, the feeling I had of all things being held in the force field of my father's moods, which was always there, even when he was at work. I felt it in the saturations of silence, in the orderliness—how the architecture magazines were arranged on the coffee table, mail stacked on the edge of his drafting table. When I pulled the front door shut behind me, I felt I was stepping free.

Summers were different. Howard vanished. Did he travel with his family, go away to camp? Strangely, I don't know. But if I squint back to those long open days, I never see him. He was never there riding bikes with me around the complex system of neighborhood turnarounds or joining us in our endless hours at the lake. I don't think I ever saw Howard in a bathing suit. I was left to myself.

What I retrieve from those summers is my sense of happy solitude. I loved Walnut Lake, loved the promise—renewed daily—of blue water and trees. I never tired of going to the beach, swimming out to the floating docks to begin the day with a repetition loop of dives and cannonballs. Out there I gulped and plunged, following the buoy anchor ropes down into the tonic green depths, holding my breath until I felt I would explode, then surfacing in the echoing hollow under the dock, surrounded by empty oil drums. Later I would work on my crawl, swimming back and forth between docks in imagined competition. I wanted to be a swimming star, to make my way through the water like Mark Henderson. I swam and swam and then, tiring, went back to floating and diving.

Whatever changes with age—almost everything does—this simple thrill remains. I still find my sweetest moments of release, of purest distilled solitude, in the water. I love the detachment from all dailiness, how the feeling intensifies the deeper I pull myself down, foraging toward bottom with both arms and then pushing up, tipping myself suddenly onto my back with a release of quicksilver bubbles, to see the sealed-off light of the whole upper world wavering dully above me.

Howard was also not involved in the great frog massacres, though again I don't remember why. These group hunts took place every spring for several years, as ritualized as marbles, as soon as the new frog population had matured. Living as we do in an era when various amphibians are under real threat of extinction, it's hard to imagine that there was once a staggering abundance of the creatures. This we contrived to do something about. Five or six of us would gather with our bows and arrows after school, either at the swampy area off Cimarron Road, in my neighborhood, or else at the so-called Peat Pond over by Bobo Spriggel's house. Arrows notched, bows flexed, we slowly paced out the mucky peripheries, all eyes peeled for the distinctive smooth wedge shape of the frog's head. And we shot. These were murderous orgies—nine- and ten-year-old boys proudly waving their skewers aloft, their prey still twitching. What an excitement! Together we accounted for dozens, *hundreds,* most of them young. But from time to time someone scored a great bullfrog, and this set the blood racing. The point of it all? The point was to rehearse manliness—to strike all the proud poses, to fill oneself up with the hunter's cruel focus, and then to nail a living thing with your own arrow. When we got a frog, after waving it around for all to see, we would fling its little body out onto the road, until, some days, the whole bottom end of Cimarron was carpeted with these carcasses. I can't imagine something like this happening in my neighborhood now. I can't imagine the phalanx of parents not swooping down to put a quick stop to the bar-

barism. But no one said a word. No concerned adult pulled over to give us a lecture about respect for living things or even to ask us to kindly stop garnishing the road with our spoils. The cars drove by, oblivious adults at the wheel, and we continued, poised on tiptoe, breath held, striking again and again until there were too few frogs for us to bother with any longer.

There were other sides to my life during these years, of course. Apart from going to school and roaming around with Howard, apart from the closed-off interludes with family about which there is still so much to be said, the long Sundays during which we worked on home projects by decree or drove all together in my father's car to check progress on some building site in Detroit—dank excavations, slowly accreting foundations—I inhabited my private world. My humming solitude. I had begun plumbing its satisfactions back in Henrietta days, dreaming my projects on the warm skirt of grass in front of our house. Older now, I still liked to spend time sitting in one of my hideouts up in our wooded hill, or riding my bike slowly around, hypnotized by whatever rhythms I was muttering, or just hanging back in my room, surrounded by family but utterly absorbed in my own doings. I could, if I gave myself over, sometimes break free, surmount that slow, roiling anxiety that still makes this one day of the week excruciating for me. I pushed to generate my own countering energy. I would spend hours looking through my nature guides, copying charts, or cutting out animal pictures from the stacks of *National Geographic*s that had been passed along to me by a friend of my grandmother's, or making labels for the rocks, butterflies, and snakeskins I collected and displayed. I was then en route to becoming a scientist.

I was happy to do schoolwork, too, working through pages of math problems or preparing reports. We were always engaged in some larger project in class—on the human body, the states of the Union, countries . . . I drew highly detailed illustrations of body organs and blood circulation patterns, agonized over papier-mâché relief maps of Oregon, my state, and Latvia, the country I chose when a vestigial chauvinism won out over my complex reluctance. Schoolwork set tasks, gave clear rules, and performance was promptly rewarded. I loved the homework for itself—attacked it in order to do it well—but I also knew that when I reached a certain pitch of absorption, I would find release from the obscure tensions of home.

The family situation still baffles me, in some ways even more now—now that we are all grown up and reasonable, now that the passing years have taken much of the edge off my father's tense impetuosity, made him, comparatively speaking, almost affable. These days when we all get together—maybe two or three times a year, around holidays—we can talk about things, bring each other up-to-date on life and work. My kids are there in the near vicinity, tokens of my maturity, my grounding in a wholly independent life. As we sit, lingering over a family dinner, I can sometimes lift my glance and through some momentary trick of dissociation see us as if through the eyes of an outside onlooker. Father and son. Two adults arranged in postures of ease and respect.

How true—and how misleading. My father and I have come through, have struggled and have reconciled, and have felt the old differences and misunderstandings recede—if only because time has moved us forward, wearing out the nerve of argument. I watch as he makes some familiar gesture, steepling his fingers while listening, sliding his hand forward as he makes an emphatic point, inserting between his phrases that ancient maddening pause—that "aaaah"—and I suddenly feel that there are no months or years, that the fond essence of family belongs to a time of no time, that everything just goes on and on in some unreal better place where all memories of dissent and conflict have vaporized.

But no—in the next instant it all comes undone. My headstrong son swims demandingly into his field of vision, shouting or flailing his arms or insisting on something, or else my mother has forgotten to put on the water for his tea, and there is the surge of his terrible irritation, the leap of that old thing that was always there, behind everything, and if a moment ago I felt outside of time, now it's as if the years have been erased and I'm back, in the then, mobilized in anxious defense.

How could I ever tell my father this—I never have—that the erratic flaring of his moods, his incessant swerves in and out of temper, created the very weather of home and are now part of the core deposit of my childhood?

To be sure, our family life was never about violence or even the threats of violence. I was never hit or cuffed, and if I earned a spanking or two, there was always good reason. What I'm talking about is a particular atmosphere, a tight hair-trigger dissatisfaction my father exuded, as if he could never relax himself into things, and a moment-by-moment awareness of that tension on my part. The explosion is nothing compared with the ongoing expectation of the explosion. I felt it, and so did my mother and sister. The awareness became part of everything. All of us moved like wary creatures, heeding signals. The least inflection in my father's tone—to sharpness, to disappointment—activated us. My sister and I pulled away; my mother moved in to placate and soothe. Only when he was gone did she allow herself to become a countering presence.

Daily life in our family followed what I sometimes think of as the upstairs/downstairs dynamic of British manor life. I don't mean to suggest that we were in any way aristocratic—we were not—only that there was a pronounced split between the formal and informal aspect of things. But where the gentry and servants divided the roles—the manservant plunking his boots on master's table when master was out—my sister and I played both parts as circumstances dictated. That is, as long as my father was home, working, having meals, doing whatever else he did when he was around, vigilant decorum reigned. We all fell in with it, making our way unobtrusively from room to room, talking in low voices; certainly we refrained from watching TV or having our friends over. Not only because my father had all but decreed it thus, but also because we had learned over the years how easy it was to irritate him and how bad everything felt when he was irritated.

I keep trying to account for it, why these moods of his, these dissatisfactions and sparking gibes, should have tyrannized us so. Regarded from the remove of many years, they appear almost laughably minor. Back then it seemed as if the whole of life were at stake. The flash could come at any moment.

I picture breakfast. My father is at his place, reaching this way and that—for bread, for cottage cheese, for his plum preserves— laying out his day for my mother, lapsing into what I think of as the adult drone. A momentary equipoise; all things are in balance. We watch it, though, none of us quite trusting it. My sister and I work at being good, taking our toast in neat bites, drinking our milk without sloshing. My mother hurries to the kitchen to refill the cottage cheese dish. My father bends forward now, butter knife in hand, looking for another slice of the dark bread he likes. "Duda—" This is his pet name for my mother. "Duda—bring more bread, please." The silence from the kitchen goes on a beat too long. I shoot a quick glance at my sister. She is watching, too. "*Du*da?" We hear the first tremor of his irritation and fear the worst. My mother will have forgotten to buy more bread. I can hear her rummaging quickly through the refrigerator. My father is already tightening up, looking this way and that, agitatedly screwing the lid back on the jar of preserves. In another few seconds he will crack his hand against the table, rear up in his seat. *"Duda—"*

But no, my mother is back, cottage cheese in one hand, a small plate with two or three slices of dark bread. My father subsides, almost reluctantly. "Where in the hell did you go?" But the sharpness is tempered with mere exasperation. It sounds almost fond. My mother laughs, not so much righteous as relieved.

What did we think would happen? I don't know. Common-sense responses mean nothing here. What it felt like, often—too often—was that we were just a hairbreadth away: one more thing forgotten, one more misplaced tool or mistimed response and the ensuing detonation would blow a hole in our world. That's what it *felt* like, and since such a detonation never really came, since we all got through more or less intact, I began to think at times that I was just crazy, misaligned.

Every so often something would slip; the feeling would come seething up against the barrier wall. Christmases were especially hard, I think. Year after year we gathered upstairs by the fireplace on Christmas Eve. The fire would be lit, the presents—more and more abundant as time went on, as my father's office prospered— would be neatly arranged under the tree. We would all be dressed up for the occasion, my father and I in ties, my mother and sister in dresses. Everything set. Except for the unease that seemed to gather and build in the corners, back behind the low couches, along the window ledges.

And then, with almost perfect inevitability, the scene unfolds. My father puts an appropriately solemn record on the turntable— Handel or Bach—and we all draw together on the floor by the tree. My sister and I rein in our greedy inspecting glances, do everything we can not to look at each other. The danger is great enough with-out any instigating prompts. I sit cross-legged and press my heels into the carpet. My mother arranges a happy smile. It *is* Christmas Eve. Then, when my father sits down, we are ready. In a moment, following some ancient Latvian tradition—or so I imagine—we will each be called on to sing or recite something. A Christmas song, something learned for the school holiday program, maybe, or, in my mother's case, a long sad poem about soldiers in the snow.

First, though, my father commemorates family, reminds us of his mother in Latvia. She is thinking of us, he says. *"Viņa jūs ļoti mīla*—" She loves us very much. I hear a slight throb in his voice, feel him pushing toward something more, some bigger emotional connection, but then he turns away, making an awkward dismissive gesture, as if we could not possibly understand what is in his heart. When my mother does not encourage him, the initiative turns into silence, an extended pause during which I know I am to be thinking of my grandmother. Naturally I fail. There are the presents, waiting. There is the song to be gotten through.

The performances are what sink us. My sister and I wait for the signal to begin. We know what is going to happen, but there is no getting out of it. The trick, we have grasped, is to look away into the distance, to focus so absolutely that there is nothing but the song. But no. Because we are nervous, full of the sadness of ceremony—because we feel my father right there, awash in his feeling—we cannot usually make it through more than a verse.

> It *came* u*pon* a *mid*night clear,
> That *glo*rious song—

And that is it. My voice wobbles and clutches. I know I should push on, get through, but some devil just then pulls my glance over to where my sister is sitting, red-faced, then to my mother, who is doing her utmost to master her expression. But I see the twitch, the slightest tremble at the corner of her smile. Before anything can be adjusted or contained, I burst into snorting giggles. I feel, at the same time, the sharp stab of mortification. My father is on his feet in an instant. "You finish this yourselves—" He is already crossing the carpet toward the bedroom. It is as if we have desecrated the very spirit of Christmas.

"Don't be like that!" Now my mother is up, following him.

My sister and I sit by ourselves, chagrined, abruptly emptied of our laughter, no longer entitled even to look toward the treasures laid up under the tree. We wait.

Remarkably, things always get salvaged. After some minutes,

my parents emerge from their bedroom, sit down again. My mother recites and my father holds still, looking past us, and then, in the flurry of opening presents, the occasion repairs itself. We are ready to go downstairs to have our turkey.

Now it seems so clear. I remember an evening—I must have been in my twenties—when my father and I were sitting together, upstairs. For some reason, my father, who is not at all a literary person, wanted to recite the opening lines of Goethe's "Erl King." He'd learned them in school: *"Wer reitet so spät durch Nacht und Wind? Es ist der Vater mit seinem Kind."* ("Who is that riding so late through the dark and the wind? It is the father with his child.") But he could not make it through. I stared awkwardly at my hands while he released a single held-in sob—the saddest sound I've ever heard—and said: "I never *had* a father."

Upstairs, downstairs. Life in the manor house. The summer days were, for so long, the same. In the mornings, after breakfast, when my father had readied himself—put on his suit, collected his papers, and rolled and rubber-banded his working drawings—we all made our way to the landing to say good-bye to him. My sister and I would hover at the periphery while he gave my mother a kiss. I strained to be unobtrusive, afraid that, as so often happened, he would pick up on some fidget or somehow divine my concealed pleasure at the prospect of the day to come and be moved to create a task.

"Pete—" How often he caught me at the last possible instant, when I was already beginning to turn away, inclining ever so slightly toward whatever plan I was hatching for myself. "Pete—" He pretended to be thinking as he searched my expression for signs of dissidence. "All those weeds by the railroad ties—I want you to clear them out." I would nod, doing my best not to look disappointed—the wrong reaction could easily call forth other tasks—feeling the stain of obligation on my day, not knowing why I minded it so, an hour's worth of work at most, except that I did.

He would then pause again, regarding me, almost goading, pulling for some reaction. Until I looked away. Because I was uncomfortable with him watching me like that, because I knew it bothered him. "Look me in the eye," he used to say. "Don't look away when a person is talking to you." He waited a beat, shrugged, conveying thus a hint of disappointment—as if I should have embraced the assignment more fervently—and then he was off. We watched from the porch as the brake lights of his Jag winked, before he made his turn and disappeared.

Whereupon the ions in the room were suddenly rearranged; all vigilance and formality were dissolved, and the day was handed over to us. In my split-screen scheme of things, this was downstairs. My sister and I could make noise and blather at each other. We could run through the rooms, play, even—God forbid—turn on the TV. We were safe.

My mother had her morning occupations—cleaning up the breakfast dishes, making up their bed, getting dressed for the day. Then, before too long, she would be putting in her daily call to Ūm, slowly working her way from a chatty report of domestic events to an ever-more-exasperated parry and assault as she tried to fend off my grandmother's needy advances. So familiar, the words, the aggrieved tone. *"Es never, Mamīt, ne šodien—"* No, not today she couldn't drive to town, there was just too much to do. Certainly not in the morning, not for lunch. If there was a chance later, then maybe. I heard the same rising intonation I sometimes heard when she tried to go up against my father. But with Ūm I heard more grit, more emotion. *"Nē, Mamīt!"* She could let go with her mother. She could run through the octaves—denying, accusing, threatening, building to symphonic exasperation, before dropping back to catch hold, at just the right moment, of the placating note that would set things right again.

I listened, fascinated, caught up in the drama. At the same time I knew this was not my mother, not really. This—like the morning kiss at the landing—was one of the roles she played; it was something she fell in with. I felt, always, that she had secrets in reserve, places she could get to where she was free.

My mother was, for one thing—no, not for one thing, *mainly*—a reader. A devoted reader. Not quite as obsessive as the mother in Lasse Hallström's *My Life as a Dog,* who reads while her life falls in around her. But watching that film, I know I made some sort of primitive connection. For my mother, too, books were so much more than a hobby or amusement. They were a passage out *and* a place to get to away from the glare of the ordinary moment.

My mother read with addictive velocity. She often said that her life did not feel quite right to her if she could not spend some time inside her book every day. I watched, puzzling, just a bit jealous, as the titles and authors thundered by: Louis Bromfield, Anne Morrow Lindbergh, John Updike, Lawrence Durrell, *Zorba the Greek,* Hemingway, *Too Late the Phalarope,* Steinbeck, Louis Auchincloss, Thomas Wolfe, Taylor Caldwell, Sinclair Lewis, biographies of the Churchills and, later, Kennedys, Hildegard Knef, John Cheever . . . Good books, classics, but also books that might speed the hour, allow for that immersion that has always been so essential to her.

My father, not at all a reader, could not understand this. He would joke about it at parties, usually turning things around so that he could affirm that he himself had enough to deal with in the real world—he did not have to add on any complications from the realm of imagination. But if my father exerted great control over the so-called real, his digs did nothing to dissuade my mother from her passion. She read past him, right around him.

Some of my fondest memories of my mother from the time of childhood have to do with reading and books, at least indirectly. On these summer days, when she finally finished her epic negotiations with Ūm, she would, almost without fail, pack us up to go down to the lake. This was back in the era of summer quiet, before ubiquitous motorboats and Jet Skis. The beach at our end of the lake was sandy and serene, raked clean every morning by the lifeguards. There my sister and I dove and swam and indulged our myriad water dreams. But wherever I was, however far I'd allowed myself to drift away from the world and its familiar contours, I had only to gaze over to the spot, up from the shore, where the sand was soft, and there would be my mother, on her stomach, sunglasses on, utterly lost in whatever book she was reading. And I would get that sensation of freedom and rightness, of the bubble centering, as if her being elsewhere certified that the world did not stop at the tarred logs that marked the far boundary of the parking lot.

In her reading she relaxed, left behind her nervous preoccupation. As long as the book was open, I knew, the rule of tolerance was in effect. We could lobby for treats, extract promises, do everything we could to extend the time, stretching the pleasure into the afternoon, until—the moment would arrive—it could be stretched no longer. The shadow line would move across the page. My mother would look up, check her watch, and let her bookish focus reluctantly slip away. With the thought of tasks and errands the corner of the page is creased; the book is packed away in the straw beach bag. "We have to go soon," she says. "I need to get groceries and start thinking about dinner."

The pure part of the day is gone. Now everything we do will be done with some reference to dinner, to my father's coming home. "You need to pull those weeds," says my mother—the gentlest reminder, but already in her tone I hear the coming of the other order, the rule of law. I feel it as a tightening, a closing off. I'm not even sure why. But later, on my knees at the edge of the driveway, I catch myself jamming the weeding tool against the rocky ground, not caring at all if I dull or damage it, flinging the pulled weeds this way and that even as I know I will have to gather them all up again before my father gets home.

With luck, if I hurry, there is time for a TV show. *The Three*

Stooges, my favorite, comes on at five. It happens to be the show my father hates more than any other. The once or twice he found us watching, he launched into his most contemptuous diatribe: "They're *idiots,* can't you see that? Stupid, loud, low-class—" That last epithet got delivered in a special intonation, the effect of which was to make it seem that these three comics were somehow tearing down all that was fine and decent in the world. I have no counter-argument—ever, it seems. But at five o'clock, before my father gets home, I sit way forward on the downstairs couch and suck in every last "nyuk, nyuk, nyuk," laughing with my sister, even more de-lightedly, maybe, as I feel our time rapidly running out. "You did your work?" asks my mother from the kitchen. She knows I did. Her asking is just another reminder that it's almost five-thirty, and that I'd better have my ear cocked to the sound of his car; that we need to be ready at a moment's notice to shut off the TV and gather near the door.

The images of my father I have recorded are all about distance and separation, which is not entirely fair. He had his less forbid-ding side, too. When I got interested in competitive swimming and began to dream of trying out for a team, my father found a con-nection. He had been a swimmer himself, and he could understand my ambition. For one whole summer he undertook to train me. I agreed to the plan. Almost every morning he would rouse me in the first light—bending over me, his hair still rumpled from sleep—and we would drive down to the lake. The mist would still be hovering over the water as I steeled myself for that first crashing dive. I would then swim back and forth between the markers—crawl, backstroke, crawl—while my father stood at the end of the dock with a stopwatch, yelling out my times when I paused, ana-lyzing my stroke. "Stop jerking your left hand like that—and don't stop kicking when you breathe—" I read his tone for signs of ap-proval, but it was hard to tell. He was a disciplinarian—there was always *better, faster, more.* Still, driving back, seeing me shivering in my sweatshirt, he might clap me on the shoulder, linger for a second to rub his thumb against my shoulder blade. *"Laba sajūta, nę?"* A good feeling, isn't it? And I would nod, allowing for a change that he was right.

There were family occasions, too, when my father would unexpectedly loosen up. I can remember all of us driving somewhere and my father suddenly singing, "Chi-*ca*-go, Chi-*ca*-go . . ." or, "My sugar is so refined . . ." I would feel buoyant, suddenly hopeful—of what, I'm not sure. Or else he might begin teasing my mother, the two of them falling into a kind of mock-serious patter that was so convincing that I wondered when they'd had the time to work it up.

Or he might decide on impulse that we needed to go out for ice cream—a swerve into pleasure. I could feel another side of his nature trying to break out. Alas, the moods did not last through. My father was simply not comfortable feeling good for very long. I knew that at any moment, even as we were all happily licking our cones, the bubble could burst. Something would happen to trigger him, and in an instant everything would shift.

"Stop slouching, for Christ's sake—and tuck that shirt in! How can we go together to a public place with you looking like that?"

It did not matter then that my mother shot placating glances our way or even roused herself to contest him. "Why can't you let a person be who he is? Where's the fun?"

No use. The momentum was in him, and the response was surefire: "Because I want him to grow up with some self-respect. Because he represents the family; he represents *us*."

We glimpse so many things growing up, but it can take decades before we know how to read them.

I am fidgeting in bed, unable to sleep. Some need drives me out into the dark area by the kitchen. Becoming aware of a faint glow of light at the top of the stairs, I make my way slowly up. It is the middle of the night; there is no sound but the tick of the house and the powdery rustle of my pajamas.

My father's drafting table just about fills the small alcove outside their bedroom. From my spot by the top of the stairs I can see in the cone of light from his lamp just his hands and the top of his head as he bends over his drafting board. I watch him sketching shapes with a thick black pencil on a sheet of yellow tracing paper— pulling a line across, pausing, marking in another just beside it. I remain motionless, astonished that he does not know I am there. He works against his lines with rapid crosshatching strokes, stopping to peel another few rounds of tape from the end of the special pencil. And then he stops again. I see him take off his glasses, splay them on the table in front of him. He rubs his eye sockets with thumb and forefinger. When he reaches for his glasses again, I step forward into the radius of light. He looks over. For a second or two he regards me with utter incomprehension. I suddenly feel the force of his removal. In that moment he is still utterly there, among those lines and crosshatchings. He is looking at me as if he can take in only my most basic outline, as if the rest of his focus is still en route.

"Pete—" His voice is low, almost conspiratorial. He is just catching up with himself. I feel in the mood of the room a strange, almost soothing electricity.

Study them as I have for years, I still do not understand the terms and hidden negotiations of my parents' marriage. There was the story world where it all began: my father visiting the little house where my mother lived with her parents in Nördlingen, to help her study mathematics. That last phrase is always delivered with a wink, a cautionary titter from my mother. Who were they? What was between them then, or else on the day, just a few years later, when my mother drove from her new home in Princeton, New

Jersey, summoned to sign for and sponsor a young fellow Latvian whose "contact" had never arrived to meet him at the boat? Destiny, says my father. The explanatory thing, whatever it is, is hidden now, dissolved into the daily commerce of family life, summoned up only when nostalgia warrants. "How I loved that pointy nose!" exclaims my father. My mother looks to the side, pleased, showing the profile. Now they seem to me such utterly different people, in their temperaments, their interests, everything. Yet they have stayed together even as marriages on every side of them collapsed. They evolved their jokes, their sly routines, and their oblique ways of being tender with each other.

Looking back, I don't remember them being especially demonstrative with each other, though my father would from time to time catch my mother up in a lingering hug, about which she would act slightly embarrassed, as if this were a display that the children should not be made to witness. No, when I think of them together, apart from the times of meals and drives, I think of them walking slowly, side by side, along the edge of the lake at Cranbrook.

The Sunday walk. This was a brightness, a release from that day's quarantine. My parents both loved the ritual of their afternoons at Cranbrook, and so did my sister and I. For here it was not expected that we would linger nearby. These times were for their important talks, for making plans and adult decisions. As soon as my father had parked the car in the small lot near the Greek theater, we were free to run on ahead. We could do what we wanted—climb trees, explore the branching paths, search for lost tennis balls down by the courts—as long as we did not lose track of them, as long as our separate ways converged by the time they rounded the last bend of the lake walk. In the larger context of Sunday constraint—Detroit Symphony broadcasts at low volume on the upstairs radio—this felt like true liberation.

I had some of my first moments of sharpened self-awareness on these afternoons. Something about sitting, concealed, high in the branches in a pine tree, or hunkered low behind some hilltop bushes, and seeing the faraway figures of my parents gave me a much-needed inner purchase. There they were, tiny, moving right past the spot where my grandfather had painted, where I had fished with Mr. Vishnevsky. Open space and distance allowed me to frame them so differently. Waiting at the last of my hiding places, monitoring their approach—still talking, still oblivious of us—I felt as if some truer proportion of things were revealing itself. I was here, their child, subject to their every determination, but in that distance, the fabulous perspective that the lake and the surrounding hills opened up, lay the future.

Something like this also happened to me when I read—it was a form of getting away that drove me, paradoxically, deeper into myself, into my sense of possibility. This happened so reliably that in time, as it had for my mother, reading became my other place, something I held like a secret, never shared, never discussed with anyone.

From the time of the fourth grade I was a devoted consumer of books. I can't remember exactly how the compulsion began, if there was some original eye-opening encounter. But the other impressions are quite vivid.

Starting that year, we had library period once or twice a week, when the whole class filed down to the little school library. We were encouraged to wander around and look at things, and we could each check out several books if we wished. I remember the covetous excitement with which I stood in front of the section of biographies. I sought out books about inventors and pioneer heroes: Thomas Edison, Jim Bowie, Sam Houston, Lewis and Clark . . . Then came all the books about Indian chiefs and warriors: Sitting Bull, Osceola, Geronimo. Animals and dogs: *Rascal, Old Yeller, Savage Sam* . . . And then, one afternoon, kneeling down in a new section, I pulled out a book called *The Tower Treasure,* one of the very first in the Hardy Boys series. And with that began a reading obsession that lasted right into the early sixth grade. I read and reread the books—there were forty-some, I think. I borrowed them from the library, requested them as gifts, used allowance money to buy them; I even asked my mother to drop me off at the Birmingham bookshop whenever she went into town to do errands. There I would stand in place and read, knocking off forty or fifty pages at a stretch, dreading the shoulder tap that would mean it was time to go.

The Hardy Boys series gave me a complete and ongoing world—a world of danger and intrigue offset by what I now see as the clichés of cheery home life, but which then seemed the essence of what I wanted. Their town, Bayport, managed to condense the whole voluptuous larger universe, complete with gangsters, police, shady establishments, boathouses, deserted farmsteads, warehouses, train stations, wilds of all descriptions—everything, in short, required for every imaginable adventure. I entered in a state of joyous trepidation. To have one of the books under way, safely secreted on the shelf by my bed, was to have a validated ticket to immunity. Then it did not matter in the least if I was passed over for some playground team or whether my father came roaring up the driveway in one of his moods. It did not even matter that, catching sight of me propped on a pillow in my bed, he sent me out into the yard with a rake or clippers or some other instrument of manual repetition. I had only to think of my book, the marker like a signpost showing me the road back in, and I would feel safe.

My absorption into the world of Frank and Joe Hardy bled into my daily life as no reading experience has since, not quite. When I now read of others growing up with loftier excitements—those mythic schoolboys devouring their Dickens or Scott or Kipling—I feel slightly chagrined. But the fact is that I don't know if I could have hurled myself into those other imagined worlds in the same way. Part of my Hardy Boys obsession had to do with my susceptibility to renderings of American boyhoods (I also loved *Penrod*,

Tom Sawyer, A Separate Peace). I was drawn by the mysteries, of course. But I was no less deeply compelled by the settings, the images I derived of an ideal boy-world. I loved the idea of these brothers with their lightly ribbing loyalty, their constant interactions with their buddies—"chums"—the extraordinary freedom with which they went about their complicated and endlessly exciting business. Nothing could have been more different from how I lived.

When Howard and I went out on our extended explorations, when we tiptoed along the dark paths in Cousins's woods, I was also, in some elusive way, moving along in my independent narrative. I was stalking clues, developing possibilities, and Howard—though himself not much of a Hardy Boys reader—was responsive. He accepted and amplified my suspicions, embellished my notions of conspiracy. That he knew how to do this—be a believer—made ours, I thought, an endlessly renewable happiness.

I was in fifth grade, I think, when my grandfather Mike died. I could verify this with a quick telephone call to my mother, but in some way I prefer to keep things a bit indistinct. For I have allowed Mike's death to take on a certain role in memory: it was my first sign that the world as I knew it was not self-perpetuating.

The afternoon my mother told me, I had arranged to go to the woods with Steve Chudik. He had a pellet pistol, and we were going to be "shooting." It was a triumphant moment in my life. Next to Mark Henderson, whom I saw only at the bus stop or on the bus, or on the playground lording it over his gang of older kids, Steve Chudik was a hero of mine. He was tall, easygoing, athletic, one of those boys who made everything look effortless. That he was on occasion friendly to me was one of the real mysteries—and gifts—of my fifth-grade life. He had invited me to his birthday party, a fantastic treasure hunt all through the woods behind their house. I had even been over to play one-on-one, had seen the room he shared with his older brother, Chris. I had gaped at their artifacts—all the pennants, trophies, balls, camp paddles, and weapons that announced their membership in the inner circles of true boyhood. And now, on an afternoon when I was waiting for the doorbell to ring so that I could rush out before my mother answered and asked him into our quiet, bizarrely European house, I saw her standing in the doorway of my room.

She had an expression on her face that I did not recognize; I knew only that it was bad.

"Mike has died," my mother said. Her expression was stripped of the usual cues—empty. I knew that Mike had been in the hospital for some time with what everyone called "stomach problems." I could tell from the way that my parents talked about the illness that it was serious. But no one had mentioned the possibility that he might die.

When my mother sat down on the edge of my bed, I knew I was supposed to sit beside her. "It's sad," she said. That was all. She stroked my hair absently for a short while. Her face was tense, but she was not crying. I tried to focus on the meaning of her words, to take in that Mike no longer existed, was not *in the world,* but I could not. The fact is that I was thinking about Steve Chudik and wondering if we would still be able to go to the woods. I sat respectfully, waiting, not wanting to seem eager, and then I asked my mother if I could still go out to play. Yes, she said. For a little while. And I vowed solemnly to myself that I would concentrate on Mike later, when I got back.

Steve and I spent the afternoon marching through an area of woods not far from our house. He had indeed brought along his pellet pistol, and he let me try it. I was delighted by the shape and heft of it. I fired off a few shots. I remember thinking that everything would be different if I could only own a gun like that. It was while I was testing the thing, aiming into the distance and snapping the trigger, that I told my friend, so casually as to have it seem almost an afterthought, that my grandfather had just died. And when he responded, said, "Oh, wow," in an appropriately serious tone, I felt that I had taxed his generosity enough. I changed the subject and led the way deeper into the thickets.

Mike was the first person I knew who had died. This was a new kind of information, and I was completely at a loss. I lay in my bed that night, eyes open in the dark, feeling that if I thought about it enough, or in the right way, I would understand. *Mike—was—gone*. This was important; it changed the world. But as I dwelled on the fact, I could not get clarity. I felt that there should be some answer forthcoming, some response to my wondering, but there was nothing. Nor did anything resolve for me in the weeks that followed. I had not been taken to the hospital to see him—my mother had thought it might be upsetting. My sister and I did not go to the funeral, either. The last images I had to contemplate were of Mike as he had looked when he and Ūm had come over for a Sunday meal some weeks before. Though I knew it was irrational—and silly—for a long time after Mike's death I had the idea that my whole family was involved in playing a sophisticated prank on us, that there would come a moment, carefully planned for, when my parents would look at each other, smile at us, clap their hands, and *bang!*—Mike would come sauntering in to join the fun from his hiding place in the other room.

That feeling receded only gradually, after my grandmother had moved from Cranbrook to the second floor of a small house in Birmingham, only a few blocks from where we had lived on Henrietta; after she had taken in a lodger, a young Latvian architect whom I remember as plumply good-looking, the proud possessor of a modern wood-and-leather reclining chair that I liked to sit in whenever we went over to visit.

The world felt diminished without my grandfather. A certain feeling about things—some set of dreamy connections to the past—had vanished. Ūm seemed isolated now, smaller and less consequential, as if there were somehow more space around her. How different it was to watch her shuffling around those smaller rooms, to see her furniture crowded together, Mike's paintings and figurines and plants arranged in unfamiliar space.

If death was set before me suddenly, with almost no warning, the awareness of sex came slowly, like the onset of some viral ailment that announces itself through scattered symptoms but then stays and stays once it has dug in. Early in the fifth grade—this I'm clear about—I knew nothing. When Bobo Spriggel one day punched my shoulder and said, "Tell Mulholland she's a cunt," I laughed and obliged, clueless. I had some vague idea that a cunt was a cow.

Later that year, though, a major item of interest was someone's contraband copy of a girlie magazine—*Vue*—and for several recess periods we all gathered at the far end of the playground to pore over the photographs. I remember enormous, pendulous, unambiguously exciting breasts—a blond woman leaning forward with a dazed expression on her face. We passed the magazine around, more and more excited, until—as was somehow predictable—we had to vent our hot frustration by tearing the thing to shreds and littering the back ravine with glossy bits of confetti. Someone marched around chanting: "Boozie, boozie, boozie . . ." By then I knew, if not the particulars then certainly the fact, that behind the bland facade of adulthood lay some kind of intoxicated fever-dream, and that the world would never again subside into its old easy contours.

It was shortly after this awakening that I found on my parents' bookshelf a dull-looking green book called *Sane Sex Life and Sane Sex Living*. And henceforth, whenever my parents went anywhere and left me alone in the house, I went straight upstairs. With an anxious pit in my stomach, I would—always making sure I saw just how the book was positioned on the shelf—sit down and start reading about the "engorged male organ" and the "stimulation of the clitoris," and I would study the decidedly unerotic drawings of the male and female sex organs, and I thought—as every child in the world thinks at some point—that it was absolutely impossible that my parents had ever done together any of the things described in these pages.

And then, in the middle of sixth grade, almost as if our lives were obeying some ancient schedule, everything seemed to change. For all of us. If there is a fine line between childhood and the beginnings of adolescence, then we moved over it in a stampeding mass. That quickly. When we left school for the weekend, we were still normally unruly little barbarians, at home in our own skins. When we returned, whatever spring day that was, the air seemed to carry a new saturation that made us feel strange to ourselves.

I recall the sensation, the wrenching sadness that was also lit up with a giddy exhilaration. One day I was sitting at my desk near the window, staring out at the trees by the golf course—at the very spot where I would a few years later stand as a caddy—and I felt, with an almost physical pressure, the idea of *no more*. The solid, chalky room around me, with its immemorial archetypes of wall maps and globes, its foot-burnished dark linoleum—it suddenly counted for nothing. There, all at once, midway through Miss Hilty's morning session—on the dynasties of the pharoahs or the discovery of techniques of sterilization by Joseph Lister—in its moment of parting, I grasped my childhood, the deep safety it had represented. I felt unaccountably, unfamiliarly, choked up. I couldn't bear the thought of changing, of never again—ever— being at Walnut Lake School, in these rooms, even as I tasted an undeniable thrill at the prospect of breaking free.

I was not alone in this. The dreaminess was there in the room. It was there in the way that kids were acting with each other. Suddenly we all understood: We were the new anointed. Now we knew why the older kids, last year's departees, had acted the way they had. We were now them; we wore the sign of departure. We could stand in big groups at recess time and make rude and knowing jokes about the girls—all the humor pointed toward sexuality—and they could band together in their own knowing little circles, sending off provoking looks our way. The younger kids, who formerly had a chance of joining us at kickball or tetherball, now stood exposed as creatures of another order. They were *kids*. They had absolutely nothing to offer us. It was for them that the drinking fountains were placed so absurdly low, for them the peeing trough in the boys' bathroom. We felt brutal in our superiority, revved up to mock what we were leaving.

Suddenly it was time for transistor radios, for mouthing the words to the latest songs, which we all memorized overnight, and gyrating with self-conscious aggression by the outside wall next to the janitor's room. Cathy Mokerski, a new girl—her family had moved into the house up the hill from us—showed up at the bus stop one morning with ratted-up hair and nylons. She sat in the back of the bus with two of her brassy friends, all three of them swaying back and forth like little pop divas and singing, "That Charlie Brown, well, he's a clown . . . ," and once again the known world shook.

Howard and I were still friends, of course. We entered in on this newness in our own way, playing along with it at school but making small retreats as soon as we got home. We still headed out to Cousins Farm at every chance, only now, rather than playing in the old way, we kept silent company or else speculated ignorantly about what life would be like in junior high.

Then, one afternoon, just a short while before the end of sixth grade, Howard showed up at my house with a stricken look on his face. "We're moving," he said before I could even ask. "My dad is being transferred to Kansas City, and we're leaving as soon as school is over."

We didn't know what to do, how to act around each other in the face of this new information. We went out and patrolled the path between his house and mine, hardly talking. Near us, wherever we turned, was the cliff edge. Nothing—so it seemed to me—had any point anymore. Why play anything, go anywhere, say anything— he was going to be gone forever in just a few weeks. The summer was suddenly a great gaping hole, an immeasurable emptiness, and there, on the far side, waited the terrifying institutional newness of Berkshire Junior High.

Howard and I did carry out some kind of pretense for those last days. We got through the sadness and bravado of the last day of school; we started the summer almost as if everything would just keep on, that the move would not really happen. But of course we could not ignore what was going on at his house—the packed boxes in the corners of all the rooms, the desolation of newly quarried space. When the day arrived, I went over early, as we had planned. We stood around and watched the moving men; we paced back and forth in the echoing basement; we both sat in the low branches of the apple tree in the backyard. Then Howard's mother called him and we all stood in front of his house for a few unbearable minutes, promising to write, to visit. Howard's mother was nearly in tears. She said, trying to make a warm moment out of it: "You really were best friends." Howard and I went through our awkward pantomimes, punching at each other, grinning, not quite meeting glances. And then I was off, dragging my way slowly along the path leading to our backyard, starting to cry and, most uncharacteristically, not caring that I did. I had never felt such emptiness before, and I had no idea what to do with it. When my mother took us down to the lake later that afternoon, I swam back and forth between the docks to the rhythm of "One-o-one-o-two Delano Lane." His new address.

I think we sent each other a few letters that summer, but we did not sustain anything more. By the time school began the next fall, I was well over the loss of my best friend. And when he did come to visit for a single afternoon, I was more irritated than overjoyed.

It was a staged surprise. I came home from my new school one fall afternoon and found my mother giving off strange looks. Stranger still, she started asking me about my day—in English. Before I even had time to confront her on this, the closet door burst open and Howard—red-faced and laughing—jumped out. "I'm here until six o'clock," he announced. There we stood. I was utterly unprepared, and somehow I hated the thought that my free afternoon had been stolen from me.

Howard and I ended up going for a walk down Indian Trail, the road that led to Cousins Farm. We stopped at the barbed-wire fence but didn't push through the clumpy briars to climb over; instead, we turned around. Both of us were self-conscious. Howard started bragging about his new school and his new friends in Kansas City, and I replied by bragging about how "cool" everything was at Berkshire. By the time we got back to my house, we had run out of talk—we really didn't know what to do next. We sat together in my room, eating a snack my mother had fixed, listening to WKNR, the Detroit pop station, until Howard's parents arrived to pick him up. We had no contact after that.

A short while back, however, after a lapse of thirty-five years, I had a disconcerting—and exciting—experience. I was part of a panel convened by the Columbia School of Journalism to discuss the impact of television and electronic media on American cultural life. My co-panelists and I were done with our short speeches and exchanges, and a microphone had been set up out in the audience. "Please give your name before you ask your question," instructed the moderator. I saw three or four people rise to get in line, and suddenly I felt a clutch in my stomach. There, big as life, balding, with a short, sandy mustache, was Howard. In a flash I aged him, gave him a life, conjuring a background that led via twists and turns toward journalism, maybe television, maybe academe . . . It made sense. I sought his gaze, wondered if he would find some way to make allusion to our long-ago friendship. I wondered if I would be the one to field his question. Would I then stop everything and say, "Ladies and gentlemen, you won't believe this . . ."? I was, at the same time, already dreading the possibility of renewed contact, of trying to become distant adult friends, with Christmas cards and yearly phone calls. When he then stepped up to the mike and gave his name—it was Alan something—the whole thing went up in a puff of relief and disappointment. The miraculous possibility that had just charged up the room was gone. It was just early afternoon now, and a guy named Alan had a question for the panel.

CHAPTER 4

THERE IS — OR USED TO BE — A HIGH, UNPROTECTED TRESTLE ON THE outskirts of Ann Arbor. Narrow, constructed of massive beams, it was straight out of a cinematographer's imagination, just the sort of place that a romantically suicidal undergraduate would think to go, though I don't know whether anyone ever did successfully—or even unsuccessfully—jump from there.

I no longer remember the string of events that got me and my friend Cal up there, but one very early morning in the spring of 1970, still somewhat high from some mescaline we had "dropped" the night before, we were balancing our way across, daring each other on, trying not to focus too comprehendingly on the Huron River moving in shadow far below us. Cal would shuffle a few feet ahead, I would follow. From time to time we would gaze at each other with the mocking hilarity of the insane. *"Ándale, ándale, muchacho!"* we sputtered back and forth in the cartoon voice of Speedy Gonzalez—don't ask me why.

Cal and I, best friends from high school, were in the last weeks of our freshman year at the University of Michigan, though I don't think it would have been possible to be any less invested in studies or college life than we were. Cal would go traveling that summer, looking for some click of connection, and would end up dangerously ill from dysentery picked up in his wanderings in India and Afghanistan. I would shortly be taking incompletes in most of my courses, scrawling what I thought were revolutionary witticisms in my blue books. I had big plans, too. I was going to expatriate my-self—simply not come back from my summer of travels in Europe. I was ready to say good-bye to America permanently, sell my passport on the black market, and live on the bum. I would sleep in fields, work for my meals. I had been reading *Tropic of Cancer,* and my brain was on fire.

During this time, still living in the freshman dorm, I was smoking marijuana regularly and taking mescaline with some of my crazier hallmates. Instead of going to classes, I had been staying up all night, sitting in the undergraduate library paging through the big world atlas, or reading my Henry Miller, or hiding away in a carrel up in the stacks with my notebook and a contraband bottle of Ripple wine. There I busied myself writing out my plans, over and over—as if writing them out would make them real—working through my fantasies and my Thoreauvian manifestos about a better, truer life.

Odd—how we make our way into our lives. Now I get a picture of that early morning—the two of us shivering and grinning and not much more than a misplaced step from terrible injury or death—and I see it all as an image extracted from a continuum or, better, as the beginning of a free fall that would only break, months later, in a cheap hotel room in Barcelona, when I sat on my bed and wept in frustration because I knew that I could not see my plan through, that I would have to return home, my grand escape a fiasco.

But at that moment, high, determined to outfox the whole mad system, I was sure that I was on the very brink of liberation and that some astonishing consummation was imminent. Cal and I, and my other great friend, Todd—we were all still buying the youth culture promise that a total revolution of being was in the offing.

The very first hints of this culture—and promise—had reached me and most of my friends by way of the transistor radios we held pressed to our ears from earliest junior high on. There were phases and stages, of course, deviations of fashion in one direction or another, but the deeper momentum held steady. For the first time in history the world was being handed to the young.

The whole business had begun in the early 1960s, with the arrival of Beatlemania and the answering waves of British and American rock and roll. The music was an environment. The Beatles were "in the air"—playing incessantly from all radios, mugging from the covers of the many fan magazines that took on mushroom life to cash in on their huge appeal. And so much else followed. I remember standing in Ed Downing's pharmacy right across from Walnut Lake School and hearing erupt from somebody's transistor the first buzzing guitar notes of "Satisfaction," knowing at that moment that some barrier had been breached and that something new and gnawingly real was out in the world, something that could not be sucked back into the radio and unplayed, ever.

I was in junior high then. All of my friends—the kids I hung out with—were getting interested in bands, starting their own, talking nothing else but guitar and amp trivia and which bands were playing at which school dances. I had the same hunger. I pushed and sulked until my parents agreed to pay for a rental guitar—an electric Gibson, cherry red—from Grinnell's. I, too, stood around posing at the sock hops (which is what junior high dances were called then) held in the gym after every football or basketball game. I was too nervous around girls to even think about dancing; I was happy to stand right up by the side of the stage, watching the musicians, studying their hair, their jeans, and trying to remember the chord progressions they were playing. I remember getting dropped off at the Birmingham Teen Center by my—or somebody's—mother and wedging in front and center to hear local boy Bob Seger's new band, finding myself queasily fascinated by the guitarist, who not only had the longest hair I'd ever seen on a male, but was as pretty as a girl.

This period, junior high school, ages twelve to fifteen, is the great uncharted zone in the life of the American male. Who were we, and what did we do? I can reconstruct easily enough the outer image, see us all milling together in our little gangs in the parking lot where the buses lined up, or coalescing in territorial patterns around certain tables in the vast underlit cafeteria. We poked and prodded, maliciously mussing each other's obsessively combed hair; we showed off hot parts from James Bond novels, sniggering endlessly over Bond's bombshell love interest, Pussy Galore; we monitored with intent, if casual-appearing, focus the up-and-down fluctuations of social status, aware at every instant of what the "cool" kids—the good-looking ones or else the genuinely corrupt—were up to, even as they moved around and past us without the merest pause of recognition. I picture us later, after school, in Kim Swift's basement or Ed Phoebus's garage, smoking cigarettes snuck from our parents, Ed astonishing us all with his gift of blowing rings through rings until one of us felt compelled to break the spell with a rushing charge of hands.

But what was the inside view? I have no specifics, only a sense of extreme intimacy, of being in a world away from the world. That we were abusive and gross goes without saying—belching, farting, joking about "boners" and "BJ's," saying, "You're hired," every time someone blew out a match. Could it be that this was most of it, this constant group friction of testing, belittling, posing, puncturing? I don't remember us ever talking seriously, without the armor of bravado. Family life was not discussed; parents were invoked only for complaint. We were huddling together to get *away* from family, from all the dullness and limitation. When we hunkered over Kim's pool table, playing yet another game of Stripes and Solids, squinting into our smoke like Steve McQueen, we were putting as much distance as we could between ourselves and the idiocy of homeroom or gym or parental rules and expectations.

The first local inkling of liberation came when Chris Chrysler, one of our little group, turned sixteen and miraculously got use of his mother's car. Now, whenever we could, most often without permission, we drove around, thrilled as could be by the sheer possibility of motion. We did all the things we did at home, goofing, smoking, knuckle-rubbing each other's heads, but everything was different. The radio blared rock and roll; we were part of the public stream, eyes peeled for kids from our school—to see, to be seen. And yet for all this movement and agitation, the time was not yet right. Something hidden from us was still ripening.

Nor had it revealed itself, quite, in 1967, when I entered upon what would be the first of my many seasons of deep disaffection. But where the later troughs were generally obscure, hormonal, without outline or obvious origin, this one grew out of a clear affront. My parents, unhappy with what they saw of Groves, the large public high school I now attended, and the kids I was spending time with—my rock-loving, cigarette-cupping buddies— decided after long deliberation to send me to Cranbrook, the all-boys private school. I would go as a day boy, of course, but I would still have to submit to a far more rigorous schedule of classes and activities.

It was then, powerless, trapped, forced to knuckle under to my father's will—"You are going, it's as simple as that"—that I let my rebellion take the form of inner separation. Shouting would have availed nothing, I knew that, and threats and refusals just excited him to greater displays of strictness. I decided I would simply carry on my real life deep inside, where he couldn't see it. Which meant, in that first isolated, unbefriended year, that I sat in my room with the door closed, listening to my records—my Peter, Paul and Mary, Donovan, and Bob Dylan—daydreaming and reading. I must have appeared to be a good kid—docile, compliant—and my parents must have thought that their plan was working. But I think now that I was just husbanding my energies, sharpening my sense of grievance. I was unhappy, terribly lonely, yet—if this is not too overt a contradiction—I loved my exile. Coming when it did—I was just fifteen—it was giving me the most intense and promissory intimations of self. I lay with my head between my stereo speakers, feeling the knife edge of sadness and alienation, but when I rolled over and saw the trees blowing outside my window, I was sure that the gift of the future was somewhere being wrapped for me.

Cranbrook was crisp, decent, imbued with the borrowed spirit of the British public school. Ivy and bricks, a central quadrangle with a fountain, and names of all the grads carved, by class year, into columns and plaques. It was a huge shock to me, after two years at the suburban chaos of Groves, to be in a place where intelligence was prized and where an essential attitude of respect prevailed. Wry and brainy, that was the tone. Michael Kinsley, one year ahead, seemed to me the "Crannie" ideal. The old Groves style of snuck smokes and withering sexual put-downs was utterly useless. For a while I felt as if I were coming into a haven of snobs from some more authentic, cooler place. It would be some time before I understood that there was nothing particularly authentic about my disaffected neighborhood friends.

Still, I used my wised-up cynicism as a shield against what I imagined was Cranbrook's do-gooder ethos. Aloof, preening myself on being "different," I wandered the halls and grounds by myself, slipping my cigarettes from my blazer pocket when I was sure I was alone, exhaling more pensively now that I had no one to pose for. In my thoughts I ran some version of the "I'll show them" scenario, my fantasy being that of beating the grinds at their own game while immured in my alienated solitude.

So intense were my imaginings, and in such a romantic light had I cast myself, that an unexpected mirror or reflecting window could ruin me for the day. My inner man was lean and forlorn, with sunken cheeks and eyes aflame with secrets. Alas, at fifteen I was a somewhat overweight kid with tight kinky hair and thick glasses. Some of my old Groves friends were beginning to go out with girls. I did not know how that miracle of passage would ever come about. There was only Kingswood, the girls' school, on the other side of the estate, but it might as well have been across the river in Windsor. I had no possible entry there. And in that self-lacerating way of adolescence, I was perversely glad. The pressure was, effectively, off—as it would not have been at Groves. I was free to conjure heroic eventualities with all sorts of impossibly desirable women.

I went through most of my junior year in this way, waking myself in the dark, hurriedly eating two Pop-Tarts and drinking a cup of instant coffee, then taking various backyard paths I knew from childhood to get to the faraway corner where the Cranbrook bus stopped. A day of classes and regimentation, and then my mother would pick me up in the auto court. At home I went right to my room, where I might nap, practice my guitar, read, or just listen to records with my chin draped over the edge of the mattress. I was left alone. There was a new baby in the house—my brother, Erik, was born right before I left Groves—and the shift of attention in his direction was welcome.

The baby made a huge change in the family, reoriented things completely, and it is evidence of my incredible self-fixation that I took this in only obliquely. Of course, I would sometimes roll with my new brother on the rug or pause to study how he slept in his crib, but mainly I went on with my business, surprised only years later that he had grown up in such strenuous bursts.

I cannot easily dramatize this long period of obsessive solitariness. I disappeared inward. The life I was designing for myself, the escape velocity I felt gathering in every recess—this was my preoccupation. I would show them, show them all. Just *what* I would show them was less clear. Indeed, I think that the whole point of this self-fashioning was that it was intransitive. It was not anything particular I would soon reveal; it was my whole dazzling self. How I would do this was something I needed to work on. At various times I saw myself stepping forward as a rock guitarist, a leather-clad biker-folkie, or some kind of writer/poet/wanderer. At this same time, I was beginning to write jarringly romantic poems in my notebooks, poems that had me as an outcast, a visionary or prophet brooding under a tree at sunrise. I read Hermann Hesse—*Demian* and *Steppenwolf* and *Narcissus and Goldmund*—and I was just catching on to the Beat writers, beginning with Lawrence Ferlinghetti. I pondered for hours—literally—over my little square-shaped City Lights edition of *A Coney Island of the Mind*. A few pages—a few lines, even—proved as formative, I'm sure, as later studies of far more "worthy" texts.

I broke out of my solitude rarely, and when I did it was because one of my old neighborhood friends thought to include me in one of their outings. I was still the tallest of the bunch, and as such I was sometimes conscripted to put on my father's trench coat and try to buy a case of beer at the Farmer Jack's on Square Lake Road. It worked more than once, though I don't know if my mature appearance did the trick so much as my instinct for which checkout girl would be most easily cowed by my brashly assumed confidence.

I remember one of our nights with special vividness—it was the first time I made myself sick on hard liquor. It was winter. A few of us—Kim Swift ("Swifty"), Ed Phoebus ("Feebie"), and I—had gone on foot to Corky Price's barn. Corky was a kid our age who went to some other school. His family had a small horse farm on Lone Pine Road, and Corky had his own private room rigged up in the barn. At least that was the story. Corky could do whatever he wanted. Corky had girls who came to visit him. . . . I cannot picture Corky Price now, thirty years later, but the feeling of that night, that space in the barn, is as clear as could be.

Kim, Ed, and I stamped around behind Corky's house, finding our way to the barn in the dark. There were no lights, no sounds. We rapped on the big sliding barn door and waited. And then, miraculously, as if this were a scene from an old traveler's tale, the door slid open and we stepped into what had to be the most exciting and manly atmosphere imaginable. In the snug recess of the barn, across the ancient plank floor, through volumes of warm air that smelled like horse, was an archetypal lamp hanging over an archetypal table, around which four or five guys—older guys of local-hero stature—sat with cards in their hands. The air over the table was, of course, swirling with cigarette smoke, and there were cans and bottles of all descriptions around. Corky, who had welcomed us in, returned to his place at the table. "Let us know if you guys want in," he said; he said we should help ourselves to whatever we wanted.

Kim may have played, or Ed, but for my part I found a place to sit in a loft just overhead. I just sat and took it all in. The jokes, the easy card-player bravado, the whoops and curses and sudden explosions of laughter. And I drank. For whatever reason—maybe there was nothing else in easy reach—I set myself up with a bottle of Martell cognac. Sipping, watching, laughing more and more as the night wore on—I felt grand, free. I did not understand drinking, really, certainly nothing beyond a beer or two, and this cognac, once I was past the wince, was not bad. Only when I finally stood up to look for a bathroom—when the room started swinging back and forth in great arcs—did I get it. I had a problem. My insides were tipping this way and that, and the time—I suddenly knew that it was late, that I was being waited for, that I had better slip out and start walking.

Which I did. And what I preserve, like a souvenir postcard from my youth, dramatically lit by a full moon, is the image of myself crossing the vast snowy field behind the Sweeneys' house, trying to take a shortcut, finding that my shoes keep breaking through the crusty surface of the snow, realizing in a moment of true anguish that the faraway lights of my house were getting no closer, that my head was not clearing but was in fact feeling worse, and that I was surely destined to die not five hundred yards from my front door.

When I did at last get to our drive, I did whatever I could to reassemble myself. I rubbed my hands in the snow in a bid to get rid of the smoke smell; I ate a handful to clear my breath. I brushed my legs off, composed a face, and then, with a pretense of naturalness that I would love to see now on film, I walked in.

Luck was running against me. My parents were sitting in the living room, watching something on TV. To get to my room I would have to get past them; I would have to say words.

We all know the comic camera renditions of the drinker's progress—the endless corridors, the ominously leaning fixtures, the jiggle of imperiled balance. My journey to the living room comes back to me thus. I had scarcely reached the bottom of the stairs, bluffed my casual "Hello," before I knew that I could not make it. My best bet was to sit down—not too close—and feign some interest in the show, their company. This I did. But try as I might, I could not get the TV screen to come clear. Sitting down after my walking ordeal was making everything worse. I knew I had to get to my room before either of my parents thought to ask me something. "I'm tired," I said, pulling myself to my feet. And then, with no warning, before I could even turn in the direction of the bathroom not ten feet away, I let fly. The whole evening—the chips and Cokes at Kim's, the cognac, the breadsticks and pretzels—everything raced through me, and there I hunched, directly between the TV and couch where my parents sat, throwing up as never before and possibly never since. And when it was over, and I sat, drooling, empty, my whirling thoughts abruptly silenced, I knew that apology was futile. I said, "I'm sorry." The silence had echoes in it. Finally, my father, getting up and stepping past me to turn off the TV, said: "I want this spick-and-span." That was all.

My mother intervened, got my father to agree that I might not be able to get more than the worst of it that night, that I could finish in the morning. Which I did. With temples throbbing and stomach still on the edge of revolt, I crawled back and forth with sponge and bucket, disgusted with myself, but feeling, too, that I'd had a real experience at last.

I did not give my parents very many such privileged glimpses into my doings. Mainly I kept to myself and practiced what I assumed were the routine subterfuges of adolescence. I hid my cigarettes—Tareytons—in my drawer and "crotched" them when I left the house or returned. I wandered around a good bit, hitchhiking the five miles or so into Birmingham to go to Discount Records to browse through albums, or to Readmore Books, the new all-paperback store, where I looked at and sometimes bought books like *The Amboy Dukes* or *Boys and Girls Together,* novels that promised not just "hot parts," but also some insight into how the whole dizzying business might come about. Mostly, I waited. Part of growing up was having the sense, stronger every day, that something was going to happen.

I became adept at this underground living, keeping myself emotionally apart. Instead of seeking out conflict, meeting what I saw as my father's dictatorial affronts directly, I closed down. Sitting with my family at dinner, I said little, responded to jabs about my appearance or attitude with a private smirk. This infuriated my father. He wanted to lock horns, I could sense it. But I kept most of my comments to myself. And when meals were over, I quickly hid myself away in my room. To daydream, to read. This, too, provoked him. My father knew that when I was hidden behind the covers of some book, he could not reach me; I was free of his will. Nor could he quite come out and forbid me to read. His own mother was one of the great proselytizers of the book.

He settled for mockery, a steady needling that went on, it seems, for all the years of my growing up. "How you can sit like that, I don't know. It's decadent. The world is going to come as a big surprise to you. You and your mother, both of you. I don't understand. If I had your time—if I could *buy* the time that you waste lying there, turning pages. Novels—who has time? The world—"

When digs and prods were not enough, when he felt the steam build up and saw that I would not be flushed from my retreat, he resorted to tasks, injunctions, and prohibitions. Suddenly every plan I made, every initiative, was countered. Go to the movies?

Forget it! The lawn needs to be mowed, the garage cleaned, those weeds in back—it was the old pattern. If I protested, or slouched, or expressed any sort of attitude, there would be more. I would feel my rage and resentment build.

"Okay, and when I finish—"

"Oh, don't worry, I have other things." This would be offered in a calm, knowing tone.

"Like what?"

"You just worry about doing this right."

"But Kim and Ed—" My exasperation would start to leak out in spite of myself.

"There isn't going to be any 'Kim and Ed.'"

I can only remember one explosion on my part, but it was magnificent. It lasted only a minute or so, but like a film loop, it flashes by again and again. The occasion? I forget, nor does it matter. What I preserve is the scene. I am in front of the house, holding the hose—watering the lawn or washing the car. My father emerges from the front door. I am aware of him, but I carry on with whatever I'm doing, allowing myself to be just a little bit slovenly, so that he won't think I'm his obedient little soldier. Now he says something, points out a spot I missed, hints at a fresh task to follow this. Whatever he says just then, it is the proverbial last straw. Suddenly I go into a frenzy. My terrible joy, my release. I start flailing like a man possessed. I whip the hose this way and that, screaming nonsense, smashing the brass nozzle against the asphalt, utterly out of control. I feel like I could smash that nozzle down forever and it would not be enough. And then, in the next instant, the watchful "I" is back. I give the elm tree a few halfhearted whacks, drop the hose, turn away. When curiosity at last compels me to turn back, I see that my father is still there, arms at his side, watching me without expression. He offers nothing, not even a shrug. When he finally turns and goes inside, I do not feel gratified so much as exposed. I have shown too much, and I vow it won't happen again.

. . .

This long period of self-submergence, this period of indrawn breath, was where my sixties began. For it was at this time, in this unstructured receptivity, when I was so focused on discerning what might be next, that I registered the first tremors, the original signals of what would be an eruption unlike anything I had known. The news came by way of radio.

I had been listening, starting with pop music, ever since I got my first transistor at the end of sixth grade. The little leatherette-encased plastic box was on all the time. When I brushed my teeth in the morning I kept my radio on the shelf; I was listening to dee-jay Dick Purtan's cynical chatter and the countdown hits of the moment. I lay in bed at night with the earplug tight in my ear. I took in Motown, the Beatles, the later British bands, early West Coast rock like Buffalo Springfield and the Byrds, Bob Dylan . . . Later, when I started buying records, though, I bought mainly folk music, which was harder to find on radio. I'm not even sure where I was getting the idea of folk. But I know I loved the album covers. I would stand in the aisle at Discount Records and stare at the cover photos: the misfit-looking figures posed with their guitar cases against raw urban backgrounds—jeans, boots, leather—the whole magic summed up for me in the words "Bleecker Street."

Then, at some point during that long first year at Cranbrook, I found my way to FM radio. Suddenly—it was like a fuzzy signal resolving itself into a clear note. Out of the blur that represents so much of this time in memory comes the bright image of myself lying on my back on the white carpet in our upstairs living room. My eyes are closed, the sound is way up high—I must be the only one home. The song is "I Shall Be Released"—Bob Dylan's song, but done in eerie high harmony by a group identified as the Crackers—the group, soon to be rechristened the Band, that had been working as Bob Dylan's backup group. This was no longer AM rock, this was something different, and I found my way in as through a door with my name stenciled on it.

At that time there were two alternative FM stations in Detroit, WABX and WRIF. I listened to the latter, especially—religiously— to a disc jockey named "Uncle Russ." I listened for the revelation of the music, the deep saturations of sound that were so utterly unlike what I had been listening to before. Here were the long cuts, the real cuts, the songs that by sheer virtue of length repudiated the whole canned ethos of Top 40. This was music made for itself, not for profit. Creedence Clearwater's interminable "Suzie Q," Janis Joplin's "Ball and Chain," "Time Has Come Today" by the Chambers Brothers, "Crossroads" by Cream, strange things from San Francisco, from the Grateful Dead, from Jefferson Airplane, Jimi Hendrix. I took to all of it, indiscriminately, perhaps, because coming in from behind the music was something else—was this intimation that I have been trying so hard to zero in on. The sounds, the lyrics, were charged with it, and I think I would have found my way there even without guidance. But Uncle Russ, consummate, mellow-voiced—"stoned-voice"—host, was there to weave it all together. The music, the culture, the sly low confiding style of talk, and the winking suggestion offered at every turn that a whole other world existed and that these songs were but its advertisement. I knew a bit about drugs, marijuana, though at that time I had never tried it—the opportunity had not come up. Russ obviously knew a great deal about it. His voice, drawing the call letters of the station forth from his deepest contemplative soul—"W—R—I—Efffff"— told the listener that he was himself irretrievably stoned. His anecdotalizing, in the same voice, put a thrilling new spin on the most mundane bits of chat: "Man, I was out riding yesterday with my lady . . ." or "I ran into some freaks, some brothers, on the corner, and they sure had a funny look . . ."

Now I suspect that Russ was an easygoing fraud, giving suburban kids what they were wanting, and that he had no special key to the doings of this subculture. But then, thirsty, I inclined my ear to his every syllable and I began to believe the story that he was telling us. Elsewhere—in San Francisco, in New York, on certain corners in Detroit—was a life, a strange new rising energy, that had absolutely *no*thing to do with the safe and affluent and complacent world it was my sorry fate to inhabit. It was a perfect cliché—my furiously judgmental fifteen-year-old's perception of the lives around me and the righteousness with which I exempted myself. The life I was being asked to live was a fraud; everything about it was a lie. But the music knew, and Russ knew, and these people he talked about—the "freaks"—whom I had begun to glimpse here and there, on street corners, driving by in oddly decorated cars on Woodward Avenue, they knew. But the distance was too great. I could not suddenly pretend to be like them.

So I simply tuned in, wandering about and fantasizing. I was alone. I had no circuit, really, no social element from which to draw instruction or get the solidarity I needed. I receded into the corner of my room, sat on my bed strumming my guitar, and if my parents went out, I quickly got my cigarettes and went out behind the house to smoke.

I continue to linger here, not quite willing to let this odd miasmic period go. I feel that if I cannot understand who I was at this point, then I will be able to make nothing of that exciting and disturbing image of Cal and myself daredeviling our way across that high trestle; and without clarity there, much that follows must also remain obscure.

When I think back on these months, the analogy that comes most readily to mind is also the most obvious: that of the metamorphic transformation of caterpillar into cocoon into butterfly. Not that I would, for an instant, liken my emergence into the 1960s to the unfurling of a butterfly. But there is something about the interim phase—that dull, inert-looking cocoon—that seems right. The thing just *sits* there, like something shat onto a twig. But no, inside the dressing room, surreptitious and powerful, the event is preparing itself. My indrawn solitude, with its music and musing, and the jottings I made after paging through my Ferlinghetti—this was my changing place. I was fifteen and knew little—but now I knew that something was coming.

Later in that school year I made a friend, a senior named Adam. His parents were both Polish, architects; the family spoke Polish at home. We got friendly in math class, and when the commonalities emerged, it appeared we had no choice but to become friends. Soon I was catching rides to school with Adam, a huge stride toward freedom. He would beep his horn at the bottom of our driveway and I would gather up my books and step free. It was as simple as that. My parents, my father especially, approved of Adam—he was a "decent boy"—and I could have gone anywhere. As it was, we just drove down Lone Pine and back, blasting his radio, talking with licentious inventiveness about what we would do with certain Kingswood girls if we ever got the chance. Adam was, or made himself out to be, a sex hound. On weekend nights, if nothing was going on, he would call and ask if I wanted to go "Woodward-ing"—which meant driving up and down Woodward Avenue with every other bored teen in the metropolitan Detroit area, drinking beer, pulling in and out of drive-in parking lots, boldly racing window to window with carfuls of girls, the driver egging his partner (me) on to make the pitch. I was terrible at this, but Adam was the only one who could drive. While I sat paralyzed in attitudes of cool—pretend affectlessness resting on a bed of nerves—he would fling himself sideways across my lap, steering wheel ready at any instant to hurl us into oblivion, and shout things like "Hey, what's a bunch of babes like you doin' drivin' around?" or "Follow us and we'll have a party," never failing to mutter, for my benefit, "A party in my pants."

Adam was split like that, shy and upstanding when in public—a real father pleaser—but readily raised to excitability by a few cans of beer. For all his persistence and bluster, though, nothing ever happened. We did not even come close to scoring—scoring a date, that is, never mind anything more bragworthy than that.

Party in my pants indeed. But those early spring nights were a good time. We would be swilling beer, looking left and right for parked police cruisers, conducting epic chases of cars Adam deemed likely, lane-shifting and light-running from Birmingham all the way down to Royal Oak and back again, and by the time Adam dropped me off at home, I was usually in giddy good spirits. There would remain only navigating the transition—stalking by feel through the dark and abruptly silent house without rousing anyone.

It was through Adam that I finally met some Kingswood girls, Elise and Francesca. They were both younger—fourteen—but their parents didn't seem to mind them spending time with older boys. That, or else a practiced glance had persuaded them that we were not the kind of boys to be worried about. In any event, we were soon spending our Friday nights sitting in the living room at Elise's house. What a change of atmosphere this was for me—for both of us. The Millers, mother and father, were easy and ironic, there and not there, well trained in being unobtrusive. Elise had two older brothers—college age—who lived at home, worked at all sorts of oddly entrepreneurial jobs, and were forever trudging through the room with cronies, partners, and girlfriends. For them everything was a scheme, an adventure, and we were pulled in as consultants. Elise just laughed her husky laugh, squinting her eyes and throwing her head back, and found everything brilliant. Francesca, shyer, could usually be won over to the spirit of things by evening's end. Mrs. Miller—Helen—set herself up as the perfect foil, providing outraged reactions as needed: "Brian—you will do no such thing!" And her husband, Jack, "Black Jack" to everyone but himself, stepped in and out of the living room, freshening his drink from the decanter next to the bookcase, looking over his half-glasses to catch my eye when he had a vocabulary word for me. "Chthonic," he might say, or "Serendipitous," certain that I would need many guesses before he would enlighten me, and then head off to whatever offstage location he favored.

It was all so easy and gregarious—as long as we sat in that living room, which was, I now fancy, like the set for some Noël Coward play. The dynamic of the nights was set entirely by the walk-ons and exits. One-liners zipped in every direction, and timing was critical. As long as the comedy was hot, there was no getting up to leave.

As things stood, Adam was slightly paired with Elise—he had taken her out to a movie once or twice—and I was, by default, more with Francesca. Which is exactly how I would have chosen it anyway. For Francesca, the Deans' daughter, was a genuine beauty. She looked, at fourteen, like a model—tall, dauntingly blond, so far out of my league that it almost implied amazing things about my personality. Her looks, especially at first, flustered me. Just to glance her way was to feel the painful bite of being myself. But I did think that I was funny, and I could be merciless if I believed it would win me a laugh. If the current of banter was running high, I could keep up with Brian and John, both mockers and raconteurs. I loved to see Elise discompose herself into laughter and call me "Sven" as she patted my knee. She was the only person who used my real name with me until I was almost thirty.

But I had only to find myself sitting outside alone with Francesca to metamorphose back into a big curly-haired kid with glasses, the vein of my wit inexplicably mined out.

One night we actually double-dated—I went with my mother to buy a seersucker sports jacket for the event—and I fell into every midmovie cliché ever passed along by the Hollywood gag writers, wondering if I should land the tips of my fingers on that exquisite landing strip of skin at her shoulder, agonizing ahead over just how I would get my lips near to hers when we finally got to the door. The evening narrowed to a point in my mind; it seemed that everything—my whole future—depended on what I would do when I reached the end of Elise's flagstone walk. When we finally pulled up it was late, too late for us to think of coming inside. Francesca was staying over, so we all got out together.

Adam and Elise preceded us up the walk, and when I happened to look over I saw that they had gone into some sort of intimate clutch in the doorway. Francesca and I stopped, faced each other. I'd been working up some initiative, but as soon as I turned, any boldness I'd mustered withered. Francesca offered not the slightest sign of encouragement, not the least inclination of the head or softness of look. I could not, will myself though I might, get my lips to move the intervening distance to hers. I wavered, maybe even winced, and got myself leaning forward just the slightest bit, at which point Francesca solved everything. She smiled, touched my forehead with a finger, and said, I kid you not, "Boop."

Boop.

Summer arrived. Adam and his parents promptly left the country, traveling to Egypt and Iran. Without my best—my only—friend around, I quickly reverted to type. I drew myself back into my brooding chamber. But now it was different. For now that solitariness was shot through with a clamorous sort of romanticism. Almost overnight I became one of those frighteningly intense young men, something vampirish in my demeanor. My inner life turned extreme. I stayed up late, couldn't sleep. It was always one o'clock in my room, with the record player on low. I had discovered Leonard Cohen, the endless mooning iterations of "Suzanne." I sat in his acoustic haze and wrote in my notebook, on and on and on, bearing down with my ballpoint, pushing on through each new page as if I were marching somewhere. What did I write? Gibberish, I think now. But then it was not gibberish, it was my life; it was what my agitated soul was capable of. Did I really think I was in love with Francesca? Yes, no—how could anyone not have been in love with such perfect beauty? I have, somewhere, these pages—sheets covered with the most mawkishly lyrical eruptions, many in which I am bent at the knee, if not prostrate, before a "you"—not quite a "thee"—which had to be at least the idea of Francesca. And there I sat, writing, fanning cigarette smoke out my bedroom window.

I must have slept at least a little, for I also recall how I was always waking myself up right before sunrise. Awake, unable to keep my agitations indoors, I would borrow the car and set off down Lone Pine Road to Cranbrook, where I parked by the art academy and then made my way through the wet grass to one particular hillside spot. There, looking down on the lake, the mists rising up off the water, I sat, feasting on the thought of sunrise— *a never-before-seen day*—making more notes in my journal, and hoping that if I focused hard enough, I would somehow summon Francesca forth: I would look up and there she would be, backlit by the sun, moving toward me through the grass.

I did not go to Elise's so much anymore. Without Adam and his bluster, I felt exposed, less able to be sociable. But I did, almost every night, drive over to Cranbrook after dinner, hoping that Francesca, who lived right there, might see me sitting in the quad and come out.

I hadn't been loitering long before my parents intervened. I had too much time on my hands; it was not healthy for me to be moping around all day. I had better think about getting a job. If I did get a job, they promised, and if I saved my money, they would sell me the red VW squareback I'd been driving these recent weeks.

That was enough to rouse me. I hit the pavements like a man possessed, and within a few days I had found a job working in the warehouse of the Barricini Candy Company in Birmingham. Excluding my long-ago stints of caddying, this was my first real employment. I took it very seriously. The hours were nine to five, and my duties included unloading trucks under the supervision of an old black man named Willie Ford, stacking boxes on shelves, and going out with my partner, Tom, to make store deliveries all over the Detroit metropolitan area.

I was finally a free agent. I woke myself up—often going to sit in my hillside spot before work—and in the evening, after dinner, I usually went to sit by the fountain next to Francesca's house. Where was my family? How was it that my father was allowing me such a long tether? Surely we were all together in the house—sitting at the dinner table or collecting around some TV show in the evening. But I can't remember a thing. There was only me—always up, always stalking about, incessantly narrating to myself the hugely interesting adventure of my life.

Late in the summer there came a change. Looking back, I find it unaccountable. But even then, I think, I was marveling—anxious and exhilarated—at new feelings I was having. The main sense was, if I can put it so lamely, that something really *was* happening. Not to me, for once, but out there—in the world, the culture, in that part of the whole big picture that somehow touched my life. Like any sixteen-year-old solipsist, I was not very deeply attuned to events out in the world. I was aware, of course, of Vietnam and would have voiced protesting sentiments with some conviction had a microphone been thrust at me. And I certainly registered the assassinations of Martin Luther King Jr. and Bobby Kennedy, even connected those tragedies to a fairly vivid sense of a national malaise—maybe crisis—in the offing. But they were nonetheless events in the larger out there, that part of the world that was so obviously in the hands of the grim-faced men in suits—the generic adults who had no feeling at all for the lyrical truth of things. I confess that I feel somewhat ashamed of my younger self. I wish that, in looking back, I could find a spark of nascent political outrage, the beginnings of some more authentic dissidence. But I find only my fixation on the claims and desires of my adolescent soul.

Then, suddenly, the flash of it all. The Democratic Convention in Chicago—the yippies and Mayor Daley's troops, his "pigs," the street rioting all over the evening news. I knew outrage, cleansing generational fury, long before I understood what these street scenes were really about. I felt a churning fascination, almost unhealthy, at the sight of so many long-haired people, such shuddering grimaces. *That* was what first stunned me and gave all of the confusion inside me a home. Everything now flew together—the television footage, the music and the covert insinuations of Uncle Russ, that imponderable something I'd felt myself inclining toward. It was as if these thousands of protesters had come streaming in full wild array from that place I inhabited when I listened to Jim Morrison, to Jimi Hendrix, to the grating guitar lines of Wayne Kramer of the MC5. They were the "brothers and sisters"—the freaks—that Russ was always invoking.

But where *did* they come from? Looking around within the confines of my little world—suburban Detroit—I did not see many traces. One would have to go farther down Woodward, down to the Wayne State University area or the grungy inner city, where the Grande Ballroom was starting to feature some of the bands I was listening to. I hadn't gotten down there yet, but every so often, when my partner, Tom, and I drove around making our candy deliveries, we spotted some psychedelic posters on walls or in shop windows.

Then, in August, Cranbrook sponsored a monthlong program called Adventures in Creativity for artistically gifted kids from all over the country. When they arrived they brought the virus with them.

The Creativity group boarded in the school dormitories, and in the evenings everyone seemed to gather in all of my usual places. They were high school kids, but definitely of the more "creative" stripe. Some of the boys had long hair, longer than anything I'd seen around our end of town, and dressed with that "freak" flourish I suddenly found so attractive—in flowered shirts, decorated jeans, bandannas . . . I saw them sitting with their sketch pads, their guitars. Several of the girls owned that long-haired waifish air that thrilled me in a way that the fresh-faced all-American look never quite had.

Before long I was inching my way over, joining them on the grass, sharing cigarettes, listening to someone play the guitar, or nodding along to the radio. It didn't matter that I was not in their program—they pulled me in. I felt—and this was new for me—

that these were my people. From that moment on, though I'd had glimmers of it before, I understood what was most desirable in life. To be like them, *creative,* making something, looking for the new—drawing, painting, writing . . . These kids were open and smart; they thought *different* was interesting. And I began to figure out how everything fit. All those feelings stirred up by Chicago, by those film clips and news stories, and now these artists. I felt that same inkling: that there was power in numbers, that there were others, many others, who were not going to play the game in the old way. I drove at top speed down Lone Pine Road, heading to Cranbrook or heading back home, and with a spin of the radio dial I found the sound I wanted, the arrogant and heady noise that caught the moment, lifted it from my restless nerves, and joined it to the world.

In the last weeks of summer—I forget exactly how this came about—I found myself connecting up with Cal. We seemed to find each other by radar. Cal lived up near the school, and as I was at this point driving everywhere in the red VW squareback that was now officially mine, I would drop in to visit him. We would sit up in his room in one of those palatial Bloomfield Hills houses with columns that my father so reviled, listening to his records—Grateful Dead, Paul Butterfield—and hatching plans to start a literary magazine. Cal was an intellectual, a thinker, or else I just insisted on seeing him as one. I know I admired the books he had stacked up by his bedside—his LeRoi Jones, Kerouac, *Nausea, The Myth of Sisyphus*—and somewhat self-consciously emulated him.

Tall and intense, Cal had a way of widening his eyes behind his glasses whenever he started talking seriously. Which was often. He was intellectually combustible, keen to take any suggestion to the next level; he wanted to *act* on things. Cal and I would slowly work each other up with our magazine plans and our "intense" insights about life, about what was happening out there. We were putting our heads together, figuring out the signals that were coming in from all directions. We philosophized. For me it was a first—having someone to trade ideas with, to read books with. We went at it until we got giddy, and then at a certain point we would have to get out. Onto the street, into the night—wherever we thought it might all be happening. We regularly egged each other into adventures—like driving down to the Bowery end of the inner city, where we sat with winos and gave them quarters, convinced that we were in touch with the Kerouackian real thing; or else we patrolled the area around Wayne State for action, sitting in campus coffee shops and eyeing the bearded characters, the "hipsters." A few times, too, we pulled off all-nighters in Ann Arbor, our idea of Mecca. I would sneak out of my room after my parents went to bed, carefully propping the garage door so that it wouldn't lock against me. Cal waited for me at the end of my street in his mother's red convertible. Together we would go tearing down the highway, beating the dashboard and shrieking brave nonsense into the night.

It was in Ann Arbor on one of these nights that we dared each other to knock on the poet Donald Hall's door. Though it was quite late, the light was still on in one of the downstairs rooms. Cal and I jostled and pushed each other up the walkway. Hall was our idea of a writer. He had come to Cranbrook once, read what we all thought was a terrific poem about the discovery of the skeleton of a pilot in the cockpit of his plane. Bearded, unorthodox, he was as close to the real thing as we could manage. And he was awake. He actually answered the door and invited us in. Sitting on his couch, we were shocked at how easy it was to get this venerable man—he must have been in his forties then—to talk about poetry. He served us each a warm foamy beer, which we treasured in small sips, gave us a few sensible thoughts about starting a literary magazine. We left, reeling with our good fortune, the boldness of our venture. As far as we were concerned, we may as well have passed the night drinking in a Welsh pub with Dylan Thomas. Indeed, Hall had dusted off a few of his Thomas anecdotes for us, ones I was not terribly surprised to encounter a few years later in his memoir, *Remembering Poets.*

That fall was senior year. From the moment of our reconvening in the old upstairs assembly hall, it was clear—I think to everyone— that there had been enormous shifts in the deep-down structure of things. How else to account for the strange giddiness, almost euphoria, that prickled through the room? A certain amount of this was to be expected—we were seeing familiar faces, checking out the new kids, catching up on summer news—but there was something else. The signs were everywhere—long sideburns, hair now touching shirt collars in back, a certain indecipherable shift in attitudes, in personal style, in the temperature of things. I saw one or two kids greet each other across the room with power salutes; I saw, flashing like a wink, the fork of a peace sign. These were but little outward indicators. What I felt, what we all felt, that morning in September 1968 was that all of a sudden we added up to a power of some kind.

For me, it was as if late that summer the edge of my life had caught a spark, and now, in the first autumn, the blaze had taken over. Everything was different. That long isolation, those brooding hours in my room—that was all part of another era. I felt like I had come through something. I was now my own person, and I seemed to know what I wanted.

I don't know that I could have spelled it all out in concrete terms, but my instincts and intuitions were on full alert. Now I drove my own car to school—my VW decorated with flower stickers and a peace decal. I had friends, the beginnings of a crowd. Cal and I gathered around us a small group of the like-minded, and we all got very serious about launching our literary magazine. *Tracks,* it was called, and the first issue (there were two altogether) featured a cover photograph of receding railroad tracks taken by Francesca's brother. People started calling us the "*Tracks* group," and that sounded good. I also fell in love—defiantly and abjectly, with nothing held back in reserve.

It was late afternoon. Classes were done for the day, and the perfect September weather drew a group of us out to the grounds, where we sat on the hillside overlooking the lake, smoking our cigarettes and tossing ourselves indolently back in the tall grass. Perfect ease. The air was soft and carried just the first receding hint of fall. From where we sat, we would watch the cross-country team loping along the Kingswood shore. Cal lay back with his eyes closed. The two Johns—Ferrier and Rau—were, as ever, needling each other about something. And the moment stretched, ill defined, open at the edges, carrying whatever scraps we tossed off, until at some point everything suddenly came to attention. The two Johns broke off, Cal opened his eyes, and I turned my head to look.

Heading toward us from the direction of the boathouse, veering off the walkway and onto the grass, so that we knew they really were coming our way, were two girls in jeans and black leotards. Nor did they turn away as they drew closer.

"Jeannie . . ." John Ferrier knew one of the girls. She acknowledged him by taking a sashaying step into our midst, her friend right behind her. I sat up.

"Hey—"

"Hey." We all shuffled a bit to create space.

"This is Beth." Jeannie was shading her eyes, looking at each of us in turn.

"Cal, John, Peter," said Ferrier. And there we were, all sitting, almost immediately—so it seemed—making an "us," confirmation granted as the first of the runners chugged by and Beth and Jeannie exchanged an amused glance.

We talked and joked. Some of us lit up, but only Cal had the wits to offer his pack. Jeannie shook her head. But Beth, who had stationed herself just opposite me, close enough that I had to think about where to look, stood up. From the waistband of her jeans she extracted a flattened pack of Newports, and when she lowered herself back I was there with a match.

She took the light, said nothing, but when she exhaled she met my glance and held it. "I'm not supposed to be doing this."

I laughed. "What—*fraternizing*?"

She laughed, too, a low, husky laugh. "No, fraternizing is okay, but this—" She held up the cigarette and studied it. "I don't mean that we might get caught or anything. But I'm supposed to be training my voice."

"For . . . ?"

"Singing. I'm trying to become a folkie." She gave the word just the deprecatory spin it needed.

I plied her with questions, filled the air with my judgments. But my energy was all in looking and fielding cues. It was work not to be rude. The whimsical gods had to be toying with me. I took in the long brown hair, the dangly silver earrings, the downward dip of her mouth as she ventured one of her sarcasms, and I felt a dangerous tilting sensation. Beth. I could feel her attention. She got my style, my humor, I could tell. I could read her laugh: she was saying, "Go on." And in no time at all it was deep dusk. The runners were sprawling in the grass, practice over, and Jeannie was getting to her feet, pulling us reluctantly apart.

The next afternoon I was back, and so was Beth, at first walking along with Jeannie, then spotting me and coming over by herself, as I knew she would. And in some extraordinary autumnal acceleration, after walking, touching, grazing, and rubbing, we found ourselves back in a grove of oaks where the leaves were already falling, and the coherence of my life fractured into long, dizzy kisses. The world knotted up into lips and tongue. We kissed until we hurt, and then, strange to ourselves, in a kind of awe, we smoked cigarettes, stretching the strangeness and also hurrying to get through it, to get back. What an astonishing certainty I felt: I had someone.

I remember driving home in the near dark that day, late for dinner, pierced by the feeling of fall—that melancholy light—but feeling behind all the mortality some counterbalancing joy that I had never thought possible. Everything was poignant, unbearably full. My mouth was wounded from all the nips and bites, and I was driving as fast as I could, massaging my lips with a wetted finger. I was hoping to get in under the wire, to avoid the laying down of the law, but that was more from habit than anything else, for all of a sudden I felt invulnerable.

Love. I dropped into it like a thief going over a garden wall. I was all longing and sensation, full of sadnesses I could not have guessed. And how readily Beth and I slipped into our togetherness, each of us hurrying down to the lake after classes, sending long daily letters through the school mail, hanging on the phone during calling hours at the dorm. To this day I cannot sort out how much it was Beth I adored and how much the vertigo, the injection of so much intensity into my life. In those first weeks I was possessed, full of an elation that gave me no peace. I realized, with a deep shudder, how alone I had been before, and I marveled to think that there was another person, just a few miles away, who had me in her thoughts. I felt the great power of that. Inside the closed world of family life I now carried my own complete other world. Life was changing.

On the home front things were slowly heating up. My father and I tried our best to be civil, but we both knew that we were never more than a sneer or a gibe away from a flare-up. If Nixon appeared on the evening news, asserting anything at all, my father might mutter, "You tell those bastards," while I would snort audibly and leave the room. Music, drugs, politics, Vietnam, ideas of liberation—it didn't matter what the subject was. Between us it was tinder. The merest shake of the head from him at the sight of some hippie on the street could get me vowing revolution. If he walked past my open door and I was playing a record, he would invariably say something like "*Turn* that bingo-bango down."

Of course, scenes like this were going on between parents and their kids all over the country just then—and with so few real variations. I realized this when I got to college and met the rest of my tribe. We had all, it seemed, tuned in to FM radio at the same time, gotten fired up by the same bands, read the same few books—*On the Road, Howl, Naked Lunch, Been Down So Long It Looks Like Up to Me*—and now we were all linked in broad solidarity against the corrupt and avaricious system of the elders.

But then it was not so clear to me. Then I stalked the same few rooms with my parents, moving away far more than I had to when I passed my father in the hall. I still did what I was asked to do—I raked, weeded, shoveled—but always with the hot fire of indignation in my veins. I had begun to dream of the freedom that was coming. I had begun to think of myself as just putting in time.

Getting together with Beth—having a first girlfriend—gave me an enormous separating momentum. For the time we were "together," my thoughts were entirely claimed by her, by the least vicissitude in our relations. Home life was little more than a dim background event. I had dinner with my family, most certainly added a few sarcastic insights to the conversation, felt misunderstood when these were ignored or rebuffed, and then fled to my room as soon as it was acceptable to excuse myself. There I sat and tried to occupy myself until eight-thirty, the time when Kingswood girls were allowed to receive phone calls. I could hardly wait to lock on, hook myself into that intimacy, begin that low, murmuring exchange that was the only thing that brought me peace.

Looking back now, from a distance of thirty years, I am shocked to realize that Beth and I were together for only four or five months, and that while we put in our time rolling around clothed on the grounds or in the back of my squareback, we never did get to the real thing. The compulsion was certainly there—I remember well the numbed frustration I used to feel driving home from one of our dates—but in another way I think that both of us knew that sex was incidental. The whole relationship was, for both of us, more about prying open our wounded souls, showing each other our vulnerability.

The easy sarcasm of our first encounter had dissolved quickly. Beth was a misfit, a sad girl from a sad family. Under her brash catchphrases were tangles and confusions that easily matched my own. We both wanted solace, balm, some dream of total under-standing—but of course these are only the realizations of hind-sight. Then we had no idea, either of us, what we wanted from the other. We were locked together in some painful stasis, sitting by the lake, pressed shoulder to shoulder, smoking. We were both prisoners. Of our parents, our schools, our society. We leaned close over coffee at Alban's, the local deli, talking. We picked at each other's moods, sulked, got tangled in labyrinthine recriminations, said, "Nothing," and, "I didn't mean it like that," and looked away into our separate distances, until at last we would arrive at some plateau of impossibility, whereupon time would have run out and I would have to get Beth back to the dorm for check-in. How many weekend nights or school day afternoons did I return home in the blackest despair, convinced that everything was done, that I was alone again, only to get home to a ringing phone. Beth, peni-tent. "I am *so* sorry," she would say. "I think I know what it is now, I understand. I'll write you all about it. You were so good and pa-tient." Pause, lowered voice. "I love you."

"Ditto."

So it would go. This was my very first relationship, and it was consuming me entirely. I was idling in school, barely getting by—and worse, I didn't care. "Senior slump." Alone, I drew into my-self, was not to be reached. When I was with my friends—Cal, the two Johns, my new friend Todd—I acted out, struck the right poses, said outrageous things. But increasingly I felt a stark indif-ference to almost everything—except, of course, the least inflection or grimace on Beth's face.

There came a desperate season of silence. Beth still sent me let-ters, as she had done every day since the very first time we kissed in the leaves. I always hurried fearfully to the school post office just before lunch. Here was the daily barometer—and what a drop in pressure I was registering. At first, during the giddy weeks of finding each other by the lake after our last period class, of hanging on the phone every night until the dorm mother started flashing the lights, the letters were grandly extravagant. Intricately decorated envelopes and frank endearments—"Lover"—that filled me with a sense of proud possession, and then page after page of jumpy, confiding prose. About her misadventures with school authorities—"Tell me, am I just paranoid"—about how she was just about to go sneak a smoke, about how she and Jeannie, roommate and best friend, were getting on, about our future together. She would be a horsewoman, a singer, and I would be a great novelist, the greatest novelist of all. I sat in the dining hall turning the pages while the chaos of lunch raged around me.

And then, quite suddenly, the letters lost their color and high charge. Beth wrote more to apologize for the previous day, for things she'd said or not said; she analyzed herself, her moods, the gloom that swept over her, which she assured me had nothing to do with me. I felt a growing sense of futility. Mr. Schultz, the physics teacher, would be double-timing us through formulas for calculating the coefficient of friction, and I would be pushing the tip of my pen into a hole I was gouging into my desk. I felt trapped, explosive. Something would have to be done. If only Beth and I could run away, if we could get someplace where we could have time to sort things out. We would think of something. I would meet her later and we would find a way to get happy again.

Beth and I reached a dead end shortly after Christmas; neither one of us could stand it anymore. We got together with each other in order to suffer. We sat in my car and smoked cigarettes. We scarcely touched. I would put my hand on her shoulder and she would shrug me off. Then she would apologize and give me a forlorn, pitying stroke on my arm or a placating kiss.

I dropped her off in front of the dorm one winter afternoon

with no idea that it was the end, that I would not see her again for long months and would never know her as my girlfriend again. Going back over it, later, I would reconstruct the gloom of our last minutes in the car, anatomize the feeling of impossibility that had been there in the air between us. I remember lying in bed as the room got dark, listening to Bob Dylan's "Don't Think Twice, It's All Right," taking what stoic sustenance I could find there. I did not expect a call that night, and there was none.

I only found out the next day that something had happened. Jeannie wrote saying I should call her as soon as school was out. Nothing more. I went through my afternoon classes in a state of throbbing agitation. I was so certain that Jeannie had been deputized to tell me that things were over that I almost couldn't take in what she was telling me.

"Beth went home." She said it very slowly. "Her parents took her out this morning." Home was halfway across the state, hours away. I held the phone, waiting.

"She got weird last night, Peter. I don't know what happened. I know they took her to the nurse." Jeannie was Beth's best friend at school, but her voice sounded strangely unempathetic. "This might be better, you know?" She then told me how distant and sulky Beth had been over the past weeks, how she kept to herself, shrugging off conversation, ignoring her work, lying in bed with her eyes wide open.

I stood at one of the dorm phones, hearing everything from a great distance, trying to connect what Jeannie was now telling me with what had been going on during these weeks. I was thinking what to do, how to make it right, when Jeannie added: "There's a kind of blackout. No one is supposed to contact her."

I was stunned. As the news reached me, as I took in the weight of it, I started to feel desperate. There was no recourse. In the next days I sat with Todd, then Cal, trying to make sense of things. Each saw it differently. Todd shook his head and donned a tragic expression, as if to say this was life, the real business, and the only thing to do was to swallow it. Cal wanted me to do something Byronic—to drive to her house in the night and somehow rescue her. Desperate as I felt, I could not quite see that. What would we do? Where would we go? I thought of all the deadness that had been between us in those last weeks. I shook my head, and Cal shrugged.

The weeks passed slowly. I was numb, but within my numbness I went from thinking that Beth might be back any day to understanding that she would not. Bit by bit, but steadily—I could feel it—my hurt subsided. I grieved as much as I was able, wandering the grounds, sitting by the lake, freezing, as I tried on poses of stricken reverie. I also, I must admit, tasted relief and enjoyed the new existential gravity I had acquired. People knew that I was the guy whose girlfriend was taken away. Even my father accorded me a certain adult respect. He had not—this I knew—liked Beth much. But neither he nor my mother made the mistake of suggesting that this was for the better or that I would soon be over it.

Many weeks later, when I no longer walked around with the shock of Beth in my system, an envelope arrived. There was no letter. Inside a tightly folded sheet of notepaper I found my ring, still wound around with a piece of blue-green yarn.

The school year passed. At some point all of the seniors let go of their grip on the here and now and began looking toward the fall. I had been accepted at the University of Michigan and took that as my sign; I did not exert myself to apply elsewhere. Cal and Todd would also be going. We cruised around in our cars, ventured off on long group errands under the pretext of distributing our magazine in various outlets in the area. Some afternoons we got loose from school and drove to Detroit. Our hangout there was a place called Alvin's Finer Deli—it had the best Beat ambiance going. We sat in the corner and checked out the serious long-hairs, some of them, we knew, members of poet John Sinclair's White Panther

Party. We put quarters in the jukebox and tried to gain points with the regulars by playing John Coltrane and Miles Davis tunes—as if we were hipsters, too. In fact the music baffled me completely.

On prom night a whole group of us chipped in together and rented a suite at a hotel in Birmingham, and instead of going to the dance we got beer and wine and had a party for ourselves. It was "*Tracks* group" and friends, and I remember being surprised that some of the more "arty" girls from Kingswood stopped by. My date for the night was Francesca, who was now just a friend—I felt romantically depleted by my scorching months with Beth, too old to be trying to date a sophomore.

Though I have very few photographs from any era in my life from adolescence on, I do have a picture from that night. I am in a tuxedo and Francesca sits demurely on my lap. We are in our upstairs living room, just getting ready to head out for the night. I am taken aback to see what a fresh-faced, horn-rimmed fellow I am. I moved about in such a cloud of loss, of romantic bereavement; I was so full of rages and schemes and conceits. How is it that none of this shows up on my face? I look distressingly like what, in a sense, I was—a college-bound senior from Cranbrook.

As for Beth, much as I wanted to hold that pain intact inside me—for it certified me as serious, even tragic—the fact is that I got over her. I wanted a girlfriend, yes, and I wanted that sense of an intensified charge between myself and another person, that rich culture of secrecy, but I don't think that I wanted to be back with Beth. For a long time she simply vanished from my life. I thought about writing her—against all injunctions—but I honestly didn't know what to say. Whatever we'd had had not been enough for her. I didn't know the person who was racked by those terrible sadnesses, though I believed I had sadnesses of my own. I had no basis now for approaching her. So I did nothing, and the relationship pretty much faded into memory.

There was one occasion the following year, when I was in Ann Arbor, when she came to town to visit her older sister and called me. We sat together over coffee, said more than a few times how "weird" our meeting was, made vague avowals about staying in touch, and parted. Then years went by without a word. When Beth resurfaced again, six years later, it was with Cal. They had gotten together and were living on a farm outside Ann Arbor. By that time Cal and I had begun to drift apart, and his connection with Beth finished off our friendship. They have since married, and I have heard nothing from or about either for more than twenty years.

But now it is a late spring Sunday in 1969 and my other friend, Todd, and I are sitting in Alvin's Finer Deli reading *The New York Times*—another pose—and drinking coffee. Todd has inaugurated this as a ritual, and I follow his cues. As was clear from the day he transferred in as a senior, Todd knew the codes. He was later the first person I knew to sport a ponytail, the first to wear a pirate's hoop, then a stud, in his ear. When the rest of us were living in designated student apartments in Ann Arbor, Todd had moved to a downtown transient hotel with his Lou Reed records, his Zen books. I would drop in and find him, goateed and in an Indian robe, drinking tea and reading *The Alexandria Quartet*. But here, at Alvin's, he has something else. He is leaning over a page of the arts section and hammering the table excitedly with his palm.

"What?" I always feel like such a dullard beside him.

"Dig this, man—" Todd loves his hipster talk. He points to the page and I take a moment, looking upside down, to make out the now iconic logo and read the roster of scheduled performers. Woodstock. It is decided, without even a pretense of mulling things over, that we will go. Not just go—make a trip, an adventure, out of it.

We ended up going out to the festival site two weeks early. We hitchhiked—Todd, my old friend Adam, who was back from his first year at Princeton, and I—riding through Buffalo in the predawn hours with an amphetamine dealer who kept opening his suitcase to show us his pill supply; scaring each other witless in a deserted farmhouse somewhere in upstate New York with stories of murdered Confederate soldiers and listening to the scurrying of various night creatures. Arriving finally in the town of Woodstock, we learned that the festival had been moved to a farm outside the town of Bethel. More hitchhiking. Then, in a bar somewhere near the new location, we fell to talking with some decidedly "freaky" characters. They said they were from the Hog Farm; their commune had been hired to set up the event and provide security. After more beers they invited us to stay with them at their camp.

It was Todd, of course, who grasped the enormous significance of what had just transpired. He actually knew the pedigrees and lineages. The Hog Farmers were, many of them, former members of Ken Kesey's Merry Pranksters. The Pranksters, and even I knew this, drove a psychedelic bus called Further, the driver being none other than Neal Cassady, the model for Kerouac's Dean Moriarty. *On the Road* still had the status of sacred text with some of us. Todd and I could egg each other on by saying things like "What would Dean do, man?" Adam, who cared nothing for the counter-culture ethos, was along for the ride; his main hope was to hook up with some loose hippie girls and get laid. Riding in the bed of the Hog Farm's pickup, he seemed oblivious to the fact that we were tantalizingly close to the real thing, the scene that was the mother of all scenes. He closed his eyes and tried to nap.

So much of experience takes the form of expectations dashed and fantasies deflated, but in fact our ten days of living with the Hog Farmers before the festival started were as thrilling as anything we might have conjured in imagination. These were indeed characters out of some wild comic book of American life. True eccentrics, true misfits—hippies who had nothing to do with the marketplace image that would eventually turn the whole lyric impulse into another piece of stand-up shtick. Cheech and Chong. But these people were the pioneers. Their leader, gap-toothed

Hugh Romney, who wanted to be called "Wavy Gravy" (and who much later ended up in this guise as a mascot figure for some flavor of Ben & Jerry's ice cream); Paul Foster, the supposed paranoid genius who used to ride with the Pranksters and whom Tom Wolfe memorably described as hiding away in a tree in *The Electric Kool-Aid Acid Test,* his book on the Pranksters; a genial character—half hippie, half redneck—who called himself Reddog; a stunning woman named Mountain Girl, who had a red dot painted on the tip of her nose; and a yoga instructor named Tom, who led the Farmers—and us—every morning in their deep-breathing exercises. Tom had, then, the longest hair I had ever seen on a male— straight, combed out, it reached most of the way down his back. A few years ago I saw a "then and now" photo spread in a *Life* magazine issue commemorating the twenty-fifth anniversary of Woodstock, and there was Tom, lean, shorn, and dressed corporate hip, and I had to marvel, as I do increasingly, at the transformations a life can hold. It had seemed so absolute, Tom sitting bare-chested on that hillside, leading us toward purity and enlightenment as we chugged along doing the "breath of fire."

There was another character, Buffalo Bob, of whom it was said routinely that he had consumed more LSD than any human on the planet. We saw no evidence of hallucinogens there, at the campsite, but at night when the bonfires were lit and the tribe gathered around, there was plenty of wine and marijuana. And singing and storytelling and silliness. So much so that Adam got unsettled and left to visit a Princeton friend. Todd and I, on the other hand, were in a state of bliss—we had arrived at the glowing center of things. We both believed, without ever spelling it out in so many words, that these people were the front-runners, the advance wave, and that the future would be communal and egalitarian in just this way.

We sat in the light of the bonfire and watched and listened. We drank from the jug when it came our way and took hits from the circulating joints until our heads grew heavy. And then we just moved a few feet over to our sleeping bags. In the morning, early, we sat on the nearby hillside doing our yoga and breathing. We waited for Wavy Gravy to produce his clipboard with the list of that day's tasks. More often than not, we were put on a crew with Reddog (by all accounts the least "together" of the crew) to dig latrine holes, haul boards, or nail together flooring for rice kitchens.

That whole period was like one long held-in breath—healthy, with long days of hard work, and loud and dissipated once the fires were lit. And then, quite abruptly, it ended—our Woodstock. The rest of the counterculture began to arrive. At first just a few, spotted coming over the hills like straggling soldiers in some Civil War movie, then in groups, vanloads, and in a blink there were people everywhere, pouring toward us from every direction. Our campsite lost its integrity; the Farmers were mustered out to other tasks—working security, mainly. We could hear the massive loudspeakers being tested and tested. And then they carried the historic message: People were here in excess of all expectations—it was to be a free concert.

I will not even try to describe the first day—the view we got from a tree of bobbing heads as far as the eye could see, the anxiety that filtered in when we realized that the kitchens and latrines were not going to be enough; the combined exaltation and misery of standing under someone's propped-up poncho, waiting for the rain to stop so that the next act could get on stage. Very late that night, Todd and I looked at each other with the same thought in mind. In a minute or two we had gathered our few things and begun tramping toward the road, among the first to counter the flow, truly astonished to see for how many miles the line of stalled vehicles and intrepid walkers extended.

We ended up—I don't even remember quite how—at the Newark Airport. We waited and waited for a flight out, passed part of the time chatting with an exhausted-looking Larry Taylor, bass player for Canned Heat, who were on their way out, too, and he kept nodding at us in the way people nodded back then, saying, as if he had not just said the same thing a hundred times, that the whole event was a "fucking monster."

Arriving at last in Detroit, I phoned my parents to ask for a ride home. Todd—who now insisted on being called Reddog—and I sat on our backpacks, so tired that we could barely keep our eyes open to watch for our car. At some point I looked up and saw my father's blue Jaguar stopped in front of our patch of sidewalk. My father did not get out. He rolled down the window and instructed us to put our packs in the trunk. When we got into the backseat and closed the door, he turned and gave us both a lingering appraisal. Then, at no pains to conceal his distaste for our whole enterprise, he said: "You guys really stink."

Todd and I arrived in Ann Arbor on the day of registration as the heroes of our own myth. These other kids, our fellow freshmen, our prospective dormmates, were tyros. They were hippies, sure, wearing their jeans and boots, and some of them had even been to Woodstock—who hadn't?—but we were the pilgrims from the source. After all, we had felt the opening of our chakras right beside Wavy Gravy, had sat on a log listening to Buffalo Bob reminisce about his epic adventures in psychedelia, adventures far beyond what these suburban "heads" could imagine. Never mind that we were ourselves suburban kids—somehow we believed we weren't. Todd was now Reddog and—amazingly—the name stuck. For several years, until he decided he was a painter—and Todd once again—everyone he knew called him Reddog. In his ear now, to add to the raffish image, a large silver hoop. Unable to venture anywhere near so far out, I simply grew my hair as long as I could, grew it so that it stood out dandelion fashion. That was my signature style, the white Afro, and nothing on earth made me happier than some black person—some "spade"—giving me the nod. I had my hair, my cowboy boots, my brown zipper motorcycle jacket (though I had never been on a bike in my life), and my new attitude, that of one just back from lonesome wanderings. I was sure I had cowed my roommate, Bob, for I would often catch him just staring over at me from his corner of the room, a look of anxious fascination on his face.

Bob was part of a whole group of friends who had all gone to Farmington High School and had requested the same dorm. I met them all immediately and then watched over the next few months as they—like everyone around them, like me—succumbed to the irresistible combination of easy-access drugs and nightly peer pressure. The Mosher-Jordan dorm was, throughout that 1969–1970 school year, all the evidence anyone would need to prove the thesis that the West was in a state of precipitous decline. We were all in it together, going down as a merry band, and it was no one's fault. Which is another way of saying that we were all to blame.

There was no supervision that I can recall. We were just a barracks of seventeen- and eighteen-year-old guys who were all confused and vying for status just as the drug revolution was reaching its first crest. In the beginning we consumed mainly marijuana and hashish. Groups of us moved up and down the halls, dropping into each other's rooms, offering a joint or a pipe, or else sitting down to share one. Great stoned parties developed, and soon they became a nightly thing. Six, eight, maybe even ten of us would crowd together into somebody's poster-decorated room, blocking off the door with a towel (just for show, really) and then just getting high and listening to King Crimson or Traffic or Procol Harum or Firesign Theater, at some point getting the collective "munchies" and pooling our resources for a pizza delivery.

Reddog lived in another dorm, but more or less the same thing was happening down his hallway. He dropped in often, seamlessly, taking a place on the floor without special ceremony. Cal, living across campus, was more elusive; he had calmer dorm friends. School? I remember sleeping through countless classes and actually convincing myself that my dereliction was a political act. The university was just part of the system, selling us the biases and ideologies of the dominant class. This same system was responsible for the bombing of the revolutionary North Vietnamese; it sponsored the ROTC program just a few buildings over. We were the "people," and our truth was getting high and being together and not hurting others. We turned out in great numbers to march against ROTC that fall, and the police came out in riot gear to break us up. We gathered—almost daily, it seemed—at lunchtime on the "Diag," where speakers got up to decry the war, where petitions were passed around. Ann Arbor was, after all, the birthplace of SDS. Political heavies like Tom Hayden, David Dellinger, and Rennie Davis were always passing through, giving rally speeches from the steps of the graduate library. I was there—we were all there—pumping fists in the air, chanting things like "Power to the people!" and "Ho-ho-Ho Chi Minh, NLF is gonna win!" I'm not sure I could have explained much about Ho or the NLF or what half of the rhetoric was about. But I was cool, and being cool meant having your body out there to swell the crowd. I had one eye on the speaker and one eye, always, on some girl in a denim jacket just a few feet away.

My sixties were not political. It is a truth I'm ashamed to concede, for so many people around me seemed to care passionately about where the country was going. My sympathies were with the radicals, of course. But I was not old enough. My self-involvement was so complete that there were almost no sympathies left over to distribute. My sixties—my counterculture years—were about striking poses, not striking. I was full to the brim with rage, but it was confused rage. I said it was against the system, against the authority structure, but much more it was against my father, the source, I thought, of my childhood estrangement from everything I wanted. When I traveled with half a million others to Washington, D.C., that fall to march, it was not U.S. involvement in Vietnam that I was really protesting, but my father's arrogance, the willful, critical way he had acted toward me when I was growing up. Probably it was not quite as neat as that. These things all flowed together. My father, once a great Kennedy man, was now on Nixon's side—he despised the unruly decadence of the whole youth movement. He was for Nixon, I might have argued, because he disliked me and my friends. Who knew how these things sorted out at a deeper level? But to march and chant and pump my fist in the air, and then to sit in someone's parked van and get drunk on Ripple wine—it was all the same thing. It was somehow getting at my father, even though he likely did not even know I had left my dorm and was halfway across the country. Busily making history.

My relations with my father were in some ways at their most strained during this year and the next, even though I was no longer living at home. I remember that he would drive to Ann Arbor every Tuesday to teach his graduate seminar at the university's school of architecture and that on some of these Tuesdays we would have lunch together at a place called Dominick's. How painful these occasions were for both of us—me desperate for the hour to be over so that I wouldn't be spotted with my suit-wearing father, and my father trying his hardest, and not always succeeding, to keep to himself his comments about the way I looked. What did we have to talk about? My courses? I was hardly there enough to know what they were about. My friends? Not likely. Did I press him for the latest news from home? I rack my brain to discover even a single little bit of common ground. What a relief I felt when he said good-bye and headed across the street to the art and architecture building and I could hurry around the nearest corner to light up a cigarette.

There is no point in trying to order events from that long year— only the general trajectory matters. And that was, certainly from my father's perspective—and even the perspective I hold now— resolutely downward. The partying continued, intensified, as the fall semester went on. I was partying every night, it seemed, and barely getting through my classes. My attitude grew more sullen, more arrogant.

It was at some point during these months that I discovered Henry Miller and promptly claimed him as the voice of my liberation. I had picked up a little paperback somewhere, *Quiet Days in Clichy*—I liked the title—and I was dipping into it while waiting for an afternoon concert to begin. Suddenly I forgot everything I was doing and intending. I went back to my dorm room and lay on my bed, reading about this soulfully heartless character. Just then, and for quite a long time after, I wanted nothing more than to be like him, on the bum, hopping from bed to bed, unscrupulously cadging meals wherever I could, living close to the street, but somehow, *somehow* also tuned in to the hidden momentum of the spirit.

From that little book I found my way to the others, to the two *Tropic*s, the volumes of the Rosy Crucifixion trilogy—*Sexus, Plexus, and Nexus*—and in fairly short order, ungrounded as I was in any strong sense of reality, I began to conceive of a plan. I would check out of this whole corrupt system, get away from Nixon and the draft and the newspaper headlines, not to mention the sneers and criticisms of my father. I would go to Europe, not to travel as a tourist, but to live. I would stay there, become an expatriate. How I loved the sound of that word. I honestly saw myself living a glorified tramp's existence—in Paris, in London, on the Greek islands, in Spain. I would drift with the stars, the weather, go where people and adventures took me; I would live on my wits, like a Gypsy, like Zorba, right up against the ticking pulse of things.

The whole fantasy sounds so outlandish now—I can't believe that I was entirely serious. But no, I filled journal after journal with lists of what I would need; I studied maps. And things were different back then. Wandering was in the air. Hippies were drifting everywhere, starting communes, living on the road, trekking toward the Himalayas. It was the romance of thirsty boots, of "goin' down that long lonesome road. . . ." I would become one of the migrants, and one day I would write about all of it.

Cal and Reddog were privy to my plans. They were unmoored,

too, working on their own fates. Reddog wanted to get to India, Cal to Nepal. Everyone we knew was getting ready to go somewhere. Student charter flights were dirt cheap, and word was already out that Europe that summer was going to be a great party.

I tried to do everything as Henry would have done it—drinking, prowling the streets, savoring the spark of the unrepeatable moment—except that Henry bounced effortlessly from one lusty bed to another and I did not. My love life was unspectacular, especially when the wild freedom of the times is taken into account. I had—technically—lost my virginity during my first week at college, to a waiflike blond girl who was as drunk as I was. And I had, with only moderate enthusiasm, paired up with Lisa, whom I had known slightly from Kingswood. I went to Lisa for solace and late night companionship. I would blunder my way to her door at the end of whatever debauch the evening had brought, and she would let me in and make a place in her bed. Why she ever put up with me remains a mystery.

I have mentioned getting high nightly, but to better document my downward slide I need to fill in more of the picture. Marijuana and hash were there, for all of us, all the time—drugs as wallpaper. Everywhere any of us went, every person we dropped in on, every group we encountered—there was a joint, a pipe, and the expectation of partaking. It was harder then *not* to than it would be now to find such an easy partying ambiance. Bill Clinton claims not to have inhaled, but I would counter that he could not have gotten away with that. We were all watching each other—you did not shrug offers off lightly or only pretend to hold down the smoke you had just inhaled. Getting a bit high was as casual and frequent as having a cup of coffee, and few people thought twice about it.

But in the basement of Mosher-Jordan—I was on the third floor—things were getting a good deal more serious. A small group there, including some of the Farmington High kids, had passed quickly from snorting the occasional nickel bag of heroin to shooting up. We had three or four serious junkies in our midst—a test for all of us who believed in maximal tolerance—and at least one of the group was carted off to a rehab program by midsemester.

Still, we made these users, our friends, welcome in our midst—it would have been hypocrisy not to. While the rest of us passed around our joints and listened to music, these others receded into a corner to tie off. I didn't draw many lines in those days, but heroin was something I was firm about, even as I stared with stoned fascination at the others, sickened and thrilled to watch the plunger draw back and the clear cylinder darken with blood.

Hallucinogens were another matter. I saw those in a Blakean light—they were keys to the mysteries of spirit. Late in the fall of that first year, the kid who lived right across the hall from me actually slipped a "tab" of mescaline into the beer I was drinking, and when I had drained it he announced what he had done. Everyone had a good laugh, and I laughed, too, only half believing what he said. And then—abruptly—I believed. I felt myself being lifted slowly up into a rich, comprehending hilarity. I started to smile and found I could not stop. The smile seemed to be flowing forward from the front of my face. And everything—absolutely everything—made sense. Profound sense. The doorknob—perfect, beautiful, what a thing to have there on the door, which was really all about openings in space, points of entry and departure. The carpet seemed to be glowing up toward my fingers—and why not? I began to say of everything that I saw or heard that it was "cosmic." Which it was.

And now a group of us—there were a few others who had decided to "drop"—headed out into the night. The whole sleeping town became the set for a movie that we were playing in. We wandered down quiet side streets and played a new game. This was to stop at every house that had a porch and then tiptoe up to sit there for a minute. Then, giggling, thinking ourselves grand players, we moved on.

What I remember, though, most distinctly of all, was the exalting realization that I had found for myself the source of happiness and higher awareness. This is what the real hippies had been talking about—now I got it. As long as I could get some of this astonishing compound, as long as I could go through the world feeling this sense of exorbitant rightness, everything would be fine. Life would be profound, a trip.

The next few times I tried mescaline I had similar—if not quite so delightfully hilarious—experiences. Thirty or so minutes after swallowing a tab, I would feel an easy, smile-inducing relaxation move through my system. With the ease came, invariably, that powerful sense of knowing. Life was a web of intricate correspondences that our normal daytime consciousness missed entirely. Mescaline reversed the perceptions, pulled them inside out. Nothing was trivial; everything resonated with everything else. I had only to direct my attention to something and I would promptly grasp its secrets, secrets that were right there on the surface. Just like God, except, of course, that it had been the beam of His attention that put everything there in the first place. Children, age, death, journeys, suffering—all things were purposeful, intended. And with each new access of knowing I was certain that I had caught hold of the secret once and for all.

But no—the frustration of my drug experiences during this period was that I could not bring the wisdom back into my life. I would awaken at whatever hour the next day, back down—"crashed"—cotton-mouthed and feeling as if my brain had been drained of its vital fluids, and I would seek in vain to catch even a flash of the insight that had roared through me just hours before. Nothing. The world now mocked me by becoming even duller than it had been before. I stared as though through thick goggles at my fellow students with their backpacks and notebooks. The pointlessness of all this preparation! For what? To end up as office fodder—become a guy wearing a suit and living in a development somewhere with wife and kids? I could depress myself for the whole day just by pushing a few ready buttons. When I got into these moods I saw no point at all in going to classes. I would, instead, take myself out—wander the arboretum or follow the Huron River as far as I could, trying to cleanse my thoughts, to recover the right sense of things. I would make a little nest under a tree and write in my notebook. Later, often as not, I would end up at Cal's door, ready for his company and counsel.

Cal understood my situation, knew why I wanted out. He was my abettor, sitting with me through the wee hours in the Wheel, our favorite all-night hangout, drinking coffee, and helping me lay the plans for my escape.

Only now, enlightened by the times, do I see that what I was going through was a fairly severe depression. Back then it was just life; it was just my recognition of how things really were—the astonishing bullshit of it all. And as winter wore on, things got worse. I could hardly stand to be in my dorm room. I would pass through just long enough to change shirts and grab my journal, and then I would head out again. The pointlessness was almost like a pressure against my chest. I looked around, aghast. Any person who was simply carrying on with the normal business of living—riding on a bus, walking along the street with a briefcase, working in a store or office—was lost, blind to both the wonder and awfulness of the world. How easily we let ourselves slip. "Shades of the prison house," I muttered, half remembering the lines from Wordsworth.

Walking, I fantasized about how it would be in Europe. Stirring together Miller with some Kazantzakis, some Genet, some Hamsun, I created my new life. I would live simply, among unspoiled working people; in their natural wisdom they would help me. I would slip through the keyhole of this fallen culture and get back to something. The sooner this could all happen, the better.

When spring came, when the weather sharpened my desire to be wandering, I bought my airplane ticket. I had a few hundred dollars saved, and I would make more over there, selling my return ticket. I had heard, too, that there was a thriving market for U.S. passports. I could "lose" mine, claim it had been stolen, and get a new one. It no longer mattered that I would finish out my freshman year with a string of incompletes—each was further proof of my determination to not look back. It did not matter what my parents thought—so I told myself—for they would get it eventually. I would write and explain everything. I repeated to myself for the thousandth time the lines from the opening of *Tropic of Cancer:* "I have no money, no resources, no hopes. I am the happiest man alive." In this spirit—ready, chafing—I scored some mescaline and headed over to Cal's place.

Of the evening—our "trip"—I remember nothing. I have only the picture I began with, the two of us having talked ourselves into the heroics of crossing the railway trestle at sunrise. The point? I'm no longer sure. It was a ritual, I think, a way we had of sealing a pact, a recognition that most of existence was idiocy, but that in our adventures, our sleepless manias, our exhausted sunrises, we had found the secret way through. I write these words and realize that nothing could sound more vague. But we understood each other's vaguenesses back then—we knew the romantic longings that lay behind them.

When we reached the far side, felt the ground come up under us, we looked at each other with that Keatsian "wild surmise." Here was another one for the books.

I ended the school year in disgrace—the first time this had ever happened to me, the first time that my intellectual vanity had not kicked in to rescue me. I just didn't care. No, I was in fact proud of my incompletes, took great pleasure in the thought that I had abandoned the pretense of college life. Sitting down to take my last exam, in Chinese literature, I stared long and hard at the question sheet. I knew that I was not going to address myself to any of the questions, but still I stared. Then, picking up my pen, smiling to myself, I very carefully drew a picture of a butterfly with its wings spread open. Below, taking care with my calligraphy, I wrote:

"Professor Crump fell asleep and dreamed he was a butterfly. Or was it a butterfly that fell asleep and dreamed it was Professor Crump?"

Gathering up my backpack, looking out over the bowed heads of my classmates, those pretend revolutionaries, I strode up to Professor Crump's desk and set down the blue book. I paused only long enough to see that he was looking at me with a pained and inquisitive expression. Then I nodded, half bowed, and left the room. And for an hour or two, abroad in the May sunshine, I convinced myself that I had never been truer to myself. Or freer.

My ticket was round-trip, and my parents had no idea that I did not intend to use the return portion. Given the finality of the step I was planning, I marvel at how normal I acted around my family. School was over, dorm life was done—forever—and I was back home. I was happy to have a few weeks to sleep and read and consider my plans. I took walks and played with my little brother, now four. I said nothing to anyone about my disastrous year at school.

The night before my flight—before I left for six weeks to England and France—my father took me out to Fox & Hounds, a fancy restaurant on Woodward Avenue. He was, I could tell, primed for a man-to-man talk, and I tried to hold up my side. I asked him questions about his work, encouraged him to explain things. We both drank wine, and the more we sat, philosophizing, the more oppressive my secret became. Finally, riding the good feeling that seemed to be between us, I let on, with great casualness, that I had some ideas about staying in Europe for a time. "If I like it," I said, "I thought I might take some time off from school, maybe find a job—"

My father did not miss a beat. He looked straight at me—into me—set his jaw, and said, "Absolutely not."

"What do you mean?" I felt a fluttery agitation all through my chest.

"I mean you will do nothing of the kind. You come back as you planned or you don't go at all."

"But—" The familiar tears of frustration—which I so rarely let him see—welled up. I was the kid in the yard with the hose, except I was no longer a kid and I had no hose. I could think of nothing more to say; I locked down, retreated inward. I was at once hurt and fortified. If *that's* what he wants, I thought. His intransigence, his refusal to even hear me out, was making it easier for me. All he cared about was preserving his authority. I would follow the plan anyway—this was better.

Then he said, apropos of nothing I'd said, following the track of his own thought: "Don't break your mother's heart." And against that there was no defense.

When I flew to London the next afternoon, I was still resolved. But I would wait to see what came my way, where I ended up, whom I met—before doing anything final. I trusted that the path would be shown to me when the time was right. That was the extent of my metaphysics then. Decision making was part of the long view, and I was bent on living as much as I could in the glory of the moment.

My itinerary was correspondingly vague. I would travel around England for ten days until Reddog arrived, then the two of us would travel around for a time. Cal was landing in Luxembourg some weeks later. And Lisa and I would write to each other about whether we might connect somewhere.

I was entirely on my own, and I was thrilled. Everything was an adventure, a story for Reddog and Cal. After spending a few nights in a cheap doss-house off Piccadilly Circus, I hitched around southern England—fancied myself quite the resourceful tramp as I snuck around residential neighborhoods stealing milk bottles from front porches. In Winchester I spent a night with an old Cranbrook acquaintance who was on exchange and fell madly—if briefly—in love with a beautiful Pakistani girl named Ela, who went to school in nearby St. Swithun's and who let me kiss her on a walk we took and gave me a copy of Kazantzakis's *Freedom or*

Death when it was time for me to go. Then I hitched back to London and met Reddog's plane, and the two of us bounced around the same basic places, carrying on an elaborate fantasy in which he was called the "Dover pro" and I was his sidekick, Billy, and we were hunting for girls to fall in love with. We crossed to the mainland, and then, after a few days in Amsterdam, during which time we frequented the legal "hash" bars and roamed along the canals, Reddog met an exotic-looking blonde named Enneka, who promptly attached herself to him and offered to travel with him to India.

Reddog and I parted by a bridge. I remember sitting down that night on my hostel bed and writing a melancholy poem about two old friends traveling in different directions, which ended with an image I still like: "Each of us / Leaving for the world from a corner." A few days later I was off to meet Cal.

Cal and I covered France, north to south, hitchhiking, walking around Paris the whole of a long night because we had no place to sleep—I remember how we debated stealing a baguette from the backseat of a car—and then hurried to get out of the city and into some countryside. There we tried to hitch and had very poor luck. We spent days walking side by side down endless rural roads, scheming, confiding ourselves, screaming insults at the motorists who blew by us. We lived on bread, cheese, and chocolate, slept in fields, and made our way in slow spurts down to the French Riviera, where we foolishly imagined we would meet interesting people who would take us in. But it was clear the moment we got there—we saw how the shopkeepers folded their arms and stared at us, how the beautiful women did not even know we were on the sidewalk—that we did not belong. So we pointed ourselves toward Spain, ending up one glorious molten evening on the Ramblas in Barcelona, stunned by the sight of so much fruit, so many birds in cages, the smells in the air. There, inadvertently, we insulted a bar filled with prostitutes (we didn't know) by refusing them, one after the next, when they sat down and asked if we might buy them a drink. There we drank with a table full of riotous Algerians, enormously enjoying our grunting and pointing until a phalanx of Guardia Civil suddenly rushed through the door and with sticks and rough shoves herded them all into the alley, whereupon they were loaded into a waiting truck and taken away. There, too, in a cheap room we rented, I broke down. Sitting on the edge of the bed, drinking beer, writing my thoughts in my journal while Cal read, I suddenly knew that I would not be able to carry out my plan. I did not have the resources, the languages, the skills. Winter would come and I would have nothing. And I missed my family. I could not sever myself from them—I wanted to try again. This was, at root, a positive realization, a step forward, but it felt like defeat. It had taken me all this traveling to find out that I was not free. I lay on my bed, turned away from Cal, tears streaming down my cheeks.

Two weeks later, after ten days of camping on a beach on the island of Formentera—Lisa had arrived with fresh energy and resources—after spending an afternoon in jail there for nude bathing (Lisa had to bribe the arresting officer with a bundle of pesetas), after being denied entry to England for having no shoes (Lisa had to buy some on the other side of customs and send them across to me)—I found my charter group and got myself ready for the flight back.

CHAPTER 5

FOR A GOOD PART OF MY ADULT LIFE, ESPECIALLY THROUGH THE long period of my twenties, I carried on with an active belief in the principle of destiny. Which meant for me, essentially, that if all the veils were to be torn asunder and the core working of things exposed, then the intricately purposeful interconnectedness of all our wishes, thoughts, and deeds would also be clear. Walking around, going through what often felt like the mere motions of daily life, I was always coaching myself to embrace the necessity of whatever I was doing. Pushing a broom along the deserted corridors of Saint Francis College, where I worked as a night janitor, or, years later, carting stacks of textbooks to and fro in Boston's first Barnes & Noble, I fought the obvious implication—that failure was my lot—with the full force of my being. These were my appointed intervals, and their value could not be assessed in conventional societal terms. These stairs, these bags of trash—I simply could not yet see the puzzle in which they were necessary pieces. On and on it went, this thinking, growing at certain heightened moments into a conviction that every gesture, every pause on a crowded sidewalk, had to be thus, not thus, that the script was complete down to the last character. But no, that was madness. That was fate tricked out as the most extreme sort of predestination, and I struggled to haul myself back from the precipice. Destiny, what I pledged to, was something else. Destiny was more like a possibility, a set of hidden doors mapped into an otherwise contingent universe. Destiny was an elusive exchange, a path to absolute self-attainment that had to be fought for incessantly; it was something we earned. These thankless menial employments were all instances of the not-yet. They were my goad, my cue to dare something lest I perish in mediocrity.

I was confused. I worked on life as if it were a mathematical equation I had to solve, as if there were a right sequence, a thought I might discover that would spring me from whatever was the latest miserable entanglement.

I don't know for sure where this inclination, this disposition, came from. I suppose everyone in my family had certain such leanings, though generally more in the direction of superstition. After my grandfather Mike died, for instance, my grandmother suddenly revealed herself to be an adept in the fortune-telling arts. Sitting with her in her dark upstairs apartment in Birmingham, left to keep her company while my mother went off to do her errands, my sister and I would watch, transfixed, as she set out the elaborate design of the future with her deck of cards, gasping dramatically whenever she turned over the queen of spades, which she called the "death card." "Soon," she would say, nodding to herself but speaking audibly nonetheless, "soon I'll be with my Mike."

And certainly my mother, Ūm's only child, was not immune to suggestions of dark influence. Through her, on a daily basis, we imbibed a somewhat diluted awareness of old world superstition. There were all the old formulas about not whistling at night, avoiding cats and ladders, throwing spilled salt over the shoulder, and so on. But more telling, I think, was the outlook that underlay it all. That the guardians of our fortune were somehow there, animate and watchful; that one could never presume. To express a desire or hope without some ritualized pause—a kind of touch-wood acknowledgment of the hubris involved in any optimistic projection—was to invite disaster. How much did she believe this, and how much was she paying reflexive lip service to her Latvian origins, I don't know. But my sister and I certainly took it in, in our younger years anyway, as fundamental life information. And to this day I cannot launch optimistically on any venture without the active rustle of caution-giving voices in my ears.

It was, however, my father who probably had the greatest influence in this matter. My father, as rational and empirical a man as one could imagine in most respects—a man who to this day thinks of long airplane flights as a form of relaxation—was at another level a ceaseless proselytizer for his own brand of destiny. Not destiny in general, certainly not destiny as it might figure into someone else's life, but destiny as it had, from the moment of his birth, dictated to him the shape of his life and career. How many hundreds of times—never without a keen vicarious edge—have I listened as he has talked us through the latest installment: how it was meant from the first that such and such a client should have come to him, or how some design solution should have announced itself in just the way it had. Sitting with him in our upstairs living room, I used to soak up these stories. I loved the feeling I got from such a contemplation—that the things that befall us do so as a consequence of innumerable invisible orchestrations; that everything adds up and at the end of one's days some marvelous revelation of pattern gets passed along. If I am less certain about this now, I remain sympathetic, provisional, unable and unwilling to rule it out completely.

All of this makes a cumbersome prelude to the story of my relationship with Jess Zachariah, but the dynamics of our encounter on the Diag at the University of Michigan in the late fall of 1971 cannot be explained—or given the proper dramatic contour—without some understanding of this particular warp in my character.

Some more background. As I mentioned before, Jess and I had grown up in the same little corner of Bloomfield Hills. We went to school together from the first through the ninth grade, frequented the same little stretch of beach at Walnut Lake in the summer. We were, I'd say—and years later she corroborated me—acutely aware of each other, even as mutual shyness and the universal behavior codes of childhood, then adolescence, kept our exchanges to a minimum.

Of these, the defining transaction took place that day by the doorway of our second-grade classroom, where, as we were standing in line to go to recess, Jess turned around and announced directly to me that she was reading *The Wizard of Oz*. I don't remember how I responded, only that from then on I carried an impression of a singularly alert and articulate human being. I was, to put it plainly, in awe. I was myself nowhere close to having such mastery. This chubby, pretty, self-possessed person was somehow striding right past me in what I had not, perhaps until just then, understood to be a race. I know that from that moment on I was somehow very much interested in Jess Zachariah.

From a distance, of course. As things fell out, Jess and I were bound through all of the remaining years of grade school in a competitive give-and-take that neither of us would ever acknowledge, no matter how fierce it sometimes became. We were both in the ranks of the so-called smart kids, and we were each, in our own way, desperate for approval from on high. When the teacher asked a question, our hands flashed up first. I didn't even have to turn my head to feel her there, in her seat by the door, tilting forward in her seat, her hand not flagging or pumping but held calmly aloft. And when we had reports to hand in, special projects, the research books we compiled on a state of our choice, a country, the human body, I always shot a glance first at Jess's desk, where inevitably there sat, thicker, more artistically got-up than anything the rest of us had assembled, her contribution.

Jess trumped me, trumped us all, but I wonder how many took it to heart as I did. I can still feel—like little drumbeats from my prior life—the thudding of my pulses as I stood, year after year, in the elimination rounds of the annual gradewide spelling bee. It was always the two of us, side by side by the blackboard, as the teacher—Mrs. Fremont, Miss Hilty, Mr. Faust—called off the harder words. I smile now. But the year I went down on the word "separate"—a word I knew—and had to listen as Jess marched through the right sequence of letters without even a polite hesitation, I felt myself marked out once and for all as a second-stringer. Was there the merest edge of malice in her smile as she made her way back to her desk? I thought so.

But then things changed. When Jess and I would sometimes pass each other in the halls of Berkshire, the shiny new junior high school we attended, along with kids from five or six other area schools, I felt a fond sort of recognition. She smiled. There was shyness—from both of us. We didn't say anything to each other, but I had the feeling that warm signals had been covertly exchanged.

It was not until the ninth grade, the year before she transferred to another school, that Jess and I had a class together. Spanish. Jess got seated right in front of me, and something about switching languages liberated us. Though we rarely exchanged words in English, we were mockingly chatty with our limited new vocabulary.

"*O, la sua falta está bonita.*"

"*Gracias. Y me gusta su camisa.*"

In these last few years Jess had lost weight and become quite pretty. Her air—amused, but also slightly embarrassed, as if by some thought she could not share—appealed to me tremendously. But there was nothing to be done. I was all braces and glasses and curly hair that I tried to Brylcreem into submission every morning—no catch. But even had it been otherwise, if I'd had the looks and moves of one of the stars who sauntered along the corridors, what could I have done? This was the ninth grade, era of Friday night football games and chaperoned sock hops after. Could we have stood in one of the bleacher alcoves, holding hands while Steve Wray and his Calientes played "Hang On Sloopy"? Maybe— but who will ever know? The school year ended, Jess moved, and when classes resumed the following fall, the rest of us were all at Groves, the big public high school.

All of this is background, context to establish the momentousness, for me, of that lunchtime moment when I sat—smoking, alienated—staring into the vast Brownian motion of students jostling between classes. I was a junior at Michigan. I had just moved back into town, into my own little cell of a room on South Division Street, after a depressed few months of living at home with my parents and commuting the forty miles each way three days a week; that after a vividly desolate summer of living in a bunkhouse on a ranch in Deer Lodge, Montana, where a friend of my father's had found me a job bucking hay and where I bore with surprising good humor the nickname "Nigger-Knots" from the snorting ranch hands.

What was I doing? I had no clue, really, either about why I had moved home or why I had returned to Ann Arbor again. I seemed to live by standing things for as long as I could, and then, when I could stand no more, changing. I was full of the sense of general collapse. It was 1972 and the party was over. What had felt like the glorious opening out of the culture now felt like a delusion. Vietnam, Cambodia—our extraordinary solidarity had achieved nothing. The counterculture was fractured and worn out. And those swarming, happy get-togethers of freshman year were a thing of the past. How could they have continued? How long could you sit with the same people getting stoned and listening to "Let It Bleed"? Cal and Todd, while still my main friends, seemed to be pulling away into their own lives—both had serious girlfriends. Todd and his new love, Nancy, had even set up house together. Lisa and I, meanwhile, had parted ways before I went off to Montana. I was on my own. I had no interest in anything but reading, strumming my guitar, and writing in my journal—and not much heart for those things, either.

And then, into the lens of my gaze, which sharpened suddenly into crisp—shocked—resolution, stepped the apparition of Jess Zachariah. Between the time I got to my feet and the moment I had threaded through what felt like a stadiumful of intervening bodies to catch her by the shoulder, an amazing certainty had arrived. This was destiny, the bolt of lightning I had been awaiting so long.

Recognition from Jess was not—as I had maybe expected it to be—instantaneous. If she was basically the girl I remembered, though evolved now into a striking young woman of twenty, everything about the way I looked had changed. My hair was the main thing, though. It was long, worn still in that ill-maintained Afro style. My face was stubbly, and I had thinned and grown a good deal taller since Mrs. Whittaker's ninth-grade Spanish class. All of which is to say that Jess stood, befuddled, poised to deliver some sharp, sarcastic rebuff, and some moments had to pass before the smile of recognition broke over her features.

"Peter?" I was still Peter then. But the name sounded odd when she said it, like a holdover from childhood years. Worse, she looked amused by the recognition. We had not exchanged a word, and already I felt like something mildly diverting that had happened to her on her walk across campus.

I can't recover much about our exchange—maybe because I was leaning down and staring so intently at this familiar face, maybe because I was all but vibrating with my feeling of fatedness. The encounter was brief, anyway. And I was frustrated, sure my intensity and seriousness were not being registered. "You look so *dif*ferent," Jess was saying. She kept looking up at my hair, smiling in that way I now remembered, as if she could never say what she was really thinking. I felt she had me immobilized in some freeze-frame memory. I was her childhood suddenly rearing up in her face. That threat, those long-ago days—it was all to be tamed with a string of quips and bright dismissals.

Meanwhile, I was searching out whatever clues I could, looking for rings, listening for the giveaway pronoun that would signal a boyfriend. I couldn't guess. Certainly it would be too much to expect her to be completely unattached. Still—

I didn't have a chance to finish the thought. Jess was straightening up, shifting her bag on her shoulder. She had to be off. "What an interesting surprise," she said. I tried to decode that "interesting." "I'm sure I'll see you around." Then, before there was any chance for embarrassing initiatives from me, she was walking, looking only once over her shoulder, putting a crisp sort of closure on this unexpected encounter.

And there things remained, for a day, two days, until on the third day it became unendurable. I had never felt it before, this roiling, joint-weakening anxiety that had me looking for ways to calm myself. I could think of nothing but Jess Zachariah. In a stroke I had become the very caricature of the smitten young man—conjuring her face as I sat in the lecture hall, idling along all of the high-traffic arteries on campus, trolling for another glimpse. I had, of course, located her phone number right away in new campus listings—Jess had told me that she had recently transferred to Michigan from Oakland University—and I kept that folded in my wallet, at first just to tantalize myself, then as a kind of private dare, and finally, on that third night, as I was wandering back and forth in front of the Michigan Union, as the trigger for a decision I could no longer not make.

Jess agreed to meet me for coffee at the Wheel, a restaurant on South University. I waited at a table in the far rear corner, doodling furiously, looking up every time the door opened, until, several blackened pages later, she was suddenly marching toward me. She had on a fur coat—raccoon, she later told me—and when she regarded me, which she did even before taking the seat opposite, it was with an expression that said, "This had better be good." I had said only that I *had* to talk to her. She turned her head slightly to the side and stared at me, waiting.

Later, when we had begun to go out, when we had found our joking mode, Jess took great delight in recalling my awkwardness to me. "I was ready to bolt as soon as I saw your face, except I felt so sorry for you." I had done the unthinkable. I had confessed my torment; I had thrown myself on her mercy. I had stared across the table with baleful intensity, waiting for something. "What was I supposed to do, abandon you? I was afraid you were going to die on me."

Was I that bad? I remember only standing on the front steps of Jess's apartment, my bladder so full that I could scarcely breathe, but not daring to ask to use her bathroom, and that she let me land a quick, wispy kiss on her forehead, thereby indicating, I thought, that we could soon meet up again.

Destiny indeed. How could I see our getting together, becoming a couple, an item, as anything else? That I should now be walking the wintry streets of Ann Arbor arm in arm with the very person I had battled so many years ago in the Walnut Lake School spelling bee—it was so right as to be unthinkable. How much had changed—both of us inhabiting grown-up bodies, complexly alert to all the signals of touch—and how much we were still the same.

It was by no means an easy meshing of cogs. I was in a state of extreme anxiety over my stroke of fortune, and Jess was not one to make the placating gesture. For all that had happened to us in the intervening years, what we carried into our new courtship were the old reflexes, updated. Bright boy meets bright girl. We sat in various bars and restaurants, sparring, styling a repartee that we both fancied was Bogart and Bacall, Nick and Nora Charles, but which was really just the nervously competitive banter of two English majors, laying on each other the tags we had picked up from our reading—hers heavy on the English poets, Wordsworth to Auden, mine borrowing more from the Beats and what someone once dubbed "the literature of exhaustion." The unstated rule was simple. If one person artfully (or not so artfully) quoted or alluded, the other would then have to, subtly, indicate that he or she knew the source. Mention of a "sawdust retreat" might invite some winking mention of Michelangelo a few sentences on. Failure to follow—usually on my part—brought condescending surprise.

"You haven't read *Mansfield Park*?" The mocking inflection of her eyebrow lowered my stock slightly. But Jess was beautiful when she was winning, flush with her own quickness.

We sat in one campus restaurant after another that season, talking. I had to work hard at not staring. I found her so beautiful and mysterious—the most familiar person in the world and yet not familiar at all. My gaze strayed and returned, alighting always in the same place like some heat-maddened insect: the slight little bump on the bridge of her nose. That was the defining anomaly for me, the thing that brought her into focus for me. It reminded me of who I was with, for so much else had shifted.

Both of us wrestled with this mingling in the other of the known and the strange. For of course those years of childhood were all still there, especially in the beginning. We could not get through a meal without some odd reprising of the past.

"What ever happened to *Bobo* Spriggel?" Jess might ask.

"You mean *Keith*."

"Yes . . ." A tart pause. "Keith. What ever happened to *Keith* Spriggel? He was a charming boy."

"He was *your* neighbor. We hunted for frogs over in your Peat Pond."

"The *Peat* Pond!" Jess looked delighted. "You remember the Peat Pond—"

"How could I not remember the Peat Pond?"

"And you were one of the little boys who murdered frogs and threw their little corpses into the road." There was a condescending shine in her eye.

"You think less of me?"

Pause. "Yes." And then there would be another pause while I scrambled to assess the damage. Was she just tweaking me? Or should I have kept my mouth shut? I knew Jess, but not completely. Behind the wall of her irony—this I sensed—were sad, vulnerable pockets. Her high spirits would sometimes rapidly deflate. She would get abruptly moody, serious. We might be walking the streets, commenting idly on things, and I would sense some darkness stealing over her. It was no good to talk then. She would say that she had work to do and we would steer toward her apartment. I knew enough not to follow her in.

We walked a great deal. When we were not having coffee or drinks somewhere—certainly in the early days—we patrolled the streets. Sex was still a question, an obstacle. We did our share of kissing and pawing, especially after we'd had a few drinks, but then we both tensed up. We didn't go back to my room, or her apartment, which she shared with a warily watchful nursing student, because that would have forced the issue. A tricky business. On top of the normal hesitations—fears of suddenness and exposure—was the more vexing problem. We never came out with it, of course, either of us, but we were both overwhelmed. We were *so* familiar to each other. One or the other of us was always declaring in an awed tone, "I *know* you." How could we ever get naked with each other without both of us collapsing under the weight of our history?

So we walked, each of us feeling our way toward an opening, a solution. I preserve an image, fairly representative, I think, of the two of us fumbling our way toward campus, coming up Liberty Street after a riotous "happy hour" at the Cracked Crab, our favorite bar. Jess had introduced me to the martini, and we both felt it was the pinnacle of sophistication to knock back several of these very adult concoctions before ordering up some beer-battered fish. After, we push-pulled ourselves up the street. It was cold, we were very near my room, but if we hesitated, it was only briefly. "Not yet"—we both knew this. The kids needed to be pushed aside, displaced.

Eventually—somehow—it happened. Jess came up to my room, sat in my one chair while I fussed around opening the bottle of Mateus I had bought. She looked around and made a few quips about Raskolnikov's room, then flattered me by giving careful study to my little bookcase stocked with orange and black Penguin paperbacks. We then drank our wine out of coffee cups, Jess still in the chair, me now sitting demurely on the edge of the bed. It *was* Raskolnikov's room. There was nowhere to go, nothing to do but think about gratuitous acts of violence.

Jess and I spent our first night together, clothed, keeping each other warm under my raspy Mexican blanket. The bed was tiny. Once we had found a position, we kept it. I lay awake, staring at Jess's nape. She had taken off her sweater, wore only a turtleneck and jeans. This seemed sublime. The warmth from all that length of contact was more than enough for me. I had never felt so safe, so rightly placed in the world.

And then, at six or so—in the dark, anyway—she was up, pulling on her sweater, hurrying out. Later, I understood. Jess was terrified that her mother would take it into her head to call about something, that her possibly sadistic roommate, Helena, would take the opportunity to stick the knife in. "No, I'm sorry, Mrs. Zachariah, I haven't seen Jess. I'm not sure she was even here last night. . . ."

Jess's mother bond, I learned over time, was profound and complex. There was a deep need for approval coupled with an equally deep need to break away and declare herself an independent adult. Both forces worked on her at once. In our daily life—Jess and I had quickly become almost inseparable—she gave a good imitation of a free-spoken intellectual with desirably deplorable habits. She drank and smoked and cussed with great inventiveness. A superb mimic, she could role-play blowsy barmaids and indolently sensuous aristocrats with tireless inventiveness. A few inspired moves with a cigarette and she could open up a complete comic world. *"Mein Schatz—"* Jess was, I discovered, the queen of kitschy impersonation, and she could shift into the mode with a single exaggerated grimace. She had an ongoing rendition of Helga, a sentimental German double agent, that could take me to pieces, except that I was supposed to step in as her dull-witted foil, Helmut, so that she could ramp up her performance. At night, jammed into my spring-shot single bed, we exhausted ourselves—not so much in pursuit of eros as in a string of comic performances. In the beginning we amused each other tremendously.

This is not to say that things were perfect. Jess would from time to time fall into her listless melancholia—hating herself, hating college life, railing against the entrapment she felt. These moods rendered me powerless. To see my riot-loving accomplice folded in on herself, her gaze unresponsive, the nerve of her humor inert, gave me deep pangs. I did not understand her situation, not as well as I should have. I assumed that her distress grew out of our relationship somehow and offered radical solutions: We would quit school, move away, take jobs . . . Jess scoffed at my innocence and credulity. And her criticisms stung. For at some level we were still in competition; I was still trying to prove myself to her. When she took on that dismissive air, making out like I was still an emotional beginner—which in fact I was—I got furious.

One late afternoon, Jess and I were in my room, locked in one of our silent face-offs. I don't remember why we were at each other—the pretexts were often laughably obscure—only that at one point she began to mock me, arching her brows and smiling to herself in a knowing way. She undid me, turned my every glowering gesture into something foolish. I was beside myself. Suddenly, inspired, I grabbed our half-empty wine bottle and flung it with all my force at the far wall. It shattered convincingly. The wine ran in drooling strings down the wall, pooled on the flat carpet. I felt a rush of triumph.

Jess looked at me with startled focus and—did I see this?—a measure of respect. "Well!" She laughed. Sardonically, I thought. But I had *done* something. I had tapped my noncerebral side, shown myself to have a streak of rage, of passion. But I had no follow-through. I looked at Jess, first with righteousness, then with embarrassment. A few minutes later we were both cleaning up the mess.

Here is an admission. As much as Jess and I later argued, and as hard as I tried to become that decisive, heedless Lawrentian figure

I thought she wanted me to become, all of my raging explosions—and there were a few—were put-up jobs. They were prompted by rage, yes—I possess rage aplenty—but they were never its pure expression. I was always there, behind the arras of it all, watching. I dearly wish I were otherwise, a volcanic Sicilian. But I'm not. My self-division is complete. The commentator is always assessing the performance. Even drinking cannot completely shatter the self-awareness. I have never been so drunk that I did not know exactly what I was saying. Hamlet, Prufrock—they are my great familiars.

As the school year wound down, as summer and the need for a plan loomed up, Jess fell into frequent depressions. More and more we just sat in my room, or out, somewhere in a public place. Idling, saying nothing. "I'm boring," she would say. "Ditch me while you have a chance." I would hasten in whatever way I could think of to reassure her. What was bringing her low, I thought, was her confusion. I was urging her to stay in town—we could work, share a sublet. Her family expected her to come home. She wasn't sure what she herself wanted. An end to pressure, tension, and guilt. "*That* would be a summer vacation," she said.

My idea, which Jess finally agreed to, was that she would rent a room and that I would visit her there. I would, of course, visit all the time. But semantics was the issue where her mother was concerned. What could she say on the phone in good conscience? This line worked.

I purged myself of everything but a few items of clothing and my typewriter. When Jess signed the sublet for a small room in a quasi-communal rooming house, I stayed away. She moved in her things, established territoriality. Only then did I lug my duffel bag up the stairs, hang a few things in the far back of the closet, and begin my visit.

It was not a good summer, and I frankly marvel that our relationship survived it. I remember long humid days with the two of us moving around each other like prisoners in a shared cell. The whole house was oppressive. The communal kitchen was slick with layers of ancient grease, and the cockroach problem was so bad that Jess could scarcely bring herself to make coffee. She would not even open the refrigerator, choosing to subsist on yogurts and Diet Cokes she bought in town.

How did we get through the days? Jess was waitressing the dinner shift at a Greek restaurant, so she would sleep as late as she could. I used those mornings, when I was not picking up manual temp work, to write at the table in the living room. Afternoons, before Jess had to get ready for work, we might walk around town, take ourselves out to lunch. While she worked, I lay in bed and read. I had no friends in town that summer, no money for going out. If the phone rang, I was not allowed to answer. I did what I could to fill up the hours. I played Beethoven's Fourth Symphony on a small turntable we'd found at a yard sale. Luther Allison. Sometimes I just lay on my back and daydreamed. Then at ten-thirty I would bestir myself, head down to the restaurant to wait for Jess.

She was in a bad way. I could see this plainly, but I was powerless. One night I stood on the sidewalk and watched her through the big picture window. She was in her uniform—short skirt, dark stockings—and her hair was pinned up in a bun. Up and back, up and back—she was vacuuming around the tables. She seemed entirely wrapped up in some private sadness. Utterly oblivious—of me, the restaurant. I vowed then, in the way of a young man, that I would do something heroic with my life. I would free her, free both of us. What that meant, I had no idea.

I did not come through for Jess, not that summer. Growing up and separating from her family—a process in which I was deeply implicated—was eating her up. But she did not consult me and I stepped around her clumsily, looking for ways to cheer her up.

Sadly, I had no resources. I would come into our little room at noon, having been drinking coffee and trying to write in the living room, and I would find her curled up, eyes open, on the bed. If she ventured to talk, it was usually something about absurdity. Everything was "absurd" that summer—the room we shared, her job, our neighbors. She saw herself as absurd, untenable, a joke of a person. Whatever I ventured in the face of this seemed insipid, was consumed and vaporized instantly by the heat of her self-disgust.

The situation couldn't last. But before we could make a move, act to change things in any way, we had to find bottom. We argued. And out of the dense funk of impressions from that time, this is what comes back most vividly: the two of us standing in some mute face-off. As painted by Munch, scripted by Strindberg.

We would drink our way into it—beer, wine, anything on hand that would cut against the heat and humidity. The more we consumed, the more tangled up everything became. Neither one of us could get at it. But there would be Jess on the living room couch, pulled into herself, mute, while I stalked the perimeter of the room, looking out the window, slamming my glass on the coffee table. I can't remember a single specific issue. I only know that I felt indicted. If I criticized her family attachment, I was attacking her. But at the same time I was failing her by not being enough of a man. A real man would have taken things in hand, emancipated her, cut the Gordian knot. I was a tyro, a mere boy. Indeed, Jess knew far too well who I had been all those years ago, and she could undermine me with the slightest cynical lift of her eyebrow.

One summer day, just as things were reaching their worst pitch, when it seemed we couldn't get through the simplest conversation without fraying further what still remained between us, we bumbled into a distraction. Coming up a leafy side street behind the architecture school, we saw a woman sitting by a tree. On the sidewalk in front of her was a large cardboard box full of evident commotion. We stopped. Puppies. Fist-size little animals of indeterminate breed. Whimpers and tongues—we could not seem to get back on our way. Jess had one of the puppies in her cupped hands and was letting it feast on her chin. When she flashed a "Do we dare?" glance in my direction, I had no will to play the cautioning skeptic.

A few minutes later we were hurrying back to the room, chattering at a clip reminiscent of our early days, gaping at our own foolishness, and rising, for a moment, to the challenge of figuring out how we might keep this mournfully lovable little dog a secret from our neighbors.

We managed, at least for a few days. "Coon"—named thus for her peculiar stripes and spots—lived in a box by the bed. She went everywhere with us, nosing her way into the bed, wetting the blankets, but not enough to matter, keening for us the instant we left her behind in the room. She was so small, I remember, that when I went to meet Jess after work, I would carry her to the restaurant in the pocket of my sport coat.

Coon helped, but not enough. When the first distraction wore off, we found ourselves moving back toward our standoff. Where the little dog had livened things up, redirected our attention, now she became part of the mess. I had the feeling, more and more, that having a puppy in bed with us was Jess's way to look past our problems, whatever they were. The truth is that I didn't *know* what they were. I knew only that whatever I was offering her was not enough anymore.

The hot nights of drinking continued, followed by harsh, hurtful mornings. We got so that we were barely speaking, and Coon's scrambles for love and attention became so poignant, such a reproach, that neither of us could deal with them. Finally, we conceded. In early August Jess called her parents and said that she was coming home for the rest of the summer. I made myself scarce the day they drove up to move her things home. When I got back later, the room was nearly bare. But somehow I stood it. I knew that things were not really over. There was a sense that this was a storm that we were going to ride out—separately. And when Jess did call me the next night—I leaned, eyes closed, against the wall in the dark hallway—I felt a perceptible lightening. She was joking again. Things were going to work out. I agreed to visit soon.

And so it was I found myself one blazing August afternoon in the Zachariahs' backyard, talking with Jess's mother and sisters, later playing catch with a Wiffle ball while Dr. Zachariah cooked hamburgers on the grill. At one point, fumbling for my catch, going for a laugh, I pretended to faint. I threw myself down on the grass and lay without twitching. I squeezed my eyes shut and waited. Suddenly, out of nowhere, Jess was bending over me, slapping my cheek—hard—calling out: "He's not dead. He's not dead." Flashing to my feet, utterly heedless of the fact that Jess's whole family was watching, poised for the gag, the comic flourish, I slapped her full on the face and walked away. It was not my finest moment.

Some events shrink, even disappear, in memory; others grow, taking on an outsize gestural life. The moment of the slap—the sweep of my open hand, the impact, the satisfaction of it—that remains. Ashamed and remorseful as I felt, instantly, I could not privately get around the little burst of triumph that delivering that slap gave me. It was for all those nights we had faced off in Ann Arbor, for all the impotence Jess had made me feel; for the fact that she needed somebody I couldn't be.

Eventually I was forgiven, first by Jess, then by her family, whose fun-loving security I had unexpectedly violated. And when school resumed in September, Jess and I were still together, living just two blocks apart. I had a new little room above a delicatessen, and Jess shared a bright efficiency apartment with her old high school friend Karla.

I see the long period beginning with the fall of our senior year and ending with our semicovert departure for New England a year and a half later as a diffuse interim. Though we were still very much a couple—we stayed together several nights a week, her place, my place—we also pulled back into our separate lives. Jess and Karla spent long hours together. They were both hooked on the televised coverage of the Watergate hearings, and if I came by in the late afternoon, it was a sure bet that I'd find them side by side on the couch, drinking diet sodas and smoking in front of Karla's TV.

This was a world I could not begin to make my way into. Jess and Karla had their own language, their own gestural codes; they were immersed in a pageant I had no real interest in. They followed the blow-by-blow, lawyers and witnesses perjuring themselves as the righteous gavel of Sam Ervin, their god, marked out the path of decorum. I was impressed. Both could talk the fine points, untangle the skein of implications, but they could also fling off into spasms of hilarity, Karla parking her cigarette on the table ledge as she yanked her blond hair back to "do" Maureen Dean, Jess screaming obscenities as G. Gordon Liddy arranged himself behind the microphone. I was there as an audience to their escalating sense of outrage, nothing more. And after a short time I usually left.

My life was elsewhere. I had just that season discovered the book underworld, that to-me fascinating network of bookshops, flea markets, and resale counters where one could swap bags of used books for other bags of used books or small quantities of cash. When I was not in class I was very likely down in the noncampus part of town, prowling through that day's donations to the Salvation Army—five for a dollar—or selling my finds to Dave, the buyer at the Wooden Spoon, a used-book shop just a few doors down. Or I was making my way up Liberty Street or down State Street, my backpack packed with the "finds" that I would then pore over for hours in my room, deciding which to add to my own collection. I was quite dizzy with the whole business, could easily pass most of the night in my chair, dipping into the stack by my feet, writing down titles and references on one of the lists I had going. I would scarcely acknowledge the little twinge of guilt I felt when I reminded myself that this was not a "Jess night" and that I could continue my obsessions uninterrupted.

Yet I did love Jess, felt in her presence a kind of happy possessiveness, which is not to be construed as an "incorrect" sentiment, for I had no thought at all about having any power over her. Rather, it was the feeling that she and I were so congruent in our understandings, our aspirations, our sense of the world's absurdity, that we were a natural fit. If Jess belonged to me, it was because we belonged together—a proposition that would probably not withstand much logical dissection.

It was a mark of our togetherness, I thought, a testimony to the durability of our relationship, that we could spend so much time happily apart. These distancings, I told myself, gave us greater focus and intensity when we were together.

Sometime that year, as our final semester at Michigan drew to a close, Jess and I began to occupy ourselves with the problem of the future. Our lives—which each of us would assume full ownership of in early June. We were both overwhelmed by the implications and spent many hours over drinks at the Cracked Crab trying to make out the outlines of what might be coming. I see us there, so much more subdued than we had been in our first months together, no longer mugging and doing our endless improvised impersonations. Now Jess is shredding the corner of her napkin, while I flick my glance to the TV screen behind the bar and then back to her profile, her agitated fingers.

"We can do anything, you know." I felt a happy righteousness: it was true. Just months ago, standing in the slushy aisle of Campus Corners, waiting to pay for my morning coffee, I found myself leaning down to make sense of the headline on that morning's newspaper: LAIRD ENDS DRAFT. My eyes were smarting; I had to stop and lean against the counter while the implications sifted through me. Everything was changed, renewed. We could do anything we wanted.

"I wish I were as peppy about that idea as you." Jess closed her eyes as she looked up. "Why do I have this feeling it's not so easy?"

"It *is* so easy. Just like that. Bang. Do it. Easy. What do you want to do?" I put on my bluster just to counter her—not that she believed it for an instant. Easy indeed. What was easy was thinking that life would just totter forward, day to day, as it had for so long.

In our better, more serious moments, Jess and I wanted the same thing—to get away from the Midwest, to go somewhere and make things up for ourselves. New England, we thought. Ocean, fog, shingled houses. Beyond that we had little notion. Our best connection for an exit was Jess's sister, Susan, and her husband, Jim. They had recently moved to Dover, New Hampshire, so that Jim could go to graduate school at UNH. We'd all spent a few evenings together before they left. They were keen that we should follow them out.

But not yet. We needed to earn money first, as much as possible. And this is just what we did. For a whole year, we lived apart. Jess moved back home with her parents and took a job as a cocktail waitress. I stayed on in the room over the deli, taking a job at Borders Books, which had just expanded into its first full-size store. This was long before the days of empire, back when the two brothers, Tom and Louis, were still to be found in the basement, unpacking boxes and sorting overstock.

I loved the job—the energy, the extraordinary group of coworkers. I was kept so busy—sorting, shelving, working the registers, mounting the learning curve—that I hardly had time to miss Jess. Indeed, when she showed up one day to surprise me, standing by the new arrivals table, I was more disconcerted than delighted. I was hoarding separate energies; I couldn't mix my lives.

At night, though, when I was alone, tired of my books and the lonely punctuations of traffic outside my window, I missed her. Then I wanted back what we'd had, that nest of codes and confidences, that wry enclosure behind which the world—the future—shone. I feared that these feelings we had might slip away, that we would lose each other even as we labored to find a way to be together.

More and more often, then, I hitchhiked home for the weekends, visiting my parents and playing with my little brother through the evening, then borrowing the family car so that I could drive to the bar where Jess worked. There I would look for a seat in the back and sit nursing beers while I tracked her movements between bar and tables and listened to the singer run through her endless covers of "Killing Me Softly" and "Bridge over Troubled Water."

As Jess did not fit into my work life—my hard-won sense of myself as an independent agent—so I did not fit into hers, either. I knew that just by sitting in that room, even though I stayed far away from her station, I was somehow cramping her style. She could not joke quite as freely with the other waitresses in the communal waiting area, taking drags off whatever cigarette was burning in the ashtray, or linger as comfortably in the after-hours ambiance, when the bartender poured for everyone and the tips were divided. But neither could I make myself wait until one A.M., warming the car in the parking lot, waiting for the kitchen lights to be turned off.

When Jess got off, I followed her to her house. There, with everyone asleep, we would squeeze together on the living room couch—displacing a now indolent Coon—catching up on things, reviewing our plans, watching the late movie while we rubbed and fidgeted under a scratchy afghan.

I marvel that we made it through a year of this and that we did then follow out our plan, our subterfuge. I marvel, too, that Jess's family bought it all so readily. Jess suffered terrible pangs of guilt every day, but she pushed on. She publicized her intentions well ahead of time. She was going to quit her job in April and move east to stay with Susan and Jim; she would find work, maybe take up her painting again. I would be staying on in Ann Arbor for a time, making my separate way east when I'd saved some money.

In fact, I was the first one out. After some nervous preliminary consultation with my parents, including several long talks with my father, who kept insisting that I could not get through life without a plan—I vowed I would prove him wrong—I quit my job, packed my books for storage, and gave up my little room above the delicatessen. The whole business took about three days. Then, with surprisingly little ceremony, carrying only my backpack and typewriter, I boarded a train leaving Toledo, Ohio, for Boston. I do remember my mother remarking as she waited with me on how strange the sky looked. But it was not until the next day, as I was making my way through Boston's South Station, that I saw the headlines. The most devastating tornado of the century had swept through northern Ohio just miles from the path I was on, very near the time I had been passing through on my way east.

In Boston I stayed—"crashed"—with an Ann Arbor friend who now lived in Cambridge. The next day I idled for hours in Harvard Square, waiting to go to the airport to meet Jess's plane. The two of us were then to meet up with Jim and Susan, who would be driving down from New Hampshire. We would stay with them in their little apartment in Dover until we worked out the next step and moved forward into our lives. Miraculously, it all happened as planned. Jess's plane arrived, and Jess, who, like me, dreaded flying, emerged from the gate with an auspiciously cockeyed smile just as Jim and Susan came hurrying toward us down the corridor.

Two years ago, I was invited to give a talk at a writers' conference in Portland, Maine, an invitation I accepted straightaway, knowing that I would drive up by myself from Boston and make the detour—just to see what tricks the past might play. I would turn in off the Maine Pike and drive down those old roads: through Kennebunkport and Cape Porpoise, then along the ocean stretch at Fortune's Rocks to Biddeford Pool. Jess and I had lived in that little corner of Maine for a year and a half before we broke up, and I knew that those few miles of shore country were still saturated.

In the twenty years since I'd left, driving away with my friend Michael in his truck, tracking my departure obliquely, on the glass of the side-view mirror, I'd been back only twice. Once with Lynn, the other time with Lynn and our two kids. Both times I'd felt cheated of my frisson. There is no way to immerse yourself in the bittersweet tides of memory with your nearest and dearest present. Rather, there is the effort to convince the partner, contradictorily, that time has, yes, rendered the past safe, *and* that something profound might indeed have transpired once in such a locale. The exertion, minor seeming, is in fact all-consuming: There is nothing left over for the Proustian encounter.

But now I would be alone. I made sure to get myself up while it was still dark. My destination was about ninety miles north, and I had in mind that I would watch the sun come up from some old favored spot or other.

And so, bent upon creating a "moment," I gunned my Toyota up the highway from Boston, through the little corner of New Hampshire, clearing the Piscataqua Bridge while the light was still just barely smudging the eastern horizon, on into Kittery. At some point, of course, it occurred to me that I was—as a grown-up, husband, and father—following the very path that Jess and I had taken that day we drove north from Jim and Susan's apartment in our just-bought $500 Saab station wagon. Then we were in our early twenties, as unconnected and clueless as could be. We knew nothing, had nothing. Crossing the state line into Kittery—this I remember clearly—felt like shattering some barrier. This was the unknown; this was freedom, the end of all our rehearsals.

Same road now, same trees, same distinct estuary smell slipping in when I rolled down the window, but what a thickness of clear glass had been laid over everything. I registered in an instant just how much had changed, how far I was from that former self. And with this came a sudden twinge of anxiety: Was I setting myself up for some massive private disappointment? Could I really stand to discover that the dearest place of my younger years was spent, emptied of all its savor?

I tested that possibility, at one moment dismissing it, in the next tightening myself against it, all the while making my way north on the Maine Pike. At Kennebunk, I exited and—as if it had been scripted—slid instantly into a dreamlike intensification. This road, this stretch between Kennebunk and Kennebunkport—I knew it even in the dark. I had driven it dozens and dozens of times. What shocked me was how little these houses and hedges had changed— and if I did not remember every tree and mailbox, I nevertheless succumbed to an enveloping sense of familiarity.

Turning into Kennebunkport, I made my way around the square and connected with the road to Cape Porpoise. Playing games now, remembering quite clearly how it had felt to be driving here before, trying in every way I knew to inject the "who could have guessed?" awareness, to make it feel like I really was driving the road back then, but with a full prophetic grasp of the future. Then I had wanted nothing more than to be a writer, to see my words in print, between covers. Now, for better or worse, I had that. I was returning to old haunts like an answer to a question.

It is all so foolish to contemplate now—my willed readiness for a sublime moment and the perverse obligingness of the situation. That I should be making the old familiar turn to Fortune's Rocks, with the sun just coming up, lighting the thickets of wild roses along the approach, silhouetting the stoical shapes of the gulls massed on the rocks off to my right. High tide. Through the open windows I could hear the dull suck of water. A perfect literary moment.

Which was, of course, exactly the problem. Here was the fortysomething writer fellow, who had once, decades ago, mooned with his writerly dreams along this very stretch, returning now, looking for some click of redemption, leering greedily at the shingled houses arrayed so neatly along either side of the deserted road, familiar in their sum, but strange, too, when looked at closely, taking a breath at the quick arrival on the right of the Woodman house and, there on the left, the little cottage that we had rented from Gertrude Woodman on the spot that first afternoon. It's precisely this literary self-consciousness, the weaving of these links and patterns, that gets in the way, makes it all feel hopelessly staged and distant. How run-down the little cottage looked. Was Gertrude Woodman still alive? Was the place still a rental?

I could have stopped, stood there in the roadside grass forcing the moment, making myself get back some of the feeling of those first spring mornings when we both sat in that shadowy screened-in porch, remarking incessantly on the freshness of the ocean breezes. But to linger, just then—to risk coming up short before any real momentum had built—did not seem like the best strategy. So with barely another glance, I continued along the stretch, following now the path from Woodman's to the apartment we'd found just three months later through divine intervention. Winter Harbor Apartments, right in the heart of the tiny settlement called Biddeford Pool, as picturesque a perch as we could have wished for, with an enormous back picture window looking down on bay, inlet, and Wood Island Light, a fully operational lighthouse, and bedroom windows giving a distinct vantage over the few rooftops of the town to the row of oceanside houses I was just then driving past.

Biddeford Pool was not much changed, either. I drove the loop just as I had so often in my thoughts. I passed on the left the battered fisherman's cottage that looked out over the "Pool"—the enormous tidal basin that twice daily swelled to lake size, with a dozen or so lobster boats riding at anchor, and then shrank again, exhaling a rich, weedy smell—paused to check the adjoining shed, where Jess and I had one day been shocked to see a huge gutted deer hanging. The pulley and hook were still there, gleaming, a token of the obscure continuities that bind us on every side to the past. And so it went. On the right, the old lobster pound. A new name, true, and some upgrades to trim and window decor, but the shingled corner building was just what I recalled. Then, across, the little gift shop—Robbins' Nest—and, just up the rise, Goldthwaite's, the market that flourished through the short summer season, catering delicacies for the well-to-do, and then abruptly shut down when they left. Next to Goldthwaite's, the telephone booth, for the longest time our one connection to the outer world. I would stand there, once a week, looking into the distance over the Pool while I checked in with my family in Michigan.

I parked the car in a space in front of the market and just sat for a time. I was not finding the transport I craved; I was obstructed. I was not so much inhabiting the past as wondering, prompted by these sudden rushes of memory, what I had become in the present. Staring at that old telephone booth, I did get a vivid sensation of our old simplicity. And intensity. How cluttered and complicated everything had become! The person who had stood in that spot twenty some years ago had been in many ways a different being. I had—with Jess—accomplished such a reduction, such a winnowing of life choices. And what a righteous drive I'd had for my verities: for solitude, nature, reading, writing—even noble poverty was included as a thing to want.

I had to get out, walk. I knew I should be pushing on to Portland soon, to my duties, but I had time for a short walk. On up the hill, toward the apartment. Stopping just in front, I gave myself a minute to stare up at the window, the white sash along which Jess had arrayed her collection of found glass, behind which I had stood so many mornings with my coffee, staring seaward, reminding myself of my great good fortune.

What deflation I felt standing down below—the great clasp of connection refused to come. I waited, ruefully ironic now—another minute, and then, suddenly aware of the need to pee, I picked my way along the side of the house to a thicket down in back.

The year and a half Jess and I lived in Maine, before I left, ending the relationship, will always be bracketed off from the rest of my life. Not because the time was an idyll, though at various points it seemed intensely idyllic, or because we had any extraordinary adventures or encounters, but rather because that period marked, for me, anyway, an open-eyed plunge into what felt, without reservation, like my own life. Everything contributed to this. The circumstances of our getting away—our flight—the distance we had put between ourselves and our families, the impression I had, so hard to reconstruct now, that Maine was the new world, the frontier, that just behind the fringe of coastal settlement was a wilderness stretching north to Canada and beyond. We got there and it instantly felt like ours, from the moment our machine-gunning Saab drew up in front of Gertrude Woodman's house and we toured her little off-season cottage, knowing even before she unlocked the front door that it was ours—meant—at least for a time.

Maybe these are the sensations of everyone's first breaking-away—absolute risk somehow coupled with a faith in rightness, of taking steps that will prove intended, destined. We were so far from everything we knew, both of us, and so new and strange to each other, too, after the long vagueness of work and separation. Each of us would at times catch the other just staring, trying to take in what felt like a new reality.

What did we do? How did we get by? Those first three months, when we had Woodman's cottage, were the most distilled sort of solitude. We were living, as planned, off our savings, which gave us enough for basic bills—rent, gas, and food—but otherwise reined us in quite strictly. We took only the odd frugal trip to Kennebunkport or Biddeford, mainly just to break the spell that we had put ourselves under. This was as close as we could come to Thoreau's ideal of fronting the "bare essentials." We woke, made coffee, read for a time, and then, weather permitting—which was almost always that season—we headed out, crossing the street and threading our way along the short path that ran alongside Woodman's property, right down to the beach, which swept in a broad crescent to the north, ending at a rocky promontory. We made that trek over and over, dawdling the long mile or so of beach, throwing sticks and balls to Woodman's retriever, Johann, who liked to accompany us wherever he could; pausing, always, to stare at the enormous Gothic nunnery rearing up on the left behind a patch of tall marsh grass, then moving on to the rocks, over which we climbed, slowly, resting from time to time beside the tiny jewel-box tidepools, watching for the scuttle of crabs while Johann curled around himself on a flat rock and slept.

The great jumble of boulders continued on the far side of the promontory. One could—we often did—follow them right to another jutting promontory, behind which rose a grassy bluff, a private area that was in fact the fringe of a wonderfully picturesque golf course. If we continued along, around what we called "the head," we saw, directly across an area of open water, the Wood Island Light. The waters there were dotted with lobster buoys. We would sit in the tall grasses and watch the lobstermen, follow the honeybee track of their boats as they checked their traps. A bit farther on, the headland path died out, brought us to private property, the lower backyards of the big summer homes that perched, one after the next, on the hill overlooking the inlet. Beyond—and there were days when we made the full circuit—Biddeford Pool, where the inlet fed the vast tidal body that gave the place its name.

Jess and I walked and walked. We knew no one, met no one, inhabited a companionable bubble inside of which we made jokes, offered each other our theories about the few people who became fixtures in our lives—the fastidious Mrs. Woodman and her daughter, Faith, who lived elsewhere but drove up to visit almost daily with an obliged velocity; florid-faced Chandler—"Chan"—Robbins, who ran the Robbins' Nest gift shop and could be seen crossing this way and that between his carefully decorated little establishment and the post office; the peculiar old woman with the wraparound dark glasses of the blind who nevertheless moved with headlong purpose down the street . . . Each of these characters occupied us at exhaustive length, while we walked, but also later, as we drove the back roads, scouting, or shopped, or busied ourselves in our small kitchen together, cooking our one staple dish—ratatouille—and drinking the one affordable merlot we had discovered.

Later, when all grew dark and quiet, we sat in the two arm-chairs—mine the one that had belonged to Paul, the late Mr. Wood-man, and still bore the brown spot from his hair oil where his head had rested—and we read. Apart, but sometimes together, too, tak-ing turns, I remember, with D. H. Lawrence's *The Rainbow*. By nine-thirty or ten we were in bed, tired, both of us ready to lie in the dark with our windows open, listening to the ocean, which seemed, no matter how we assured ourselves of the rational impos-sibility, to be advancing minute by minute over the road and across our small grassy yard to beat against the very side of the cottage.

Were we happy? I think so, even as I hesitate to offer a simple yes. We were, for those months, enfolded entirely, no margin left over, in the moment-by-moment process of our living. There was nothing to break the absorption, the extraordinary mutuality. We had exiled ourselves from the old setting; our families and all that might have reminded us of our growing up had been banished by distance. A curious calm grew up between us, fed by the silence, the clarity of the air, and the constant heaving of the ocean. We remarked it in a thousand ways without ever naming it. It was there in the way we sat together over coffee, in our jokes and routines, how we kept them up until they collapsed of their own absurd obscurity. The least excursion, a drive into Kennebunkport for some minor neces-sity, grew large, became somehow charged with extra possibility, became a major side-road exploration. Every new find, fix-it shop, or barn made this particular seacoast bump more our own.

I want to say that we were very happy, that we stayed poised for a strangely long time in a dreamy exception. Indeed, at some level it was hard to believe that the easy flow of things would not just go on and on. Jess may have had a better intuition about things. She spoke often of her belief in what she called "packets of time"—condensed, self-contained epochs that were embedded in the larger scheme. But she, too, carried on "as if." We did not yet have much sense of our own undercurrents; we could not have identified the shifts and stirrings that would lead, just a little over a year later, to my abrupt and wounded departure.

Jess had always been artistic, but I had no real sense of the instinct and know-how she could bring together when she got inspired. I had never seen her do anything more than the odd sketch or caricature. She had not felt the pull. But now, sitting at the kitchen table with colors and sponges, she took hold of something. From the humblest materials emerged stunning beachscapes: bent seagrasses and rosehips, the pewter glaze at the waterline at low tide. I saw the world of our walks being built up in slow stages. Not in front of my eyes, for Jess did not like to be watched while she worked, but at intervals, when I broke my reading or stepped into the kitchen on some pretext or other. I would lean in over her shoulder and feel the pang of it. This was the real thing.

My road felt harder. I had long ago settled on writing. This meant, for me, stories, a novel, some ambitious thing of words that would make good on every inkling I'd had since childhood. Subject? I didn't know. Myself, I supposed. But my mind was barren of narrative ideas. My own rival bouts of work produced only the most skeletal results—compressed descriptions of breaking waves and ocean atmospheres that were dispiriting in their uniformity. There was nothing to be done. Whenever I opened my notebook, no matter what my original impulse, I ended up with the same basic flock of images.

That long-ago frenzy of competition—the spelling bees and class projects—what had become of all that? Jess and I hardly ever talked about that part of the past anymore. It was as if we had somehow finally neutralized it when we brought our separate lives together. Though at another level, of course, we hadn't neutralized anything. To stand by, admiring, praising, as she filled her portfolio with studies, each more venturesome and accomplished than the last, had to rankle at some level. I loved her, wanted her success and happiness, but no less did I want to be worthy, to be achieving my own gains. No such luck. At day's end I had sputters and scratches, and the sense of the ocean encroaching was as ominous as it was thrilling. I had so confidently assumed that with a new life everything else would follow. Not so. And if I ask the happiness question again—reminding myself of the long, uncontaminated days, the wanderings, the closeness we sustained—I still have to hesitate before answering.

It was inevitable, I suppose, that after such complete immersion in one another, we should begin to move apart again. Which was real—the idyll or the aftermath? Jess and I had, after a long period—intense, but also desultory—as a college-aged couple, put ourselves into a situation where we had to be everything to each other. And we had succeeded. We moved into the future—it really felt that way—as a team, protecting each other, keeping ourselves buoyed up. We had somehow surmounted the crisis of separation, stayed intact through the phone calls and ticking silences that followed immediately after our arrival at Jim and Susan's, when Mrs. Zachariah discovered, as of course she had to, that Jess and I were together. Once that crisis had been weathered, a great sense of release followed, and it carried us during those early months at the cottage.

It followed us, too, in our move from Woodman's to our apartment at Winter Harbor. We sailed through the rest of that summer—the summer of 1974—on the momentum of our adventure. We had solitude—together—in a place of great beauty. We continued our long, foraging walks, though now they took us more out along the paths that meandered through the open terrain behind the golf course. We worked, too, each in our own fashion, Jess with growing confidence and output, me ever more anxiously. I felt caught at times in some terrible spiral, as if my subject matter were in flight from my ambition. I had dozens of beginnings in my notebooks, each a dead-end foray into the consciousness of some young man trying to create a life for himself in some new locale.

As long as our relative successes and failures were just between us, confined to my envious exclamations over her progress and her supportive assurances that my muse would be arriving at any moment now, the imbalance was bearable. But there were larger changes on the way.

One afternoon late that summer, Jess arrived home from an errand in Kennebunkport in a state of suppressed exaltation. She was, like me, a great believer in the jinxing power of hubris, so it took a while for her news to come out. First she just fussed and muttered around the kitchen table, stuttering her unlit cigarette against the counter. Her face was shining, though, and she looked embarrassed. Finally, before I could begin to lean on her, she came out with it. "They took 'em." I knew right away what she meant. I had been urging her, as had Susan and Jim whenever they came up, to bring her work around to the local galleries. Jess had always shaken her head, demurring. But now she had ventured it on her own. And the response had been immediate. One of the first galleries she visited took three of her pieces on consignment and would take more if they sold. Jess was thrilled and terrified. "This is all a mistake," she said. "I'm a fraud. I'll never work again." We laughed. But she fell into a brooding melancholy against which I felt completely powerless. She lay on her side in bed and cried.

But then the next day she was back at her table—Diet Coke and cigarettes at the ready—working. Somehow she knew. In a matter of days those watercolors had sold and she was ready to deliver more.

Jess's first success was providential. Summer was waning, and suddenly—these discoveries always feel sudden—our money was running out. While the first infusion of cash from the gallery made us feel unexpectedly flush, that money disappeared quickly and Jess's new pieces did not sell right away. The day of reckoning drew near. We sat together at the kitchen table, making our basic calculations. The numbers could not be stretched, that was very clear. We had to find jobs if we were going to make it through our first winter.

We knew nothing at that point about the seasonal economy of a place like the one we lived in. In a month or so, the summer people would be boarding up their homes for the winter. No one was hiring. Jess toured the local bars and restaurants and came up empty. I tried the Kennebunk-based newspaper, the *York County Coast Star,* and the local bookstore. Nothing. I put a sign up at the post office offering my services for manual jobs and got just one bite: a man painting his mother's house needed somebody to do the high-ladder trim work. I spent three hours grappling with my just then discovered terror of heights, then gave it up. What would we do? Going back to Michigan was not an option.

Now began another phase. It could not have lasted very long— by midfall we both had jobs—but when the money goes and there is no prospect for more, when the houses are boarded up everywhere and people are clenching for winter, three or four weeks can feel interminable. We got our first taste of poverty and failure. I don't know how we could have miscalculated, been so cavalier about the basic requirements of life, but suddenly there we were— broke.

At one level, of course, everything that follows here reflects the posturing of two grown children from well-to-do families. Jess and I may have run out of money, but we were certainly not without recourse. Either one of us could have made the call home to ask for money—and we knew this. It's a mark of how determined we were that this life should be ours—that there be no voice able to say, then or later, "I told you so"—that we never even mentioned the possibility of turning to our families.

No, we continued to read the local paper, following all leads.

Jess continued to check the restaurants and bars, hoping that something would open up. In the meantime, we did what poor people do. We lived on canned goods bought at an outlet that sold only generic and damaged goods. We spent one hellish day delivering telephone books through the rickety French-Canadian tenements in the nearby mill town of Biddeford. We were so demoralized by late afternoon that we took the money we'd earned—enough for a week's groceries—and drove to Portland, where we dined on steak teriyaki and draft beer at the Rusty Scupper, until now our special celebration spot.

I was just getting ready to take my phobias in hand and sell blood when I came across an ad for a night custodian position at nearby Saint Francis College. I went in to interview, and by evening the job was mine. At the same time, almost like a nod from the gods—*Let them stay*—Jess picked up a few nights waitressing at the Lion and Unicorn, an upscale restaurant just outside Kennebunk. We could hardly believe our good fortune. It looked like our imminent financial disgrace would be averted. We would be making our rent, buying gas, paying our bills.

But now—it was October, we were six months into our new life—the spell of our mutual solitude, our intimate absorption into each other's lives, was shattered. We rejoined the larger world, though how different were our respective ways. For me it meant, essentially, being solitary for long hours in a deserted public place. From four in the afternoon to eight in the evening, every weekday, I followed my route through the buildings of this small denominational college—sweeping halls, emptying wastebaskets, mopping offices, scrubbing toilets . . . After my supervisor showed me the ropes on the first day, I scarcely ever saw another person. But I hardly minded. Despite my years of bucking the tasks my father assigned me—the *fact* of them—I actually enjoyed the rhythms of manual work. I carried my mop and broom from hall to hall, lost in reverie. Sometimes, when I got ahead of schedule, I went to sit in one or another of the professors' offices, reading.

Jess, meanwhile, had found her way into whatever nightlife there was in York County in the off-season months. She had instant rapport with Jacques, the charmingly bibulous owner, and his crew of cooks, bartenders, and waitresses. For Jacques, everything was about the sporting life, the party that went on and on.

A new pattern started for us. Jess would drop me at the college and then return home—to nap, to shower, to get ready. I would lock up at eight and hike the two miles back. Jess's shift would be half over by the time I got home and made myself a sandwich. The quiet hours were all mine. Sometimes I tried to work. But if the work was not going well—and usually it was not—I would sit on the couch and read, working my way slowly through my wine, getting up every so often to check the kitchen clock.

The rooms were so silent, nothing but the low purr of the refrigerator. Our neighbors, quiet anyway, would have long since gone to bed. There was no phone yet, no expectation that whatever mood I had woven around myself would be punctured. I read and mused. If I looked up, I could see the periodic stroke of light from the Wood Island Light—it cut through the picture window and ran a diagonal slash through the corner of the room. Otherwise, nothing.

In the first months, through the winter, I usually stayed awake until Jess came home. At a certain point in the evening I would go to sit in the dark bedroom and watch the straightaway that skirted the Pool. I could pick out the distinctive close-set lights of the Saab instantly. I loved how Jess would then clatter up the stairs, bearing in with her a cloud of cold air, perfume, and smoke. I would join her in the kitchen for another glass of wine while she counted her tips and flexed her toes in the air. Her project still felt like our project; her stories were part of our adventure in Maine.

This all changed—slowly, not dramatically. Over the long winter months Jess got more and more involved in her restaurant life. People liked her. She was able to be a character—mimic, party girl—among the cast of other characters: "Highrise," the manic cook, Annie, the hapless vixen ... She stayed later for the after-hours fun. That was part of the deal. If you worked for Jacques, you almost *had* to stay and party. There came a time when I no longer expected to be awake to see the lights coming down the stretch. I would hear the car door, her steps on the stairs; now, often, I would turn back into sleep.

Of course, this meant a certain distancing, and to this I contributed. Some nights when I wasn't working, Jess would invite me to come along—to meet her friends and join the action. But I didn't have the heart for it. I was too locked up in my frustrations, my bitterness. Whatever work I thought I was doing had come to a standstill. I still put in my hours at the desk, but now it was with no expectation of result. More often than not I turned my energy to other writing, long letters to my old bookstore friend Tom, or self-castigating journal entries. I was no longer sure of what I wanted; my life felt arbitrary and insubstantial. I berated myself on paper for as long as I could stand it—at least it was writing—and then I very often headed out to walk. I wanted to wear myself out, to regain my sense of physical boundary. When nothing else availed, I turned to the wine, sitting by the picture window and sipping merlot until the lacerating edge of my self-recrimination was smoothed down.

In the early winter my job situation changed. Working my way through the administration offices one evening, I all but collided with a thin man—worn tweeds, longish gray hair—holding a wastebasket. I gave a start. He quickly apologized, introduced himself. His name was Dave, he said. He did the public relations for the college. We talked for a few minutes, and I told a bit of my story. How I'd moved to Maine with my girlfriend, that I wanted to write. Dave heard me out, then asked, point-blank, if I had a college degree. When I nodded, he flashed me a conspiratorial smile and asked me to stop by the next day during regular office hours. He had some ideas, he said.

By week's end I had a new job—assistant to the dean of college relations—a desk, a typewriter, and a lengthy typed list of possible leads to pursue. "Your task," Dave had said when he handed me the sheet. He then shrugged, suggesting with this gesture that nothing could be easier for a young writer like myself. "Just write whatever you can think of that might get the name of the college into the papers."

I took my mandate seriously. I strategized over lists of faculty, looking for any possibilities for a human-interest story; I talked to coaches about their teams; I tracked down students with special backgrounds or skills. And while the job lasted—from midwinter into spring—I felt almost purposeful. My write-ups made it into the Biddeford paper, faculty nodded to me on the walkways, and I was drawing a real paycheck.

The change in hours meant that I saw Jess even less than before. I would drive off after breakfast, and when I got back in the late afternoon she would already be showered and dressed, ready to leave for the dinner shift. On her worktable I would see evidence of her productivity. When things fell out right we might have some time to catch up on things; otherwise I would kiss her, inhale her perfume, and then watch from the window as she backed the car out into the street and swept around the corner leaving a wreath of oily exhaust in her wake.

Now, from a distance, I see that this was the first real phase of our separation. I'm not sure what I thought then. While I was certainly aware of an estrangement, I probably viewed it as a temporary detour, a necessary consequence of our having to solve the puzzle of earning a living. The residue of our solitary months was still there. I imagined, I think, that with the coming of warm weather we would recover something of that original thrill of arrival.

We did not. Subtly, at first imperceptibly, everything between us changed, and in the long period of heartbreak that eventually followed, I spent many sleepless hours combing through what I could remember of those days, trying to find the flaw, the protruding splinter, whatever it was that diverted us from each other.

Outwardly there was the obvious split in how we were living. My day life versus her night world; my growing sense of isolation set against her triumphs—her art, her emerging status as after-hours raconteuse. I was at once proud of her and resentful. I still felt as if her success were our success, but I saw so little place for myself there.

Did I shut myself down? I wonder. For as I later began reexamining all that happened back then, I discovered what I once, only half-jokingly, characterized to someone as the "neutron bomb" effect of romantic trauma. I mean, I could restore in my mind every last detail—Jess's bobby pins fanned out on the bathroom counter, the jars and brushes lined up on her worktable, the reluctant chirp of her dresser drawers—but I could not retrieve, no matter how I clenched to the task, the stuff of our daily conversations and interactions. How were we with each other? How did we talk? What words did we use to get at our thoughts and feelings? I cock my ear and I hear nothing.

Almost nothing, I should say. The one thing that I can still get back intact from all that time is a piece of silliness, a bit grown into an ongoing routine that became, in retrospect, almost weirdly evocative.

Out one day, on one of our now infrequent drives along the back roads, Jess suddenly pulled the car over. I looked her way. She had on her old mock-serious face. She was fixed on something, waiting for me to catch up. I tracked her glance. There, nailed to a tree in the yard to our right, was a large hand-lettered sign: BABBY PIGS FOR SALE. I gave an obliging snort. Jess continued to stare. I felt her pushing back her smile, waiting for her moment.

"Daddy?" It came out of nowhere, a querulous little voice, at once plaintive and obnoxiously demanding. "Daddy, I want a babby pig."

My role here was easy. Old reflexes kicked in. I was the straight man, the mark, the well-meaning father. I fed her a line. "Honey, where would we put it? Who would take care of it?"

"I want a babby pig!"

Jess's character—"Hank"—a little tomboy of indeterminate age, became like a tic, a conversational obsession far outstripping the obsessions of old. Jess quickly gave her a life, a back story, a repertory of vices. She would intrude herself without warning into our conversation. The squawking voice:

"Dad?"

"Yes, Hank?"

"Dad, I took a drink from your brown bottle and now I feel dizzy—"

Desperate, inspired, Hank seemed to find her way into whatever was between us; that voice cleared a space and helped us to muffle some of the awkwardness we were beginning to feel.

"Dad?"

"Yes, Hank?"

"Are you ever going to get me a mom?" It had never been established what had happened to Hank's mother.

"You want a mom?"

"No."

"Well, why do you ask?"

"I want a little brother."

"Hank, that's a lot of work, having a little brother."

Pause.

"Dad?"

"Yes, Hank?"

"If I can't have a little brother . . . can I get a babby pig?"

With warm weather and the return of the summer people—suddenly Goldthwaite's was open again, the front steps crowded with returnees greeting each other—Jess was busier than ever. She had more shifts at the restaurant as well as the gratifying request for new work from her gallery. For me—the reverse. Just as school ended for the summer, the college suddenly underwent emergency fiscal reorganization—it would reemerge the following fall as the New England College of Osteopathic Medicine—and my position disappeared. Dave called me into his office to tell me officially, though unofficially I had known for weeks that trouble was in the air. We spent a rueful afternoon brainstorming about what I might do next but came up with little. Then he shook my hand and I was done; I packed the odds and ends from my drawer into a plastic bag and walked slowly home.

Looking back, the trajectory of our relationship seems clear. But Jess and I continued on for some months, working hard when we were together to recapture some hints of our old domestic calm, but also giving in, more and more often, to sudden explosive arguments that recalled for both of us that one Ann Arbor summer. I can't remember the whole fever chart of our ups and downs. There were the intensifying silences; the cracks and insinuations I jabbed her with when she found her way to bed after a particularly long night at the restaurant; there were closed doors and abrupt disappearances as one or the other of us snatched up the keys to the Saab and drove off. Clearest of all for me, though, was one still scorch-marked episode, the real beginning of the end.

It was late summer and Jess was working double duty, not only waitressing at the restaurant, but also filling in behind the bar at a little roadhouse that Jacques had some proprietary interest in. For some reason—this was uncharacteristic—I had gone to wait for Jess. Also—and this was unusual, too—I had a roll of bills in my pocket. I sat at a table in the corner, drinking beers and feeling a certain titillated satisfaction about the fact that my drinks were being brought to me by the attractive barmaid who also happened to be my girlfriend.

But at some point in the afternoon, the crucial balance shifted. I found it harder and harder to sit still while Jess—very good in her rowdy, wisecracking mode—delivered drinks to the obviously appreciative gang of men at the bar. Suddenly, inspired, I got up and made my way over to the far end of the bar. Signaling for another beer, I fingered the bills in my pocket, and when Jess came over I launched into my own ill-advised performance. Pretending to be a teetering lout—and it was not much of a stretch—I wrapped one arm around her shoulders, and then, deftly fumbling, I jammed my free hand, full of bills, down the front of her blouse.

What was I thinking? What did I expect would happen? Whatever I intended, Jess foiled me. She wrenched herself away, barked a rough laugh—just in case anyone was watching—and was at the other end of the bar before I could come up with any follow-through. The gesture—the insult—collapsed around me, and when Jess continued to avoid my eye, I left.

That was, psychologically anyway, the end of something. We could carry on a pretense—and we did for some weeks—but our relationship, which had in some ways begun when we waited together by the door of Miss Carpenter's second-grade classroom, was played out. Some long and defining cycle had run its full course. We could feel it; it was there in the way we dodged each other's looks.

It was another month before I left Maine and moved back to Ann Arbor. Jess and I never formally broke up. Instead, ever oblique, we carried on the pretense that I needed to take some time away, that after a winter in Michigan, recharged, reconnected to books and writing, I would come back.

I drove away one early September day with an Ann Arbor friend, Michael, who had come out for a visit. His presence in our small apartment made it all easy. We didn't have to get through the long silences. As long as the three of us were together, clowning around, cooking meals, I could view my preparation for departure as just another temporary expedient. It was not until the very end, really, when my few things were lined up by the door and Michael was outside making room in the back of his truck, that Jess and I, honoring all that we had been through, allowed the sorrow of the moment to register. We did not, either of us, admit that this was really it, but we did stand together in the kitchen. I put my hand on her shoulder. She looked at me and then past me in that way she had, and then we hugged. "It'll be okay," I said, and she said the words back: "It'll be okay." The top of her head nestled just under my chin. I kissed her there and took in her smell, and then—neither of us fans of the long good-bye—we picked up the bags and guitar and made our way down the stairs. And it was not until Michael's truck was taking the turn down by the lobster pound, heading toward the stretch, that I felt all of a sudden gutted, sad beyond anything I had ever felt before, convinced in a sharp wrench of realization not only that I had made a fatally wrong turn in my life, but also that I was not going to make any move to undo it, that I couldn't.

These are our moments of truth, and they disclose their implications slowly over time, not like the poker hand slapped down— voilà!—but excruciatingly, card by card, until the combination is at last revealed. Rounding the bend in Michael's truck was the matter of an instant, and as we talked, even as I confided some of my heartsickness, that instant receded, fell in behind the succession of shifting scenes outside the window. In truth, emotionally speaking, anyway, the world should have jerked to a stop then, just as my friend turned the wheel to clear the bend. There should have been an extended interval—some vivid recap, if this were possible, of all the arduous maneuvers, the hoping and wanting that had brought us to this place. There should have been, too, a frame-by-frame motion study of our moment in the kitchen, cutting repeatedly between our faces, lingering close focus on hand movements, little reflexes of hesitation. But those pauses are never given just like that. What turned out to be our last real interchange vanished abruptly in the rush of the moment, a rush that somehow expressed the foolish assumption that there would always be more time later.

. . .

As for the theme of destiny, which I saw (and continue to see) as no mere embellishment of what transpired between Jess and me, it played itself out with one last flourish before the years, now decades, of silence arrived.

As I had first run into Jess on the Diag in Ann Arbor in a stroke of pure coincidence, that sighting changing everything about my life, so it was fitting that my very last glimpse of her should also have come about by chance.

I have not kept track of the dates, and I no longer remember if this was Christmas or Easter or some other holiday during that first year back in Michigan. I remember that it was long enough after our breakup to allow for my hearing, in close sequence, from Jim and Susan, that Jess was with someone; that she was engaged; that she had married. It was all too unreal to credit. I kept waiting for some sign that the joke was over, that we could be together again.

Then came our encounter. I had been home visiting with my family. Andra and I were on our way back to Ann Arbor (she was now a senior at the university), and we had stopped in a drugstore before heading out to the highway. I was just getting into the checkout line when my sister suddenly materialized at my side. "I can't be quite sure," she muttered, her teeth strangely clenched together, "but somebody who looked a lot like Jess just went down that aisle." I felt immediately shaky, stunned through knees and shoulders. There was no need to calculate odds. Of course it would be Jess. I headed down the nearest aisle, preparing myself, even as I knew there is no preparation possible in moments like this. A drawn breath and a quick turn at aisle's end and we were face-to-face. I had a moment's slight advantage, and when Jess looked up and saw me looming toward her, I caught a spark of panic in her eye. Just a flash—quickly buried by our awkward, scrambling friendliness. "Here's a surprise—" I tried to make it casual. In the months we'd been apart, I'd forgotten how I towered over her.

"Hello, Peter." There was the subtlest of ironic undertones in her voice. Then she looked up at me and I was utterly torn from myself, too stunned to do anything but smile and nod. We stood like that. It was as if we were both auditioning for a play—and failing, hitting our marks wrong, dropping our lines. Who were we now? We rushed to draw and underscore our new boundaries, suddenly formal. She was asking me about my family, and I was answering with great animation. I tried to fix her in my gaze—this was *Jess*—but I couldn't get focus. Mere months had passed. But in that time—it came over me—she had transformed herself, had entered another orbit. She was, I had to remind myself, someone's wife now.

I stood there in the aisle, bobbing my head, not daring to lean close, taking everything in. The changes. Jess had cut her hair—short, neat—and she was wearing a new brown suede coat. She looked more adult, more solid. But whatever signs of change I was reading, whatever picture of things I was coming up with—in an instant it was all subordinated to her news. I forget her words, how she said it, remember only that the air seemed to grow dense with motes and little flares when she spoke. There was a muffled undersea moment. And then she gave me the strangest glance—pride mingled with something else, some vestige of our old comradeship—and made a shy little gesture. It was almost like a curtsey. She took half a step back, paused, and with only the faintest trace of a smile outlined her belly for me. Her babby.

CHAPTER 6

CONSULTING WITH A FRIEND ABOUT THIS PERIOD IN MY LIFE, THESE early years of romantic travail, about how I might find for them a viable narrative shape, I was startled by the sudden certainty with which she declared: "It won't really work unless you show how you hit rock bottom." Rock bottom? At first I wasn't sure just what she meant. I was not writing a recovery story. What was she saying? I should have asked, but I wanted to appear sage and didn't. Maybe for this reason her words have stayed with me, chafing my complacencies.

Rock bottom. I found myself musing about the phrase, the concept, while I did my long teaching commute or in the middle of the day's errands; I rolled it slowly back and forth in my mind as I drifted into first wakefulness, which has always been my best time for pouncing on the more elusive implications of things. And I ended up living with the idea of rock bottom long enough that it became not only a possible, but the necessary way to move my story forward.

That said, I have to admit that I speak of no epic devastation here, merely the average kind that most of us experience at one time or another—if we are lucky. I add that last phrase not to be coy or merely paradoxical, but because I believe it's true. We all need to know—if only briefly—what life feels like, and what we feel like to ourselves, when all of our props have been kicked away; when we are, simply, right up against it.

I had my time of it—I'll admit it now, taking up my friend's prompt—when I returned to Ann Arbor from Maine that fall. "Washed up" in Ann Arbor might be a better way to put it, though without any connotations of safety or rescue. It was more like I had ventured out into life, and life had tired of my hubris and sent me back. I tried on a face-saving posture, carried myself as a person who had some plans. I stopped by home just long enough to sell the idea of my temporary return—though it would soon come clear that I had fooled no one with my story that Jess and I were taking a break. From the bookshelf in what my parents still called, touchingly, my room, I reclaimed a beautiful two-volume leather-bound set of Tobias Smollett's *Humphry Clinker,* which I'd once bought from Tom Borders when he and his brother, Louis, still dealt some rare books, and which I needed to resell somewhere to get a damage deposit for whatever room I would be renting back in Ann Arbor.

I ended up, as I always seemed to, in a small top-floor room with a window fire escape on a side street not too far from where Jess and I had lived three summers before. I paid my first month's rent—in cash—to a thin, shy young grad-student type who lived with his wife, also thin and shy, on the ground floor. Moving in meant walking up the stairs, twice, with my things.

I was set up almost immediately. I arranged my armful of beloved paperbacks—*Tropic of Cancer, Hopscotch, Hunger, One Hundred Years of Solitude,* some Balzac and Dostoevsky—neatly along the top of the deal dresser, taped up a few photographs, and laid my orange-and-black Mexican blanket over the small mattress. Done. Still riding the momentum of transition, I hiked up the street to Borders, which had moved during the time of my absence from its old location into a massive new space almost directly across the street. I found Tom Borders in the little warren of upstairs offices. He remembered, of course, that I had left town to make my way as a writer, but he did not prod me to find out why I was back. Instead, he gazed out into the middle distance, as if to consult the family plan for world domination, and then, settling on something, looked over and offered me a job. It was that simple. I would start in a few days' time. I would be presiding over the remainders area in what was called the "mezzanine."

As long as I fancied myself in motion, creating the outlines of my independent new life, I could manage. I could even pride myself on my resourcefulness—I had found a place and a job in a matter of days. But then, just as I finished pulling together the rudiments of my new life, the truth came crashing through. If I had thought there was something romantic, or "bluesy," about a guy getting out of his friend's truck with just a duffel bag, a guitar, and a typewriter—and I had—I could not sustain the fantasy. Alone in my room, without even a phone to call someone with, I sat on the edge of my bed and took inventory. Here I was, a man in his—dear God—mid-twenties, without enough money for a full-course meal, without a career, having written nothing at all for months, without Jess, more or less nowhere. Alone, aware of a kind of seashell echo behind my thoughts, feeling it as the sound of nothingness, I tipped over onto my side and lay utterly motionless, watching dusk, then darkness, move in over the rooftops. I began to have an inkling of what lay in store for me.

Long years ago, when my friend Cal and I felt what we thought were dark times descending, one of us would sometimes turn to the other and say, voice freighted with implication, "Must be the season of the witch." The line was from a drugged-out song by Donovan, and we took it to mean that the whole crazily spiraling counterculture had been put under a malign, withering spell.

But those funks, those troughs that had once seemed so terminal, were as nothing compared with what I felt now. A day or two after setting myself up, I felt a blow catch me straight in the gut. I had taken a step, two steps, and suddenly I was in torment. I felt that I could not stand to be inside my own skin, and I could find nothing that would offer anything more than a short-lived reprieve. The days and nights before I began my job were unbearable. I could alight nowhere; nothing engaged me. Every thought turned me back to Maine, and every thought of Maine was a thought of Jess. The only thing I could do was to get outside, to walk. I covered the streets of the town and the surrounding countryside, logging miles every day. I thrust one foot in front of the other, and in the rhythm of that, the grinding repetition, I found a way to just endure. Equilibrium.

The idea, if there was an idea, was to wear myself out, to get it so that I could return to my room and get some minimal amount of sleep. I did not want to go mad—I'd heard of the homicidal explosions of the sleep-deprived—but it was hard to get into the right state. When all else failed, when I had twisted the sheets into a knot at the foot of the bed, I would turn on the light and pull my one chair up to the low dresser. I would then write—long, free-association rants, letters to Jess that I never mailed, bits of stories that were just my life transposed, pages and pages, until my eyes began to hurt and I had to lie back down.

I had put myself into a condition of near impossibility: I could not endure the decision I'd made, and I could not—this I knew—go back and try to make things right. Of course, I thought about taking the risk of that all the time. I was a two-hour flight and a two-hour bus ride from my old life. But it was a trip I could not make. Not only because I would not humble myself, would not admit that I had been wrong—I didn't even know about what—but because I knew, with absolute conviction, that Jess would not have me back, not now.

Still, I tormented myself. Picking times when I knew she would not be home in our old apartment, I would go up the street to a phone booth and dial the number. Turning the rotary dial felt like playing some kind of Russian roulette. My heart would beat furiously until I was sure there was going to be no answer. Then I would stand there, eyes closed, listening to the ring, picturing slowly, like a panning camera, every room, every empty space resounding with that shrill pulse. Were Jess ever to pick up—so I told myself—I would hang up quietly. But of course she would know.

The job, when it finally began, helped, but not enough. I would arrive at the front door of the store every morning with an absolute will to eclipse myself, and in this spirit I did my work. Carrying, stacking, arranging—trying to assert dominion over that small area of remaindered books. Alas, the tasks always ran out. No matter how carefully I arranged my day, the moment always arrived when there was nothing, when I sat alone behind my register and felt the awful sucking sensation start up in the pit of my stomach. I took deep breaths, squeezed shut my eyes, and tried to focus on some person or book cover to get steady. Sometimes, I remember, it got so hard that I had to ask my floor manager if I could take a short break. Outside I would walk around the block, trying to shake off whatever mania had me in its grip. A few times I even stopped at the corner package store and bought a tall beer, which I then chugged while standing against the wall by the parking structure. That helped. Helped enough, indeed, so that I felt a flicker of worry. For in these moments I understood perfectly what drove the drunk along his odyssey of obliterations. I never had before, quite. Now I had to ask myself if I cared. What was the long-term consequence beside the instant sweetness of hurt dissolving away?

But I steered myself away. While I did drink my beer and wine at night to blunt the edge of hurt, I knew not to carry it too far. I forced myself to go out walking, pacing out the side streets from one end of town to the other. Or else I looked again to my books. Literature *does* console—I began to understand that. I remember I copied out long passages from a little book by Cyril Connolly, *The Unquiet Grave,* passages that seemed to catch just the note I needed that season:

A love affair is a grafting operation. "What has once been joined, never forgets." There is a moment when the graft takes; up to then is possible without difficulty the separation which afterwards only comes through breaking off a great hunk of oneself, the ingrown fibre of hours, days, years.

I discovered, too, the tormented love poems of Joseph Brodsky. Brodsky's long arc of dissent, imprisonment, and exile had landed him a few years before in Ann Arbor. Jess and I had been in the crowd at Rackham Auditorium when he gave his first public reading. Now I would sometimes spot him coming along the sidewalk or standing by the downstairs registers, buying a newspaper. As I got to know the poems, the laments for the loss of one M.B., I imagined for him a saga of great romantic suffering. "And if you're hoping for a smile," he wrote in "New Stanzas to Augusta," written during his period of "internal exile" in Russia's remote Arkhangel'sk region, "just wait, I'll smile! My smile will float / above me like the grave's long-standing / roof, lighter than woodsmoke." Those words somehow soothed me. This man, if anyone, would understand my condition.

What a wonderfully ironic moment it was when, years later, after I had gotten to know the poet and was officially interviewing him in his apartment in New York, I asked him a question about the identity of M.B. I can still feel the duration of his pause, every excruciating beat of it, before he answered, a hint of irritation in his voice: "M.B.? M.B. is M.B." End of story.

The greatest solace, though—and it was greater for being unexpected, unlooked for—came from the talks I had with my father. I don't remember quite how we got through the old barriers, but we did. Every three weeks or so I would hitchhike the forty or so miles home for the weekend, and on these occasions—newly and somewhat awkwardly positioned as "man to man"—we would talk. In those days my father still enjoyed a cigarette or two with his after-dinner drink, and my visit home became the perfect occasion for him—for both of us—to savor our vices. After years of sneaking cigarettes, going through such contortions not to get caught, trying to bluff my way past his interrogatory sniffs of my clothes, I delighted in our new manly collusion. Ever the ritualist, my father would deliberate carefully over what records we should hear in the background—Sinatra, Viotti, some fado singer he wanted me to hear—and we would sip, pause, light up, and talk.

What a surprise this was. For so long I had lived with the countering blows of his will, or else his disregard, what I saw as his dismissal of me and, in effect, the struggles of my whole generation. How tense those dinner table conversations had been—for years. Every look or sigh or impatient twitch signaling, from each of us, not just disapproval, but outright disgust. His for my hair, my music, my friends, my sardonic bookishness, my utter refusal to face what he saw as the real-life facts. Mine, no less intense, for what I saw as his smug European sophistication, his lack of tolerance, his inability to engage with anything except his grand passion, architecture.

But here he was now, sitting right across from me on one of the soft, streamlined leather couches, asking me about my breakup with Jess in a way that I knew was sincere, letting me tell my story, speak my heart, without interrupting or moralizing. Something about my condition, my evident pain, seemed to trigger him, and we sat for long hours, first over wine, then cognac, "philosophizing." That's what he would say whenever my mother appeared at the top of the stairs, or at their bedroom door. "Leave us alone," he would bark. "We're philosophizing." And she would retreat, putting on a petulant expression but in fact glad, I sensed, of this newfound camaraderie between us.

I can't now reproduce what I said, or how my father led me on with questions, or how he worked in stories from his own life. He seemed to have a great many views about female psychology and the often perverse dynamics of love. He spoke with great authority about what women wanted and needed. Where had he come by all of these understandings? I was respectfully surprised, forced to grant him a richer past than I had before. And when I left at the end of my visit, I usually felt better. Not cleansed, of course, but lightened in my sorrow and feeling, too, that something had begun to heal between my father and me.

What heartened me was the acceptance I felt in his presence on these occasions. To confess a wound, a vulnerability, was to change the energy flow between us. And if ever my life seemed mired, headed for failure, it was then. I was a man in the first flush of maturity and I had absolutely nothing to show. I had a job selling books, that was it. I had written almost nothing—this after my arrogant rejection some years before of his whole cult of discipline and practical attainment. "Physics, Pete," he used to say. It was almost a joke between us, this coded expression of his disdain for my dreaminess. It meant: The world runs on the principles of physics; it will crush you. But he was not saying it now. He sat there, glasses in his lap, fingers lightly massaging his eyelids as he listened. There was not a breath of "I told you so." And no well-meant offers of rescue, either. He was, and I cherished this, allowing me my life on my own terms. Man to man.

I exerted a great deal of will to get through those first months back. And if the first desperate feeling of loss had abated slightly, I knew the hard times were not over. I felt myself moving through the day with great care and deliberation. Sometimes all it took was hearing one song on the radio and I would be immobilized in the middle of whatever I was doing, forced to draw deep breaths to steady myself. I also had Jess sightings. All the time. I would be coming up the street or walking through the Diag on my lunch break, and I would see her, just turning, melting into the crowd as she had that long-ago fall afternoon, walking away with her distinctive sideways tilt of the head. And each imagined glimpse brought a split-second fantasy, the circumstantial construct that would make it all possible. She had come home to see her family, had driven up unannounced to see if she could find me. I hurried my step, maybe thought of calling out. But we all know what happens next, how cruelly the sudden flash of profile mocks our credulity.

I did get involved, distractedly, in a kind of numbed slow motion, with one of my co-workers at the store, Marcie. She was kind, easygoing, able somehow to chide and cajole me out of my more sullen silences. She worked downstairs but made it a point to find errands up in my part of the store. A few times she brought me coffee. As we got more friendly, we would go for beer after work at a place called Thanos' Lamplighter. Marcie let me talk, get my story out, and she didn't seem irritated that I kept reverting to my Maine saga without ever seeming to exhaust it. She had an expressively dusky look, a way of eliciting confidences; she was tolerant. Gradually she got me to start looking past my wounds, at her. We ended up staying together for the next few years. We were not a match for the ages—we were far too different in deep-down ways—but there was a soothing lack of deeper claim that we both recognized and wanted. Being with Marcie did not dispel the darkness, but it did dilute it. Having her apartment to go to late at night made an enormous difference.

I had my first encounters with death late that fall. Except for my grandfather, whose dying had been kept from us by my parents, I had never lost anyone close to me. Nor had I ever seen a dead body, a fact that marks me out as a child of privilege. Now that changed.

First came the death of my grandmother Ūm, who had moved through the world with such steady persistence that we often forgot to think of her as a very old woman. We took her vigor for granted. The day before she died, she had walked from her little house in Birmingham—she now lived alone, without boarders— into town to have her usual cup of coffee at Machus's bakery. Only when she didn't make her regular morning call to my mother the next day did my parents start to get concerned. I happened to be home for a weekend visit at the time. My father left to go to his office after breakfast, but he must have driven right to Ūm's house, for a call came shortly after. He seemed relieved that I was the one who answered. "I want you to come over here," he said, explaining nothing but also adding that I shouldn't say anything to my mother.

My father was waiting for me on the front steps of Ūm's little house. He seemed strangely calm. When I got out of the car, he said, "Come upstairs, I want you to see what it looks like." I knew. I clamped my back teeth together and followed my father up the narrow wooden stairs, joined him in the doorway of my grandmother's bedroom. There she lay, half on, half off the bed, eyes open, mouth open—extraordinarily matter-of-fact somehow. We stood side by side for the longest time, saying nothing. I felt that I should be taking it all in, but—and this is the thing that later becomes so haunting—there was nothing larger to catch hold of just then. A long life, dense with struggle, dislocation, fought-for successes—fate—was gone. In time that absence would filter through the family in various ways. But at that moment, nothing. Morning sun brightened the rumpled-up sheets near the open window. I had the sudden sharp awareness that the house, the space we stood in, was just a constructed thing—beams and boards and skimmed plaster.

My mother had a hard time taking the news in. When my father and I drove home to tell her, she seemed to know already. She was restless in a way I had never seen before. As she sat and listened to our account—this I see vividly—she fastened on a loose button on my father's coat and began to worry the threads as if there were nothing on earth more important. "I'll sew this for you," she said. "Let me sew this for you."

It was just a few days later—I was back in Ann Arbor after the funeral—that I got up from my bed in the early morning and, putting on my glasses, felt what I can only describe as a violent visual blow. Something so strange, so unexpected, and at the same time—this is what is horrible—so viscerally familiar, that I gaped for a long time before telling myself that I needed to turn away. It was my landlord, the shy, skinny grad student I would encounter on the stairs or find doing something with his toolbox in the front hall. He was hanging in the tree just outside. His face looked purplish, almost black. The rope and body were still, still beyond acceptable stillness, except for the slightest turning of the rope.

I had just turned away, had not even taken a step—to get my pants on, to get to the door, to tell somebody—when I heard a scream from the room just below mine. At once there were doors opening and shutting, steps, voices. And I decided, just like that, to get quickly down the stairs and slip away. I remember turning my head from side to side as I walked up the street, talking to myself, doing what I could to unseat the picture from my mind.

Certainly the police came, asked questions, noted down relevant observations. I missed all of that. But I did not manage to escape altogether. For I saw, in the space of a few seconds—as much time, I would say, as it takes me to type this sentence—a story that would probably never be recorded in any officer's notebook, that maybe would never be known, except by the surviving principal.

I was on State Street, not an hour later, sitting in the window seat of a coffee shop, staring with willful mindlessness into the intersection, when, as if conjured up by some overheated imagination, I saw—just a glimpse—my landlord's pretty young wife, her arm hooked tight to that of some partner, her face lit up with whatever she was saying. And that was all. But so much was delivered in that flash: her absence, his night of anguish, his insane initiative, and the terrible obliviousness that she still moved in. It did not occur to me to intervene, to chase her down and say the thing that would speed her back home. I felt coolly removed from myself. I was seeing the human drama just then with the eye of a Balzac.

And grim as it all was, the instantaneous recognition of the tragedy delivered a slight frisson.

I told my wife this story just the other day—she claims for the first time, though I can't believe I kept it to myself. Her response was immediate: "You were looking at your own situation," she said.

"No." I shook my head. It was not my situation. Jess had maybe met someone, but she had not been *with* that person. I had not even known there was another person, though later it came to seem that I had. Besides, we had not been married; there were no vows of any kind between us. "That was not my situation," I said. But it was, in a way that I can't completely deny, the feeling of my situation. I mean, I knew some of what my landlord had gone through that night. I could guess at his dead-end sadness. But I was fighting it and slowly pushing it back.

Experience—and *only* experience—teaches us that time passes and urgent feelings fade and the demands of the immediate moment begin to dissipate even the most obsessive focus on the life of the past. Moving in my bubble, inside the dramatic story I was renewing for myself every day, I would not have believed it could happen. But of course it did. I had the friendship and comfort of Marcie. I had a few old friends I was slowly reconnecting with; I had my sister nearby. I had the daily distraction of working in a busy store in a college town. But the real shift came early one January afternoon when Tom Borders signaled me to his office as I was coming in from lunch. Louis was already there, watching me with an expression that gave nothing away.

We all got on well. I'd worked for the brothers in their first store. We'd gone out for beers once or twice after unpacking big shipments or doing inventory. We joked easily with each other. But there was no small talk on this occasion. Tom came right out with it: Did I want a better job? They still had the lease on the old store across the street. They'd hired two book dealers to manage the other store—the Charing Cross Book Shop—selling used and rare books. But things had not been working out. Tom slowly rubbed his jaw, as he did whenever things got serious. He and Louis wanted to give the business one more chance—they had started with used books and wanted to keep the connection. One new person had already been hired. Would I consider being his partner?

"Co-manager," said Louis. He was smiling now, reading my reaction. "It would be more money."

"But"—Tom was coming in right behind him—"you'd be working your ass off."

Tom and Louis walked me across the street that evening. They unlocked the door of the old shop but left off the overhead lights. There was a light on in back. I heard the creak of a nail being pried from a board. Moving forward, I saw a stocky man in a T-shirt. He was holding a crowbar and addressing himself to a wall of empty shelves. There were books piled everywhere.

"Gene—"

The man waited, gave one last yank on the bar, then turned. Beard. Red face. Glasses.

"Gene, this is your new partner."

And that was it. Tom and Louis stayed just long enough to set up a meeting for the next day and then left. Gene regarded me for a moment with ill-concealed skepticism and then turned back to his demolition. I moved around slowly behind his back, inspecting the piles of books, eyeballing the sections, taking in the dimensions of the place with a freshly proprietary eye. I knew every dent and crevice from having worked here before, but now it all looked unfamiliar.

"So you like books—" Gene talked without turning around. I caught the irony in his tone and tried to respond in kind.

"I do."

"Here, hold this, would you?" I caught the end of a teetering board. "What's your specialty?"

I hesitated. "Fiction, I guess. Modern stuff."

At this Gene laughed. "Modern fiction—" He looked briefly in my direction. "You know, they don't even offer courses on that in English universities. That's something you're supposed to get up on your own."

I snickered, as if this were self-evidently preposterous.

Gene inspected the structure of the next area of shelving, then—abruptly—turned. "What else?"

I was caught off guard. "What else what?"

"What else do you know?" Now I heard an edge in his tone. I surveyed my attainments and came up with nothing. Finally, looking at Gene, then past him, I shrugged.

"How about you?"

Gene didn't miss a beat here. "I'm ABD in Renaissance lit," he said. "I'm just taking a break."

"Oh." I didn't know what ABD meant and was suddenly afraid to ask.

We stayed there awhile longer, Gene tearing out sections of shelving, stacking boards neatly against the wall, while I perched on a stack of green geological survey volumes and smoked. In the short time I sat there, I got the first inklings of his erudition. Gene loved the Latin poets—Propertius, especially—and tried to read them in Latin. He was a student of radical thought, from Marx to Raymond Williams; adored jazz, Indian raga, Italian opera, the chamber music of Haydn. Anything, of course, having to do with the Renaissance: the works of Frances Yates, E. R. Curtius, R. R. Bolgar; Dante, but not just *Inferno* . . . I stopped listening, felt the suck of imploding ignorance, and wondered if I could still back out without losing face completely.

But I didn't. I went to the meeting the next day and paid very close attention as Tom and Louis explained the operation from start to finish. They were, they said, willing to inject a certain amount of fresh capital. Our first task, aside from making the sorts of cosmetic alterations that Gene had already begun, was to build stock. We were to advertise for books, buy libraries, go to estate sales and book fairs. They believed that Ann Arbor could support a high-quality used- and rare-book shop. There was, both brothers kept affirming, work to be done.

I loved books, and though I was not a scholar, I had imagined myself to be fairly well read. Needless to say, my self-image, already somewhat shaky, suffered a serious decline when I began to spend time with Gene. Which I started to do that very day. Indeed, for the next six months or so, I saw more of Gene than any other person, including Marcie. We were on a mission, chained together. We were going to make this store work. Gene took the lead, set the agenda, and I followed. Something about his certainty, his energetic clarity, compelled me. He had a vision of Charing Cross as a circulation center, a hub, a daily "must go" for all members of the town's sizable intellectual community. Interesting, affordable books, good taste, an environment that would make people want to come in and, once in, to linger. As a man in need of a vision, I was easily sold.

I campaigned hard for Gene's approval. After I had recovered from the shock of the first meeting, my crisis of intellectual inferiority, I decided that I wanted to learn things, to know. I would take in everything I could from Gene. Once he sensed this, Gene changed. The more I deferred—asking questions, pushing for minutiae, nodding interestedly—the warmer my partner became. Together we hammered, nailed, varnished, stacked, and sorted. And then, armed with the store checkbook and a generous allowance, we traveled around the area in the store's pickup truck, going to book sales, buying libraries from retiring professors or their widows, all the while talking. Mostly, of course, it was Gene talking. My role was to audit, to keep the line of questioning alive. And that I was good at.

We were both in flight, using this unusual opportunity to redirect ourselves. I was a would-be writer who hadn't written for most of a year, who was just beginning to put his life together after an emotional catastrophe. Gene was a brilliant, willful perfectionist, a scholar who—I gradually understood—could not abide the vocation he thought he was training for. The more we talked, the more he spun his stories, the more vividly I saw his situation. Gene was not so much ABD—all but dissertation—as he was all but ready for desertion. He was a proud misfit who was unable to abide the lockstep procedures of academia. He was too contentious, too impatient for the life that he had imagined for himself. Charing Cross was more than a civilized amusement—which he liked to pretend—it was a way out.

Gene was an aesthete, a man for whom quality of life, down to the last detail, meant everything. He would linger over an assortment of shoelaces in a store, considering his choices. We could not have been more different. My life was so simple, so without fuss. When I opened my eyes in the morning, I got out of bed. I washed my face, rooted around for a wearable shirt, fixed a cup of simple coffee (instant if need be). I could be out the door in five minutes.

Not so Gene. On the mornings when I was supposed to pick him up—if we were scheduled to go on a buy, say—I would very nearly lose my mind waiting for him to get ready. The shower, the beard trimming, the fussing with the cappuccino maker ... I would patrol his library, trying to fall in with this more civilized pace. Certainly the books were there to be admired. Gene had them sorted by subject, perfectly alphabetized. Each edition, each translation, was, naturally, *the* one to have. Dust-jacketed editions wore a clear plastic wrap; pages were marked with little slips of paper, though it was true—Gene was sheepish about this—that books from an earlier era were still decorated in the margins with his immaculate tiny script.

Gene's apartment—the floor of a small house—was a world reared up defiantly against the messy world outside. What care he had expended building narrow shelves over the doors; how the morning light glittered off the wineglasses arranged in the kitchen cupboard. But it was almost impossible to get out the door. First the cup of cappuccino, then the croissant, then I would have to restrain my twitching impulsiveness while Gene introduced me to whatever was the latest prize—an Elly Ameling recording, a new edition of *Daniel Deronda* he'd found somewhere. And so it went through the day, as we hunkered over boxes in someone's garage, treated ourselves to lunch in a new Indian place Gene had heard about, or unpacked our spoils in the basement of the store—my education.

People would sometimes ask me confidentially if Gene was gay, and I unfailingly said, "No!," though at the very beginning it had occurred to me to wonder. But once the store was open and the daily pattern was in place, I saw that Gene had relationships with a great many women, involving everything from lunches to which he would disappear, returning hours later to find me fuming at the register, to more intense drinks-and-meals events that required him to dart out to various specialty shops throughout the afternoon. Yes, Gene was also a superb cook, specializing in Chinese cuisine, though I have forgotten from which region. And his cooking extravaganzas usually heralded the appearance of a new woman in his life. He would plan, shop, fuss, including me in every part of the deliberations. I would hear about Myra or Audrey or Julia—all of them, it seems, graduate students in some recondite discipline. And then, with a twinkle and a "Wish me luck," my partner would be off. By now I knew him well enough—he did not really need to pop his head back in the door to ask me if I'd open the store. I always opened the store.

I did marvel at Gene's conquests. Though he was not an especially good-looking man, he paraded through the store with some very attractive women over the months we worked together. The relationships, however, seldom lasted more than a week or two. How quickly these girlfriends went from being "amazing" to being too this or too that. I would see Gene coming back from the kiss-off lunches, see him standing on the sidewalk outside the store making the gestures that signaled regret. If there was any brooding, I didn't see it. An hour after the end of something he would be calling me over to admire a stack of philosophy books he had just bought from some professor.

For all that amatory expenditure—all the public flourishes—I never had the sense that Gene got on with women. Those weeklong relationships were, I think, very much about Gene finding out, yet again, that he could not talk himself into falling in love, and the women recognizing, after the blitzkrieg of Mozart and handmade dumplings, that this was not a man who was going to be giving his heart away.

My life at Charing Cross lasted for a year and a half. Working with Gene, discovering for the first time in my life the satisfaction of applying myself to something and having it pay off—this pulled me out of the melancholy I had been floundering in. I had never thrown myself at anything so zealously before, nor had I ever let myself be quite so consumed by anything. As soon as I woke up in the morning, I was off to the store. I bought a muffin and a large coffee at Kresge's across the street, turned off the alarm, and let myself in. Often it was hours before opening time. I liked turning on the classical station and then drinking my coffee downstairs at the sorting table, looking over our recent acquisitions. There was always work to be done—pricing books, looking up values in catalogs, arranging the display tables . . .

More and more, too, I was taking inspiration from Gene, picking up books in areas outside my immediate literary interest—books in history, classics, anthropology, art history. It was inevitable that I would begin to amass a library of my own. And this I did—at first almost reluctantly, as if this signaled that I was settling down—then with growing zeal. My new apartment, just around the corner from the store—I moved out of the other room shortly after my landlord's suicide—had space for bricks and boards. And foot by foot I covered the bare walls with the spines of my new finds. It would be a long time before I was anywhere near being in Gene's league, but I was making a start, somehow reconnecting with those afternoons I'd spent years before at the Wooden Spoon and the evenings I'd sat in my dilapidated armchair perusing whatever I'd found that day.

I was doing many things, putting out tremendous energy—educating myself, learning how to be a public person in a place of business, and apprenticing myself to the arcana of the antiquarian-book trade. I was also spending time with Marcie, with my sister, who lived in an apartment in the same building, and with various new friends I'd met through Marcie or Gene or in the context of work. It was—and I often stopped to remind myself of this—a full, exciting life. I felt like I was breaking into adulthood at last.

The one thing I was not doing, which would cause me deep pangs of remorse when I lay awake in the early morning and contemplated my life, was writing. Whatever path I had originally started along had split. I was on some new track. It felt different. Before when I went through phases of not writing, I always knew, however frustrated I became, that there would be a moment of recovery. An idea, a quickly growing desire to be making sentences. But now, except for a few bitter rants I'd coughed out soon after getting to town, I really was dry, dry in a way that felt more permanent. I could not, living as I was then, imagine getting any sustained project under way. I began to allow the hitherto impossible thought—that I could be happy without writing.

But life finds us out again and again, making a mockery of just such easy rationalizations. Does this have anything to do with that destiny notion I used to tantalize myself with, the gist of which was that some plan or imperative lay concealed behind the facade of daily life, out of reach of the "short views" that Sydney Smith urged upon all of us? I don't know. But I have to wonder: Did I really believe that I might pass the rest of my years in some cozy hive of books, buying, selling, and sitting awake by a good light converting printed signs into the honey of knowledge?

One rainy Sunday that first spring back, when my entrepreneurial pride was just cresting, I wandered around the corner to Borders to buy a Sunday newspaper. As I was walking through the door, I noticed Joseph Brodsky standing by the front counter. He was trying to explain something to one of the clerks and judging by his expression—and the clerk's—was not having much success. I ventured closer, at first just eavesdropping and then, as soon as I made out what the poet was looking for, butting in. "You want a copy of *The Education of Henry Adams*?"

"Ya, that's it." Brodsky flashed a vindicated glance at the clerk.

"It's out of print," I said.

"How 'out of print'?" He looked genuinely baffled.

"But"—and now I felt the rush of things falling beautifully into place—"I can get you a copy. Follow me."

Brodsky made a startled surmising grimace but asked no questions. I pointed out the door and across the street. He followed me in the drizzle. How can I convey the pride and self-importance I felt as I fetched forth my bundle of keys, first deactivating the alarm, then unlocking the heavy door? "Come in."

The poet waited at the front while I loped through the dark room to the American history shelves, where, for some reason, we usually shelved the Adams. I was now hoping fervently that my memory had not played me wrong. I had such a clear picture in my mind of that oversize blue volume.

My luck held. The book was there. I could see it protruding from the top shelf even as I crossed the room in the dark. And it

was with a sense of lordly beneficence—as though I were further-
ing some collective cultural project—that I presented it to Brodsky. "On the house."

"What house?" He looked puzzled.

"A gift." I paused for a second, then added, "From a fan."

He smiled sheepishly, accepted. And then we stood together
awkwardly in the darkened front of the store.

"You know this Adams?" he asked. I wished more than anything in the world that I could say yes, strike off some startling ob-
servation. Gene could have. Gene could have kept the poet there
half the afternoon with his striking observations. I could only
shake my head.

"Well, do read him," said Brodsky.

To which I could only nod. I had lost all powers of speech just
then. Here was one of life's gift moments: I was alone, in my store,
with one of my heroes, a writer I had read and pondered, whose
terrible sorrow I thought I knew, and my speaking powers were
suddenly vaporized. But then, as I was turning to unlock the door
again, I had an inspiration.

"I live around the corner," I said. "Would you like a cup of coffee?" And before I could even begin to worry about what he might
be thinking of me, Brodsky agreed.

It was a strange two hours that followed. We did not break all
the barriers of awkwardness and have the conversation I would
have dreamed. But we did talk. I had only to mention a poet, any
poet, and Brodsky would promptly assign a ranking. "Terrific!" he
would say, fishing out another L&M from his pack ("Wystan
smoked these," he said at one point). Or else: "He's shit." I was
nervously matching him smoke for smoke, until it looked like we
had been burning leaves in the apartment. When my sister walked
in halfway through our conversation, she made a big show of fanning the air with a magazine.

With the arrival of a young woman, Brodsky's mood changed
instantly. Where he had been tersely intense before, he now grew

voluble. Everything turned comic. He began to laugh eagerly at his own gibes, eyeing the two of us with a kind of mischievous encouragement. Until it came out, as it was bound to eventually, that we were Latvian.

"Latvia . . ." He scrunched up his brow in mock concentration, and then, bright with malice, said: "In *dibens*."

My sister and I looked at each other. "In" was English, we got that. And *dibens* meant "butt" or "ass" in Latvian.

"Up your ass?" I ventured.

"Ya, exactly." Brodsky guffawed. I had no idea how to take this. I knew there was no love lost between Russians and Latvians, but there was no love lost between Brodsky and Russians, either. Was it a slight, or was the poet simply offering us his only half-remembered idiom? As he was sitting in my apartment, drinking my coffee, I went with the more charitable explanation. "In *dibens*," I repeated, and Andra and I both laughed.

But then, later, I did ask Brodsky if he knew any Latvian poets.

"There are no Latvian poets."

"Rainis—"

"*Rainis . . .*" He laughed cruelly and I cringed. "Ya, Rainis." That was all.

At that moment I surprised in myself a spark of ancient chauvinism. I felt the ancestral culture being mocked, and I—who had so resolutely refused all things Latvian—felt hurt. I wanted to rush forth in defense. I should have, though I can't imagine what I might have said. But instead I let it go. So eager was I to claim the poet as a friend that I let his cynical posturing silence me. I carefully steered the conversation back to safer ground.

Brodsky would have been in his mid-thirties then. He had not yet gone stocky and still had most of his hair, which was then reddish brown and wonderfully disheveled. But it was the face that held you, the strong blade of the nose and the wide, ironic, sinisterly sensuous mouth. I watched it at every moment, how it worked its way from cruel Caligula to what could feel like an unrestrained comic rapture. It was the mouth of an old Jewish sultan, if there could be such a hybrid creature.

Though Brodsky and I never became fast friends, our paths did begin to cross more often. He would stop in the store every so often. I would set aside odd volumes of poetry to show him. Sometimes he would ask, encouragingly, whether I was writing anything. And though I had, since meeting him, written a few pleasingly desolate lyrics, I shook my head. It would be a very long time before I would dare show him anything.

But that encounter in the bookstore was the first link in what became, with the gradual addition of other links, a chain of chance. Naturally I was oblivious to any such possibility.

Gene and I continued to spend a lot of time together. As soon as we were able to, we hired an assistant to watch the register and allow us to go on longer buying trips. These missions took us all over the Midwest, to book fairs in Missouri and Minnesota and estate sales in Illinois. As we drove we talked, about books and store business—Gene had enormous ambitions for Charing Cross—but also about ourselves. I had a bit more airtime now. While Gene still filled hours with his pedagogical ramblings—which were, to me, fascinating—he did also get me talking about things. About my family, my years of struggling with my father, about my time in Maine, about my writerly ambitions. He would listen and then he would prod. He did not mind making me uncomfortable. Why had I stopped writing? Did I really think I would resume? Didn't everybody at some point want to be a writer? What did I imagine I would be able to add to the great conversation? And so on. His questions often had a sadistic edge, and I wondered why he went at me thus. Until, at last, it dawned on me. Gene was also somehow talking about himself. Not just the abandoned dissertation and the scholarly career, but writing. My partner had—it got clearer and clearer—a long-simmering desire to write articles, even books.

This came out during one of our many celebratory dinners. We were out on the town, flush on good steak and wine. Gene had that sparkly distracted look in his eye. I noticed that he kept cleaning his glasses with the special cloth he carried in his shirt pocket. I could feel a wave gathering. In a minute, I knew, he would find the theme, the nest of connections, and he would be off. The black migration and jazz; the Renaissance ideal and contemporary urban design; Catullus and love—something was coming. And I was right. Only when Gene did start in with the gesturing fingers, the explanatory hand and arm movements, his subject was not any particular set of connections, it was himself. His middle-class childhood in Staten Island, his early discovery of books, art, music, and then academia. Through it all, identified for the first time, in my hearing, anyway, was his unhappiness. I thought of my own adolescent desires to get away, to remake myself—they were nothing compared to what I was hearing here. Gene had put his whole early life to the torch—he never went to see his parents, never even called. Everything had gone into the dream of knowledge. Gene was only a few years older than I, finally, but he had been on the scholarly track from the first. He had performed brilliantly, had won the accolades of his professors and mentors. And then, suddenly—he tried for a certain sarcastic casualness here—it all fell apart. He couldn't make himself do the writing.

"I don't mean that I couldn't *do* the writing," he said. "I could do that in my sleep. But I couldn't make myself want it, that way of talking about things." He had taught himself to love the maverick scholars, the odd ones—Auerbach, Blackmur, Frances Yates, Lewis Mumford, Hugh Kenner, Charles Rosen . . . *That* was what he wanted. He wanted to write a book of genius, a synthesis. About everything: Duke Ellington, labor unrest, cities, the secular ideal of love, radical traditions . . . I can't begin to recall all the strands that he spun together. But I do remember that as I listened, I formed a picture of Gene in his apartment, brewing his coffee, deliberating over his turntable, moving this way and that among his amazing collection of books as he thought of some new link, some reference he needed to make, and I knew—with a strange, sad certainty—that he would never write that book, or likely any other.

Meanwhile, we prospered. Through spring and summer the store changed and grew, adding elegant shelving islands that Gene designed and built himself—a superb sound system, and a stock of books in all disciplines that had new customers from all parts of the university coming through. As things stabilized a bit, as I had more time each week to myself, I began to revisit the writing question. I was tentative. I had no novel taking shape in my thoughts, no clamor of stories. But I did, more often now, take occasion to wrestle with one or another of the poems in my notebook. This was odd, and I knew it. I was not a poet, and didn't think that I would ever be one. But something kept pulling me in that direction. For the first time in my life I was reading poetry, really reading it, and finding something there that was not to be gotten elsewhere. Auden, MacNeice, Roethke, Yeats, Vallejo, Tranströmer, Milosz, Cavafy—the stranger the name, it seemed, the stronger the appeal. The books claimed a central area of my bookcase. And reading them made me want to write.

One outcome of this awakened interest—prompted in no small part by Brodsky himself—was that I decided to ask the poet if I could audit his modern poetry seminar. He greeted my question with a conspiratorial laugh, as if, by letting me attend, he were putting something over on the system. And so, come September, I left my bookstore perch two afternoons a week, crossing the campus to a sterile brick building where I joined a small group of nervous others around an enormous conference table.

If we were nervous, it was because our instructor made us so. Whatever extracurricular connection I had with Brodsky counted not at all. There was only the poem and the dynamics of the encounter.

Brodsky was at one and the same time the worst and the most vital and compelling teacher I've ever had. Worst because he did nothing, *absolutely nothing,* to make our confrontation with a difficult body of poetry pleasant or conventionally instructive. This was owing in part to his inexperience—he had never taught before—and in part to the fact that his English was still very much a work in progress. But mainly it was an expression of who he was and what he believed about poetry. Poetry was not something to be "gotten," mastered, and regurgitated in paraphrase. It was not something one notched on the belt of attainments. It was, rather, a struggle waged in fear and trembling, an encounter with the very stuff of language that might put our core assumptions about existence into jeopardy. Brodsky would bring his students—us—into the arena, but he would not fight our battles for us. It could feel almost sadistic. All of us, at times, felt utterly exposed, not only in our ignorance or the blandness of our assumptions about poetry, but in our way of reading the world.

"What do you think of this one?" he might begin, pointing to some poem we were to have read. The poem would be by Mandelstam, or Akhmatova, or Montale. Brodsky's tone on these occasions carried—I don't think I imagined it—a slightly bored, contemptuous edge, but also, to quote Auden (his favorite) quoting Serge Diaghilev, a sense of "astonish me." He made each of us want to say the brilliant thing, to earn that rarest of accolades: "Terrific." But anxiety was usually more powerful. The question would be posed and the room would grow silent—a deep, sedimentary silence.

Somehow we all pushed on, even managed to forge a certain prison cell camaraderie—one that, oddly, included Brodsky himself. Which is not to say that he relaxed one whit his vigilance, his insistence on adequate response to what we were reading. But he somehow—bored sighs notwithstanding—made himself a part of our collective grappling inadequacy. How did he manage it?

Class after class, Brodsky would arrive in the room late, after we had all begun to fidget. He would be fingering an unlit cigarette, conveying thereby that he would much rather be alone somewhere, smoking it, than in our midst. Then, almost invariably, he would heave up from his depths a shuddering, groaning sigh. But there was humor in it. For a moment later his beaked, tragedy-mask expression would loosen. He would look slowly around the room and, taking us all in, smile, as though to communicate that at some level he knew what it must be like for us, as though to forgive us for our blandness.

But then it would start again, the relentless kneading of the language. A line from Mandelstam, a question, silence. Only when the silence had become unendurable would he lead us into the thickets of sound and association, with asides on the logic of poetic images, abbreviated lessons on the ethics of utterance, on the metaphysics of nouns, of rhymes . . .

Brodsky was not yet famous as a poet in these years—not as famous, anyway, as he was for his public persona, that of a young man who had stood up to cross-examination in a Soviet trial and had proclaimed the utter freedom and entitlement of the artist; who had been imprisoned and sent to a labor camp for his impertinence. I read and reread his first book, not just for itself—because of its undercurrent of romantic torment—but also to try to divine the soul of the man who was having such a strange and powerful influence over me. For I could not deny it: I came away from those sessions around that conference table feeling that there were great invisible forces sweeping about me—about all of us—and that the life I was then living was in some primary way denying their power in my life.

I realize that I have not said much about my relationship with Marcie through all these months. In part this is because I was deeply consumed, morning to night, with the store. But my reticence also has to do with the nature of that relationship, which was so resolutely nondramatic. Whatever agitations we each lived with in private, we did not often allow them to ruffle things when we were together. It is as if we had agreed from the start that our duty to each other was to offer comfort and distraction. We spent evenings together, making dinner, going to movies, reading, watching TV, or having drinks with friends. I stayed over so many nights that eventually it made sense for us to find a larger apartment to share. But there was no deeper excitement. Ours was a comfortable adjacency. Marcie's life, during this period of my involvement with the store, was gearing up for the next step. After she left Borders, sometime after I did, she took on various jobs, started saving money. Her plan was to go back to school, to get a degree in social work. And that was as much shape as the future took for us then.

Yet this account dodges and trivializes what went on. More likely I was too numb to register the emotional content of our relationship and Marcie was too accepting, too sold on the myth of my suffering, to bring this forward.

I had a dream about Marcie just the other night, the first in many years. The writing obviously called it up. In the dream I was standing at the counter of a campus restaurant, now long gone, called P.J.'s. I was with my old friend and bookstore crony Tom Frick (who had, actually, written to me about Marcie back when I was still living in Maine). I noticed two women sitting at a nearby table, and when the dark-haired one turned I saw that it was Marcie. I sidled over, saying nothing but leaning down in an insinuating way, waiting for her to look over and recognize me. Which she did. But instead of the surprise, the smile of recognition, I saw an expression of deep—and intimate—sadness. We regarded each other. She said something to me about a book I had never returned, and I answered that I had been in this very place a year ago, waiting to meet her, to return the book, but that she had never come. And that was it. But I woke up with a terrible pit in my stomach, a sense of missed connections that haunted my morning and lingered on through the day.

Back then, though, Marcie and I were living together in a breezy top-floor apartment. It was in that place, one late spring afternoon, that I had my next great moment of realization. If I can now pretty much trace out the alignment of forces that prompted it, then it felt abrupt and overwhelming.

I had been working long hours, as usual, on what was coming to seem like a project that never ended, never would end. For even as Gene and I had our routines in place, we also had a series of long-range plans for expansion and change. These were mostly Gene's initiative, though I shared his enthusiasm and, I thought, his commitment.

But now, increasingly, I registered passing moods of reluctance. When I opened my eyes in the morning, my first impulse was not always to get dressed and hurry to work, as it had been for so long. I would now lie in the early light and contemplate other scenes, other avenues. Travel was one. I felt it like an itch. I wanted to pull around me the atmospheres of other places, wanted new smells and sounds, as well as the thrill of pure mobility. But I was also feeling the urge to write. I did not know what, exactly—that would come, I thought—but I craved something internal to counter the strenuous outwardness of these last months.

Brodsky's influence was everywhere, of course. The poetry, the classroom conversations, but even more, the man. His restlessness and intensity had to be felt, at some level, as a judgment, just as, under his tutelege, reading these various poets—Milosz, Mandelstam, Akhmatova, Herbert, and others—*was* a judgment. At some point the reader—the serious reader, anyway—was forced to ask: What about me? How squarely have I turned myself to life and how much am I living a shadow life? The more I read and listened and absorbed, the harder it became for me to take my place at the bookshop counter, looking up prices of old editions, tuning in the late afternoon quartet on the classical station.

My life changed suddenly, definitively, on that spring day. I recall the scene perfectly. I am alone in the apartment, sitting on the edge of the bed in the little back room we used to sleep in. All around me, on the walls, in stacks on the floor by my feet, are my books. I have been sitting and arranging, weeding. The light—I remember this especially—is yellow, almost buttery. It swirls with the dust I've raised up by shuffling, opening, and closing books. In this excerpted moment, this retrospective intensification of everything that has obscurely been building up in me, I have suddenly stopped whatever I was just doing and now sit transfixed, staring into the slow rotation of the motes. For in this moment—click—I have been presented with a clear understanding. A feeling of being at a crossroads.

What I grasp, fully, emotionally as well as intellectually, is this: that I can stay on, doing what I've been doing, buying and selling books, and have a pretty good life for myself. But that if I do this, those very enticements will ensure that I never find out whether I do have the drive, the nerve, to write. But if I choose the other way—and in my heart I already know that I have chosen—then I will somehow have to break from everything that I have built up around myself.

I imagine now that I sat thus, entranced, testing scenarios in my mind, until the shadows began to close off the light. By evening I had made up my mind.

I knew there would be no easy way to tell Gene about my decision, so I just told him. We were unpacking books in the basement, while Tom, our assistant, was minding the upstairs register. However I said the words, they tumbled out too casually, putting Gene in the position of having to respond in kind, the result of which was that we ended up treating the whole business with a near jocularity that had nothing to do with how we felt. That was easy, I remember thinking as I walked home after work. But then the next day and the next I was up against Gene's rigorously appliquéd cheerfulness, which I had learned was an impenetrable defense, for the other person had a very hard time asking what might be wrong. *"Wrong?"*

These were hard days between us. Gene would not come out with his real reaction, and I could not get myself to ask for it. The man was wounded. I had betrayed him—I was bailing out on our project. But we could not get to that, or to the terrible split I felt between guilt and my building need to get moving, to put everything

familiar behind me and start yet again. In the two weeks that remained—he promised to find a new co-manager by then—we cir-
cled around each other, ribbing and jousting as we always had, but
hearing, both of us, the hollow ring of it. Later, looking up, I would
see Gene regarding me from across the room.

My plan slowly coalesced. After I left the store I would be moving my things—books, mainly—to my parents' house. My sister
and I, at my father's strong urging, were going to take a trip to
Latvia to visit our grandmother Mērija. Then we would travel for
a few weeks in Italy. On my return, I would fly directly to Boston.
For in this cycle of accelerated change, Marcie had applied to graduate school in social work and had been accepted at Boston University. I would stay with her in the fall while I deliberated my next
move. I had enough money saved now to buy myself, I reckoned,
six months of writing. In my last conversation with Gene, I joked
about starting up another book business, somewhere out east, at
which point he turned to me sharply. "Seriously," he said. "Count
me in if you're going to do that."

This story has a sad epilogue, which I need to fit in here, even
though it leaps forward some way into the future.

After I moved to Boston, after several years during which I tried
to find my way as a writer—writing first fiction, then essays—I began to publish some work in a local literary journal. Gene and I
had kept in touch with each other fairly regularly during this period. After a half year more at Charing Cross he had decided to
move on, though he was not sure what his next direction ought to
be. Going back to school was no longer an option. At one point, for
a period of about six weeks, he moved to Boston to see if there
might not be some possibilities for a business dealing used scholarly books. But he found Boston and Cambridge too oppressively
academic—too tightly wound, he said—and left again, settling after more wanderings in a small town in Oregon.

During the period of his stay in Boston, we saw each other often.

I helped him move his things into a tiny room he rented in the North End. We sat over cups of espresso in his various neighborhood haunts. It was from these conversations that I first got the idea that Gene was floundering. It may have been obvious, but I'd had long training in discipleship. Now things looked different. I wasn't sure exactly what had changed, but somehow he was not the same fearless maverick intellectual I'd been so cowed by that night in the bookstore and in the months after. He still talked a good game, but everything had a different backdrop now. Instead of seeing him as the ultimate discriminator, the man who would settle only for the best, I now saw him more as a person who could not get himself to fit in. Anywhere.

When Gene moved to Oregon, he found work in a bookshop. In his letters he reported how he was scaling back, getting rid of all his excess books, eating simply. He wrote of being in a steady relationship.

I kept Gene apprised of my writing ventures, sent him my first few essays. He wrote back to praise, to offer detailed commentary on parts of my exposition, and—this surprised me—to ask if I might mention him to the editor. He had an idea for a series of articles on jazz. I did make the connection for him, and he did subsequently publish two or three of these pieces. I found them formidable in their reference but very stiff, constrained, with none of the associative magic that drove his best flights of conversation.

Then a more curious thing happened. I had the good fortune to get several reviews published in the *Nation*. I sent copies along to Gene, though I was sure he would have seen them anyway—for as long as I'd known him, the journal had been his bible. But now, silence. No answer to my letters, no response to my terser inquiries. The better part of a year elapsed, and I began to think of our connection as severed. Then a letter arrived. It was short—for Gene—and perplexing. Gene wrote that he had made a vow not to write to me until he, too, had published something in the *Nation*. He was breaking his vow, giving up that foolish idea. His life had changed again. He was now working as a carpenter, living with his girl-friend. More to come, he promised.

Except there wasn't. That was the last word I had from my friend, the last inkling I had of what he was doing. I got no more responses to my letters, and though I wondered quite often what he might be doing, I stopped thinking of him as a person in my life.

Then, in 1985, I was visiting my parents and we all drove up to Ann Arbor to have a look around. My father took us to see the law school library he had designed. I took my parents to Borders—the same location still—and showed them where I had tended remain-ders on the mezzanine. Joe Gable, the manager, saw me browsing and came over. It seems to me now that we talked about a great many different things—about Tom and Louis, Joe's marriage, my writing—before he paused, lowered his voice, and stated: "You heard about Gene."

I felt the dread of it even before he had completed the sentence, and I knew what would be next as surely as I've ever known any-thing. I shook my head, aware of a ringing silence around me. "I saw his friend Frank awhile back," said Joe. "I guess Gene killed himself." Joe did not know many details. Gene had broken up with his girlfriend; he had been depressed. He had hanged himself. The afternoon fades out at that moment, except that I recall sitting in the backseat of the car while my father drove us back. I was think-ing about Gene, of course, but in the strangest way. I was not won-dering why he had killed himself. I was wondering, rather, why I had not seen all along what was so clear just then—how sad he had always been and how superbly he had acted the other part, that of the bon vivant, the arbiter of taste, the weaver of brilliant connec-tions. In the staggered way of things, my Ann Arbor phase really ended that afternoon, years after I'd handed over my keys to my ex-partner and said good-bye.

CHAPTER 7

I ARRIVED IN BOSTON ON A CHARTER FLIGHT FROM LONDON IN SEP-
tember of 1977, fresh from a month of traveling, pared back down
to essentials. Marcie drove out to the airport to pick me up in her
red convertible, a low-idling fixer-upper she had bought in Ann
Arbor just before moving. It all felt like a colossal adventure. We
drove into the Callahan Tunnel with the top down, the high buildings rearing up as we emerged. I loved everything I saw—the old
clock tower, the ramshackle coziness of the North End, the gleam
of the State House dome in the distance. I could hardly believe it: I
was being given a new life. The particulars all had to be taken in,
absorbed. I already envied Marcie her navigating ease, how easily
she gunned through the intersections, clattered over the embedded
tracks where Commonwealth Avenue swerved toward Allston, and
jockeyed all those feet of car into what barely looked like a
space. We were home.

Marcie had rented a small one-bedroom apartment, and she
welcomed me. That we would cohabit seemed natural, an exten-
sion of the old Ann Arbor pattern, though both of us knew, I think,
that we were on the habit end of coupledom, not quite "just friends,"
but certainly not jealously passionate lovers. Looking back, I'm
amazed that we both accepted this strange limbo for as long as
we did. The point, never made explicit between us, was that we
kept each other safe, took the edge off the relationship question

while we tried to get on with our lives. We were not exactly surro-gates—we had genuine affection for each other, the relationship was real—but neither of us, insofar as we conjured the big future, when everything would begin in earnest, imagined a lasting to-getherness.

I felt the sadness of that at times, and I knew that Marcie had similar pangs. I would look across the table at her as we sat in the tall narrow kitchen in her tall narrow apartment, watching her as she studied—her fish-lip pose of concentration, the hair pushed messily away from her forehead, the cigarettes lit, gulped, and stabbed into the ashtray beside her (I never once saw Marcie savor a cigarette)—and I would think: This is a person who will be with someone else. How odd: to be with someone even as you know you will one day stop knowing her. I registered this either as poignancy or futility or some combination that would make me want to es-cape my mind by heading out into the street.

I had never lived in a real city before, and this was my romance. As I had once filled page after page with descriptions of waves breaking over rocks and seagulls hovering overhead, so I now hoarded urban details: the screech of trolley wheels, the sparking of the overhead wires, the wet garbage and piss smell at every alley mouth. Boston seemed endless, clustered densities broken up by the sudden sprawl of the common, the slow descent from the State House to Louisburg Square, its Mary Poppins vista of chimney pots straight out of my imagined nineteenth century.

I spent my first week or so just wandering, finding my way to Park Street and then riding the Red Line to Harvard Square, where I thrilled to mount up on the ancient wooden escalator (now long since dismantled) into the sunlight, where the wall marking Harvard University from the rest of the world fronted Massachu-setts Avenue. I knew Harvard Square slightly. Back when we lived in Maine, Jess and I had, a few times, chugged down Route 1 in our Saab to spend a few hours dosing ourselves on good coffee and bookstores. Now I had leisurely access—I wandered, sampled, convinced myself that I was feeling the jolts of a more potent and purposeful energy. This was where the vectors converged; this was where it made sense to become a writer.

For that was now my mission, clear and simple. I was going to hole myself up without distraction and write my novel. I knew, of course, that both my ambition and my approach were a kind of cliché: young men heading out to write their great novels. But these secondhand narratives—and anyone young trying to make his way doing anything is living one of these narratives—can fire us up as easily as they can mock or daunt. I felt the pull of the image, the unsophisticated brashness of it. There were all those photogenic predecessors: Wolfe, Kerouac, Mailer, Agee, or, raising the gaze slightly, Faulkner in New Orleans, Joyce in Paris . . . The bar never seems too high when you are still in the dreaming stage, which I manifestly was.

The writing itch had always been there, as had a strangely proprietary sense about everything that pertained to the vocation. I can't say for sure where this originated. Was it that my mother was a great reader and admired writers like Hemingway, Steinbeck, Hamsun, Remarque, and others, weaving their lore into her conversations? Or that my father's father, whom I never met—indeed, whom my father himself had never met—had been a writer, the handed-down myth being that he had left his family in order to devote himself solely to his work, his books of psychology, his folklore studies? Was *that* somehow attractive? Surely the notion of a man leaving everything behind to pursue a calling had appeal for me when I was younger. But how did the calling itself come to matter?

Whatever planted the original seed, it was helped along by my reading and fantasizing strenuously what it would be like to *be* a writer. Never mind concern for the actual work, for having something to say—all that would follow later. In the beginning were the fabulous seductions of image.

I don't mean this to sound quite as superficial as it must. The fantasies that we all have at certain periods in our lives—fantasies about ourselves being something we're not—are profound, too. As profound, anyway, as they are later embarrassing and heartbreaking to contemplate. For they are, of course, garishly backlit portraits of who we aspire to be: ourselves as magnified through the lens of our strongest yearnings.

What, then, did I imagine that a writer was? I think I had the obscure intuition—this from the devoted consumption of novels and aggrandizing biographies—that a writer was a creature of almost occult powers, a ruler over crucial portions of the realm of the invisible. He (I naturally featured all my writer heroes as male) was the shaman who gathered and arranged words into suddenly arresting combinations; he caused images and scenes to shine forth on the back screen of the mind's theater. Yet, and this was the most attractive paradox, he was, for all his traffic among ineffable signs, very often reassuringly physical, rugged even, pictured on most of his book jacket photos as one ready to have an adventure at the drop of a hat.

By the time of my early teens, I had fallen hard for musk-exuding figures like Wolfe, Steinbeck, and London. These were writers who seemed to embrace the whole vast span of human possibility, and in my typically absolute ambitiousness, I resolved to be just like them.

The desire was, of course, entirely out of scale with any demonstrated aptitudes. But so strong was my belief then, in my teenage years especially, in my exceptionality, my powers of will, that I felt no need to underwrite the fantasy with any actual output. That would naturally follow, as would my whole charmed existence.

True, I had always taken great pleasure in school assignments that required writing, and I did do well on my various reports and essays, sometimes still called "themes." In the seventh grade I even won a citywide writing award for a two-paragraph sketch I had written about sitting in my grandfather's lap and playing with his beard while he smoked his pipe and told me stories. This was, I can now confess, the baldest sort of fabrication, since my grand-father—Mike—who had died a few years earlier, had been clean-shaven and reticent and had probably never touched a pipe to his lips in his life. But though I won a tiny gold key and got my name in the paper—in microscopic letters—the honor did not stoke my grandiosity much; in my literary self-image I was already far beyond anything that the junior high world could offer me. Contests and gold keys were the sorts of things we writers trifled with only to keep limber.

This outsize dreaming was all secret, of course. Not a soul on earth would have guessed it to look at me—that I was walking down the corridors of Berkshire Junior High entirely installed in the bubble of what was to be. How can I possibly convey what this was like? Only bits and pieces from that time come back to me. I do remember one fairly emblematic moment, though. I am at school, moving down a wide stairway in a crowd during a class break. In my other world, at home, I have been reading Irving Stone's somewhat overheated biography of Jack London, *Sailor on Horseback*. Not just reading it—more like tailoring its romanti-cism until it fits me like a second skin. Suddenly it breaks over me, my illumination: *This is not my life*. These people on all sides of me—stringy guys in surfer shirts, formidable girls in braces and penny loafers—have nothing to do with who or what I am. In some clear, lit-up other existence that hasn't happened yet, I am a writer-adventurer just like Jack London. The terms of this yet unknown life are not clear to me. I see the sketchiest whirl of im-pressions: intrigues, combats, great loves, and far-flung wander-ings. Writing? Oh yes, somewhere surely there is room for the clatter of an old portable, for sheets of immortal manuscript to gather on the floor.

I did not write and I did not write, and still it was all on the way to being a writer. The dream of the vocation was purer without the stain of faltering expressions on the page. Until my junior year in high school, that is, when seemingly out of nowhere an almost frightening sensitivity welled up in me and built pressure behind my pencil point. Now—I was at Cranbrook—I carried my brown spiral notebooks everywhere. I sat by the lake after school, writing about sunsets and webs bejeweled with dew. I don't remember quite if it pleased me to put these images on the page—it must have— but I do know that I felt an odd sense of security having these note- books with me, as if they represented some sort of ticket out.

In college I was still filling pages, though less now with poetic imagery, more with extended assessments of my situation, "mean- ing of life" sorts of ponderings, many of them ultimately asking what I would do with myself as a grown-up, trying to imagine how one lives a life, always goading myself to step further out on the writing branch. Only "writing" was not then about the laborious discipline of getting words onto the page. It was about being free, unencumbered. A writer was, by some then almost self-evident logic, a person who did not get tied down or caught in any of the expected traps of family or career. A writer, to borrow from Thoreau's well-known opening to *Walden,* was one who found a way to live fronting the basic facts of existence—unprotected and without illusions.

On it went, the evolving fantasy. At some point in the early years of college, after prolonged and redundant feasting on writers like Kerouac, Henry Miller, J. P. Donleavy, and Salinger (the basic counterculture syllabus of the times), I encountered Hemingway. Not for the first time, exactly—we had read a few shorter works of his in high school—but now I was ready. I read the stories and *The Sun Also Rises* and *A Farewell to Arms* with wide-eyed adoration, as if this, at last, were the true real thing, life lived at the proper pitch of seriousness, tragic encounter, and stoical restraint. Here the adults were all free of boring jobs and classroom inanities and the ticket punching of dailiness; they could occupy themselves full-time with danger, drink, and conversations dusky with innuendo. Where I had once guided myself around in a cloud of Kerouac and Miller, now it was Hemingway who possessed me. And this he did as much through diction as narrative event or stoicism of outlook.

It was the Hemingway of the Nick Adams stories who got me thinking that I could write fiction. Here was the first real chattering of typewriter keys. My characters and cadences stepped forth fully formed from his, the miraculous thing being that I recognized so little of it at the time. I had my own Nick Adams stand-in, Peck, and over a period of about two years I gave him a world, a life, more or less coextensive with my own. Peck lived in a college town, as I did; he had a girlfriend, Angela, who was, I must say, somewhat more jaded and sophisticated and Brett Ashley–ish than was Jess, whom I had begun to see around this time. But he also seemed to sit around a great deal, drinking coffee and smoking cigarettes—just like me. If nothing finally ever happened to Peck in any of the stories, it was because nothing fictionworthy had yet happened to me. Or so I dully assumed.

But no matter. The main thing was that by writing this series of stories, I had started the drive wheel turning. I became, if only in my own eyes, a writer—and that was almost enough.

I remember with special intensity that long humid summer before my senior year. Jess and I lived together in our narrow cage of a room on a leafy Ann Arbor side street. But what should have been relaxed and casual somehow turned malign. Jess and I were not getting along; we drank far too much beer on those airless nights, and then we argued, pitting silence against silence, while the almost constant heat lightning pulsed over the rooflines.

Two or three mornings a week, I would rouse myself in the dark to get a place in line at the local Manpower office. Body for hire. This was how I bought my freedom from full-time work: I economized with an immigrant's cunning, and then, a few days a week, I did whatever I had to do to get a paycheck. On most of those days I wound up taking the call from sanitation, riding the back of a garbage truck for six hours, hopping down every few feet in the incinerating heat to tip another fetid barrel into the crusher. Nowadays when I hear people talk about soul-killing work, I remember how it felt to come up the street in the late afternoon, exhausted, enraged, and reeking. No solvent could reach deep enough. I was full of insights about the working life and what it does to a man.

But then I had my free days, the mornings when I could brew myself a pot of strong coffee and then sit in the sunny communal room at my typewriter, pushing on with my stories. This was my first real taste of the *un*romanticized writing life. I mean the workaday version in which one sits in place for long hours, caught up—or not—in the world unfolding on the page; in which to look at the day's labors is invariably to be shocked at the discrepancy between absorption and expended energy and the actual tally of lines on the page.

I wrote a good deal over the course of that summer. Most of the work was imitative, and I would wince to read even a few sentences of it now. But doing it, day after day, week after week, established a new rhythm in my life, one that I would not forget even during the long periods when the writing did not come or when I ceased trying. But maybe "rhythm" is not the best word for what I want. It was more the foreground/background inversion that writing makes possible, that absolute rearrangement of the proportions of things through the absorption in creating narrative. I would get pulled in so deep by my struggle to put the best words in the best order that the persistence of the world around me—a car horn, a mother calling to her child down the street—would seem utterly miraculous. Which, of course, it is—though how often do we think of it?

I wrote my Peck stories, collecting them toward what I hoped would one day be a book, and when summer ended and my last school year began, I carried the momentum with me into my new life. I rented a room above a delicatessen, just minutes away from where Jess settled, and when I wasn't visiting her or traipsing back and forth on my various book-dealing initiatives, I was at my desk, away from everything, caught up in the situations I was building around my character.

Alas, after school ended, once I took my first bookstore job—to save money so that Jess and I could move somewhere, so I could begin my real life as a writer—the work tapered off. I was busy. I was learning the book trade, suddenly overwhelmed, as I never had been during my four years in college, by what there was to know. Where before I might have sat over my own writing, I now skipped anxiously from one book to another, making lists of titles, of things to know, even contriving once to chart on a large sheet of paper the complete web of disciplines and their connections, a process that at one and the same time filled me with consternation and allowed me a superficial but still faintly gratifying sense of control.

Now I was in Boston. Three years had passed and I had written only fitfully. There were those painstakingly crafted descriptions of waves, those dozens of botched beginnings, a few morose lyrics written under the Brodsky inspiration. Otherwise, very little. Indeed, how did I *dare* to think of myself as a would-be writer?

I'm not sure how to answer that. I know that I still felt a special charge around books. When I read, it was covetously; I was always looking for tricks I might use and moves I might one day incorporate into my repertoire. But at this point—I was now twenty-five—I pitched toward writing because I had so systematically refused anything else—everything but dealing books. I almost *had* to become a writer. I could not seem to get interested in anything else. I don't know how many times my mother suggested to me that I go back and get a degree in library science. But while the idea made perfect sense—and my parents were certainly willing to finance further study—I could not get past a core inertia. My imagination would simply make no place for an image of my pursuing a higher degree. And that inability, that refusal, was decisive.

So now I had put myself in a corner. I had moved to Boston, away from all entanglements. I had saved up some money. The next step was to rent some kind of a place. This may seem odd to some, the more so because Marcie's apartment was empty most days. But I had my idées fixes. One was that to write a book—as opposed to a mere story or article—one needed an environment. A space that would somehow sustain and preserve the extraordinary energies of solitary composition. How could I write in Marcie's apartment, where the phone might ring or Marcie herself might decide to come home to work on a paper? No, I wanted a place that I could consecrate to the task.

I was lucky. On the very first day of answering ads in the *Boston Globe,* I found a room in a large Brookline brownstone. The rent was a flat $25 a week, payable on Mondays. For that I got the bare minimum—sooty windows, clanging radiator, and a bed so narrow and loud on its springs that one would have to be desperate to get some sleep in it. I felt the power of the archetype. There was the ancient carpet with the life track worn in—generations of tenants moving from bed to window to dresser to door. But the best feature of all, what decided me, was the great empty closet. It was almost a third as big as the room itself. And when I moved in—carried up my typewriter and paper—I immediately put the chair and tiny bed table into that smaller space. There, enclosed in a room within a room, I sat for the next four months and wrote.

During that long season I learned, again, the saving power of artistic compulsion. Had it been my fate to live in that space, alone, without the consolation of a project, I would have fallen rapidly into despair. Everything around me—the walls, the bargain warehouse furnishings, the cataract sound of the hall toilet—spoke of failure. But to me, unlocking the front door, making my way slowly up the stairs with a large cup of take-out coffee, it was the site of great hope. By the time I opened the door to my room, I had my next sentences lined up and was eager to scrawl them on a sheet of paper so as not to lose them. I didn't have time to focus on the warped veneer of the dresser top or the van Gogh aspect of the bulb that hung almost directly over my head. I only needed it to work when I flipped the switch.

My other idée fixe was that I was going to write a novella. Somewhere I had seen an advertisement for a novella competition—the winner would have his work published as a book—and that was all the prompting I needed. The deadline was in the late winter. I had five months.

I also had a story. Finally. I would write of a young man returning home to Maine to live with his parents. In his recent past, a trauma, though I would not explain what had happened so much as build by way of small recovered flashes toward a revelation. The memory narrative—and I worked on the logistics of this incessantly, while walking, while cooking, while sitting in front of Marcie's tiny TV set, watching *Kojak*—would be counterpointed by a developing story. For my narrator would get caught up in a crisis involving his old boyhood friend, a lobsterman caught up in a local feud, the whole design being that as events of the present built toward their violent consummation, his understanding of the specifics of his betrayal by his lover would fall into place, and everything would resound together, the now and the then, the private and the public. . . .

In the work—and here I took some creative license—the narrator would actually walk into a restaurant and discover his girlfriend with another man. In real life I had merely tormented myself with the imagining, and then only later, after everything was over. Indeed, the further I got from the end of things in Maine, the more clearly I grasped that there had probably been someone in the wings, poised to move in, for some time, possibly during all the months of our summer disaffection. The sheer velocity with which things happened once I left—in less than a year Jess was married, pregnant—made it seem increasingly likely. But I could do nothing with my hindsight realization except twist it around to my writerly ends.

I started my project with a great rush of energy. What profound satisfaction I felt, first in filling up page after page of the cheap, narrow-lined tablets I favored with my story, and then, as soon as each chapter was finished, typing everything up neatly in my high-speed two-finger style. I got accustomed to the coffee cycle, letting my morning take-out cup propel me into the first deep immersion, then breaking for lunch, during which time I'd cross Beacon Street to a sandwich shop; then, returning with another large carry-out cup, I'd push on into the afternoon drive, which would usually leave me, at about four o'clock, with an agitated exhaustion—a feeling that all but propelled me out the door, away from all evidence of my labors (another reason to write away from where I lived, I thought).

But the brain would not shut off that easily. I remember so many afternoons coming down the front steps of the brownstone, shielding my eyes against the last blaze of the afternoon sun, gaping at the Boston skyline as if it were a decal someone had pasted up over the horizon.

I was haunted. For the first time in my life—and in a sense the last—I entered a project of the imagination so deeply that I felt the characters acquire their own volition. My settings were absolutely vivid to me. I could be trudging up Beacon Street toward Coolidge Corner so taken up with the fine points of some problem I was trying to solve that the world around me became filmy, something I almost believed I could puncture if I put my strength to it. A wonderful feeling in some respects, but the grandiosity is more than a little misleading. The world cannot be punctured. Moreover, when the energy drains from the figments of the imagination and reality reasserts itself, the dreamer feels radically diminished. This might help to explain the depression that often afflicts writers right at what should be their moment of greatest triumph—completion.

What a process it was, the writing of this little novella. I don't know how most novelists go about their business—rearing up a structure, a world, and trying to infuse it with the complete illusion of life—but I quickly learned that it was not, as I had imagined it might be, a matter of putting one foot in front of the other, amassing pages, scenes. For me the idea of linear progress, of patient augmentation, was a chimera. It was more like trying to play four-dimensional chess. A character's action or remark did not take place in simple time—as our own actions and remarks often seem to—but was always potentially consequential. A bit of business on page twenty might presuppose the (yet unwritten) conclusion, which would put that moment in a new, perhaps truer light. Here was the real laboratory for those ideas of destiny I had so cherished. The composition process—which, if filmed, would look like the dreamiest sort of distraction, thumb and forefinger slowly twisting a lock of hair—was in fact the most exhausting sort of calculus, a constant extrapolating of possibility within the constraints of imposed dramatic structure.

Here I was on my own. I had nothing to guide me except the intuitions I had honed for myself as a longtime reader of novels. How to get inside a character, represent a moment of strong feeling or the incursion of a suppressed memory; how and when to touch in the detail that would confirm the inevitability of a scene for the reader? I made my way forward erratically.

Still, there came a moment, I don't remember exactly at which point, when I crossed some unmarked threshold, when the project became fully real to me. The premises were all set out, as were the tensions and character conflicts, and I no longer wondered if it was a book. From then on it became a matter of following through, of tracing out the various arcs I had inscribed and hoping that they would converge in figurative space as I intended.

And they did. Rather, I *thought* they did. I was fully in the grip of what I had fished out of myself. Now when I left my room for the day and slowly made my way back to Marcie's apartment, stopping to buy something we needed for dinner or a bottle of wine, the fantasies would encroach. I worried less about scenes or tricky patches of dialogue. I began to imagine what it would be like when I finished. I would have a book, a novel, like I had always dreamed. The thought was almost overwhelming. What if it really *was* good? What if I won the contest and got published? What—and this was the imagining that quickened me most—what would Jess think if she was to read it? For of course she would. There were moments, I confess, when I lost all sense of proportion. I imagined the writing of this book as a sublime intervention in the workings of fate. Jess would read it and she would understand. She would apprehend in a flash who I really was and, against all odds, she would signal me back. The sidewalk swam away under my feet as I walked along.

"So . . . ?" Marcie would prod me with casual intentness over dinner. "How's the work?" She knew how much my life revolved around those hours in the other place. But I never knew how to respond. I did not feel that I could let her in past a point. I could say things about the substance of the plot or the daily travail—if I had made progress or not—but I could not get myself to confide anything about the real process, either the feelings that prompted the whole enterprise or the fantasies that ran riot whenever I imagined actually finishing the thing. I told her as much as I could without giving an account of what really occupied me. I was pained by the lie, felt it as a kind of loneliness, but I could not get over my own barriers. I remained mired in the unstated and unrevealed, afraid, most likely, of what would happen if I began to unfold my real preoccupations.

Anyone who writes knows, of course, that you cannot write anything very substantive—certainly not a novella—in a period of three or four months. Even the most practiced professionals, writers who can get a scene on the first or second take, need more time than that. But I had my compulsion, and my colossal ignorance, and I was going to push the job through.

I will give myself credit for staying with it. Day after day I went back to work like a miner returning to his tunnel, his seam of coal. I saw nothing but what the cone of light from my headlamp showed me. And work got done. Pages mounted in a little pile on the floor by my feet. At day's end I would indulge myself for just a minute—fanning through the accumulation, pausing here and there to read a sentence. Then, every bit as orderly as Flaubert's writer-bourgeois, I switched off the light and turned the key in the lock. I might as well have punched a clock on my way out the front door.

Finally the day came. There was only one short scene left to write, and linger as I would over the sentences, the cadence of the finale, the words got set into place, the book was done. With some self-consciousness I typed "THE END" in caps at the bottom of the last page. Then I sat and riffled through the pages for a while, and with a self-satisfied little sigh I put the stack neatly in a ream box. The pages did not even fill it halfway. But no matter. This was something. I had set out to write a book, and I had done it. I took myself out for a milkshake at the luncheonette, and leaning back into the window light, I savored it like some elixir of pure possibility.

Two nights later I gave my first and only reading of my new work. It was in Marcie's living room. Marcie sat on the low couch, and beside her sat my friend Michael, just recently moved to town from Ann Arbor, the same Michael who had driven me away from Biddeford Pool that long-ago afternoon. They waited quietly while I fussed with my pages. I had no idea how much I might read or how long any of it might take. I was trying to situate myself, to connect with this prose. It suddenly looked all wrong. I felt a flinching sense of exposure.

Michael muttered something, and I saw Marcie swat him on the arm.

"Okay, okay . . ." I waved my arms around to banish the demons and poured myself a big drink of wine. Then, as if stepping into a dark room with my eyes closed, I launched forth.

"It's called *The Glass*," I said. "You'll see why if we get that far."

I began to read, quickly, trying to make it easier for my friends. I read as if from a great distance, so focused on the sound of my words, their cadence, that I forgot to listen. The first ten or so pages flashed by in a blur of articulated sounds. I was afraid to look up. I moved my character Victor from the waiting room of the bus depot to his parents' house; I walked him through his first stages of anxious arrival. When I did at last glance over, Marcie and Michael were both stock still, each of them staring into some private listening distance.

I pushed on, and as I did, I gradually found myself tuning in to my own words. But the realization was still slow in coming. At first I registered only slight discomfort, a chafing I thought might at any moment dissolve, become something else. But no, the further I went, paragraph by paragraph, then sentence by sentence, the more that sensation grew to become a sick certainty. And now I really was afraid to raise my eyes from the page. At that moment I could hear it from the outside, and I knew. It was wrong, off. My words were mawkish and overblown, and depressed. The whole project—it was suddenly as clear as could be—was nothing but a long aggrieved letter to Jess. She was the only intended reader.

I didn't know what to do. I could feel my face getting flushed, my breath coming in shallow. I forced myself to go on. Finally, pausing, at chapter's end, I looked over at my listeners. Marcie had drawn herself into the corner of the couch; she had a cigarette going and was fanning the smoke away from Michael. Michael was focused on his knees. Both looked up.

"I don't know how much more to read," I said.

"How much more *is* there?" Michael chuckled in Marcie's direction.

"Two chapters, but—"

"Aw, hell—we want to know what happens." Michael looked sincere enough.

Marcie nodded, though I thought I sensed already the silences that would come later.

"Okay." I was at a loss. My big climactic scene was next, but now, paving the way toward it, I felt none of the escalation and tightening I wanted. But I still held out the slight hope that I was wrong. Maybe I would finish up and find I'd been wrong about everything. I continued on for another forty minutes, right to the end. I let the final phrases die away. I did not have to look up. It didn't matter what expressions Marcie and Michael would put on or what they might say; I knew the truth. And for a brief instant, before the gloomy certainty of failure took over, I felt a sharp, masochistic pang of relief. I had freed myself of the burden of writing.

My situation had suddenly become serious, and I knew it. This was more than just an ill-judged first venture into novel writing. It felt like failure, the real thing. For I realized in a stroke how much everything about the future—how I thought of my life—depended on the view I had of myself as a serious writer. Which I manifestly was not. I had been trading without any collateral, and now I was exposed. To myself. And once again I deflated, crashed. I was finished as a writer. I had been lying to myself: my life was a botch. It never occurred to me that I might try again, make some effort to salvage the project. No, this was absolute.

Now it truly seemed that my life was a pattern of downward spirals. The first of these had dropped me—through my own blindness and brute obstinacy—from the paradisal simplicity of my life in Maine to a second chance in Ann Arbor. The second had lowered me from my hard-won career independence as a book-seller to this: the near indigence of a would-be writer who could not turn any of his wounds to account. I thought of Words-worth's—or was it Lowell's—poets, who "begin in gladness" but come around, unfailingly, to "despondency and madness." Well, I was not yet mad. But despondency was right. My funds were gone. There was no showing my face in Ann Arbor anymore. Boston, so picturesque and promising when I arrived, when I netted it in my fantasies, now showed its fabled cold insularity. Those towers would go unconquered; those people swarming past me in the midday surge would remain strangers, all of them.

I was lucky, though. My paranoid fantasy of a complete free fall was cut short when I applied for a job at the Brattle Book Shop in downtown Boston and got hired. From my glory days at Charing Cross this was a chastening comedown—certainly in terms of pay and responsibility—but it was something. I resolved to give it my best. Now every weekday morning I took my place at the trolley stop on Commonwealth Avenue near Marcie's apartment. I rode in to Park Street with the secretaries and young bankers, getting my muffin and coffee at the Pewter Pot on the Common, bracing myself for the myriad "gofer" tasks my boss, George Gloss, would devise.

George was the patriarch of Boston's used- and rare-book dealers. His shop on West Street, which advertised itself as "the oldest continuous book shop in America," was Dickensian in every respect, from its ancient sooty-brick facade to the jumble of volumes that filled three floors and a dank basement, which George and his son, Ken, seemed to track with the paranormal instinct that the very best book dealers possess. Indeed, George adored Dickens and loved to tell whoever would listen that he had married his wife, Dorrit, just for her name.

The man ran his business with the strangest blend of acumen and whimsy. Buying a lot of books, haggling over the price of some old volume, he would be as intractable as any dealer I've ever encountered. But then he would compensate for that side of his nature with an endearing foolishness, buying a bag of worthless romances because he couldn't bear to disappoint the old woman who had brought them in to sell, sending one of us workers out midmorning to buy a box of chocolates because he had a sudden craving, bantering lasciviously—even shockingly—with an old queen named Eddie who shuffled in every other day or so to offer the latest outrage on a certain Judge Bonin, whose name he pronounced with exaggerated emphasis as "Bone-in"—compelling George to drop whatever he was occupied with to correct him.

As George's employee, I joined the others in dancing to his whims. I did everything from parking his car in the morning to going on sweet-tooth errands, to putting in long shifts in the dark claustral basement at the shipping table. Every so often—but rarely, considering the context—I got to put some small bit of my book background to use, helping some customer track down an elusive title or going along on a buy. More often, though, I would act as George's chauffeur, taking him to one or another of the places where he addressed small gatherings on "trash and treasures" or "riches in your cellar" or some such—occasions I enjoyed not only because I got to banter with George while we drove, but because I could then wait outside in the parking lot with a book.

Dickensian distractions aside, I was not particularly happy. Though Marcie and I had left her cramped Allston apartment and had moved to a bigger place in Cambridge, the move did not feel like a liberation. We seemed, in fact, to be growing rapidly into our separate lives, Marcie occupied with school and new friends, I with work and—I honestly don't know what else. Reading, watching TV, drinking beer. My dreaming, aspiring self had gone underground. I could almost feel the first calcifying cynicism starting to set in.

At work I started to spend more time with my co-worker, Paul. A graduate student in philosophy at Harvard, Paul was, as my old partner, Gene, had been, taking a break. As the son of an old leftist friend of George and Dorrit's, he enjoyed a special status at the store. He took long lunches with impunity; he could jokingly shrug off George's task assignment and busy himself with things that interested him more. I eased myself slowly into his orbit. And for a time—for as long as we lasted at the shop together—we were brothers in mockery. I don't even know what exactly we mocked—the customers, George's eccentric autocracy—it didn't matter. We crisscrossed past each other in the store, and the gibes and puns flew. Before too long, banking on George's distractedness, we instituted the Friday "happy hour." Having gone out to lunch together, we returned with enormous take-out cups in which we had fixed ourselves gin and tonics. On these we sailed through the afternoon. And when even the drinks could not get the time to move fast enough, we took turns nudging the minute hand on the big store clock. It was a great sport. One of us would sashay over to the front counter, George's perch, to engage him in discussion. The other would edge over to the clock and, with a quick glance to confirm that George was not looking, would advance the time by a minute or two. This would happen over and over through the course of the afternoon—that is, until the culminating day when a handful of irate customers confronted George as we were padlocking the grate, and we all ended up back inside working unpaid overtime.

George loved Paul but recognized after a while that the two of us were a deadly combination. And then his tolerance for our antics faded. To Paul he suggested a break, a leave of absence—as "family," of course, he could come back at any time. Everything changed now. Without my friend, I found the days almost unendurable. I could hardly make myself descend into the basement to contend with another stack of book shipments. I hated patrolling the aisles during the busy lunch hour, watching for shoplifters. Whatever relief and distraction the job had brought me were now gone.

I had a way of egging myself into decisions back then. I remember the day I abruptly decided to quit the Brattle. I was on my lunch break and found myself hiking agitatedly back and forth along the edge of the Common. It came over me with a sudden dramatic emphasis that I couldn't bear another afternoon of work. One more errand to the second floor or the basement would finish me. I was not using my brain, I was not writing. I heard Cal's long-ago voice, quoting Bob Dylan, trying to irk me out of some slough: "He not busy being born is busy *dy*-ing." And I saw myself grown stale and compliant. By the end of my break I had built up a serious head of steam.

After returning to the store, I stood by the door, next to George's desk, and waited. He was in the middle of one of his byzantine negotiations. I watched him write a column of numbers on a brown paper bag. It was all I could do to stand there.

George sensed and correctly read my agitation, for when I finally stepped before him he was ready. "You need to go?" he asked. I nodded, suddenly feeling weak and disloyal. But George was making no discouraging motions. Did he think I was just asking to leave for the day? I was about to say something more, but George did understand. He was digging down into the bag he kept by his feet.

"You'll need some money."

"Yes, sir." I smiled now.

"I hope you're going to write something." He fastened me with a serious look.

"I hope I will." I drew myself up. I could hardly believe my good fortune. George was letting me out; he was giving me money. "I will come and visit," I said. We shook hands. And that was that.

An hour later I was sitting in the backseat of the Peter Pan bus, watching the husks of Boston fall away outside the window, on my way to visit Jim and Susan in Vermont. The idea had come to me before I'd even reached Tremont Street. That they should have been there, welcoming, when I called, proved I was charmed. I was shaking the mixture, watching the clutter of the city—my old life—disappear. For a moment I understood everything—how to free oneself one had only to act with a total sense of necessity. No daring is fatal. Though on the face of it this was to be but a long-deferred weekend jaunt, in some way it was also going to be the beginning of the new. I would be remaking my life from the ground up.

. . .

In a way I was right, but things fell out nothing like I might have imagined. What happened was that riding back that Sunday afternoon, after a long weekend of hiking and drinking and philosophizing with my friends—brimming, as might be expected, with memories of Jess and our times in Maine—I found myself back on the bus, sitting beside a young woman. My usual response, especially after noting the fact that she was attractive, would have been to retreat into a kind of hypervigilant detachment, offering not the slightest hint that I was aware of her appeal or had any intention of letting it sway me toward conversation. This time, however, was different. I was in the first hectic stage of changing my life, becoming a new kind of man, and I turned in my seat and led with the obvious.

"Are you going to Boston?" And instead of giving back the snub, the hands-off of mere politeness, she turned in her seat and shook her hair back and smiled. It was like clockwork; everything was right. Within minutes we had shouldered past the boilerplate—her name was Terri, she was headed back to the city after a visit to her family, she worked as a textbook editor—and we were really talking. About Boston, editing, writing, our families . . . She had a quick teasing sarcasm, a way of sparring that once or twice made me think of Jess, especially in our early days. But there was the feeling, too—and this became something I tested and explored as we talked—that she was interested. It was as if she were inclining ever so slightly toward me, looking for something.

I found as we rode on, talking, that I could not stop myself flashing back and forth between her eyes and mouth. I was hooked—between the challenge of the stare and the wryness of the expression. In any other context my staring would have been rude, but this was different. We were after something. I had been running full sail on a sense of rightness for days, and now I saw what I'd been moving toward.

Boston encroached. We were just getting to our real stories—our pasts—when the bus made a sharp right swerve and docked in the depot bay. We sat for a moment adjusting to the deflation, and then we rallied, keeping on with it, riding the subway together to Cambridge, neither of us saying anything when I rode past my stop or got out with Terri at Porter Square.

"Can I just walk you?" I asked. Terri laughed. We were already walking. I was weak, almost light-headed, from this feeling I had of being pulled forward, of not quite being able to guide my own reactions. I was doing what the moment dictated, heading down a quiet side street to her apartment, following her up her stairs, into the living room, into the kitchen, where we ended up crushed against her refrigerator, never getting to the beer she offered, kissing and kissing until Terri had to push me back gently, and I remembered—with a strange, detached objectivity—my life with Marcie.

It was with a frustrating sense of "not yet" that I reversed my tracks and headed to her stairs. "I'll talk to you very soon," I said, this time restricting myself to the merest brushing of lips.

I walked slowly through the back streets of Cambridge, wanting to take forever. I was not thinking or scheming so much as just remarking how strange I felt. It was as though I had rapidly inhaled some soul-expanding ether. Try as I might to make a thought, to figure out what might be next, I could not get my mind to stick. Things were, I was convinced, running along just as they had to.

I now knew that I had to put an end to my relationship with Marcie. But how? I made no announcement at first. On my first night back I essentially perjured myself, telling a great many things while avoiding the main thing. And it's likely that I lied the following evening, too, after I got in late from waiting for Terri outside her building downtown and once again rode home on the subway with her, again submerging myself in a dimensionless kiss, this time on her couch, staying until she made a show of tearing her hair and forced me to look at the stack of manuscripts she had on her kitchen table.

But then I could stand it no longer—the sound of my voice as I stumbled through the day's lie for Marcie, her credulity, the terrible ease of it all. I could not keep on with it.

There is no adhering to plan in these matters. No matter how I scripted things—my lead-in, Marcie's likely response—everything was scrapped as soon as she walked through the door the very next evening. She had only to see me across the room, the way I was lying on my back, staring at the bookshelves, to pick up that something was wrong.

"Hey—" One syllable of interrogation, but she was tuned in; we were already moving toward it.

I sat up, my temples throbbing. I waited until Marcie sat by me on the couch. I could feel the anxious sway of decision in my gut. Suddenly, without preamble, I blurted. I was a mess; I'd met somebody; no, nothing had happened; I didn't know what it meant—I said the new name—and when I had, I looked at Marcie's face and I saw there, for a moment, like a shadow passing, that expression, that melding of sadness and regret, that I would locate twenty years later in my dream.

"I'm sorry, I don't know what's going on." I did not try to defend myself or to make things better. I asserted what little there was to assert blankly and then waited to see what Marcie would say. How graceless and unfamiliar we become—to each other, to ourselves—at such moments. We sat at the kitchen table, not eating or drinking, just smoking, in silence. I may have taken her hand, or she mine. But the comfort was as nothing beside the feeling that something was ending, that we had at last reached the point of divergence that we had both always known would arrive. Did the knowing, however obscure it had been, help? Maybe. But it offered nothing at all against the larger sorrow, the sudden poignant dimming of our history together in the certainty that it was now ended. If we locked our hands together, it was to give each other a moment of support before we unlocked them and decided what was now to be done. Though nothing had yet been said, I knew that I would be moving out. When I ventured the thought, Marcie did not protest. There was no discussion at all about working things out, not that I recall. The whole episode was so clearly the culmination of changes and shifts that we had long been ignoring. Distance had been seeping in since I arrived with my things a year before. We had found explanations, ways of accommodating each other. Marcie was in grad school; I was writing a book. But now we both knew not to pretend—it would only make everything worse.

In a matter of days I was gone. I answered an ad in the *Boston Phoenix* and ended up sharing an apartment some five blocks away. "Cambridge poet seeks housemate." That was how Richard had advertised the situation. He might just as well have said "thin, anxious chain-smoker." When I told him in our "interview" that I had some interest in writing myself, he immediately offered me the room. Done. What this literary brotherhood ultimately meant was that I got to see and comment upon every variation of every poem he wrote during the time we lived together—and he wrote incessantly. But I didn't mind. In fact, Richard was a gifted writer who published two books of his poems eventually.

At that moment, however, when I stood up from the living room couch and fished in my pocket for a check, I was just relieved to have a place to bring my things. The painful avoidance rituals that Marcie and I had been practicing could end now. I would need only to borrow her car for an hour or so to move my books and shelves and a few bags of things.

I imagined—in the way I always imagined then—that signs and symbols and elegant cues about my destiny were scored into the very fabric of my life. Though my sudden departure from the Brattle Book Shop had seemed to mark the very nadir of my recent life, I believed that my meeting with Terri was a meant thing—indeed, that it had been called forth by the desperate resolve with which I had acted. I had wrenched myself off one track onto another. "No daring is fatal." I had this adjuration from the French poet René Crevel taped to the wall over my desk. Quitting had led to meeting Terri; meeting Terri had led to the end of my habit-bound life with Marcie. New revelations were surely in the offing.

But I was wrong in my arrogant optimism. That nadir was a false bottom. My foot broke through and there were great open spaces just beneath. For one thing, the prospect of a relationship with Terri was a chimera. No sooner was I alone, free to pursue that most tantalizing promise, than everything seemed to change again. The day after I moved in with Richard, I hurried down-town to present myself to Terri as she emerged from her building. I accompanied her home as before, but suddenly everything felt different. The charge was gone. We talked and joked, but now it was merely pleasant. I stared at her and confirmed and recon-firmed how pretty she was. I kissed her, but without that urge to make that kiss some absolute melding. Then abruptly—I don't think I exaggerate—we each took a half step back. Into a perfectly safe and circumscribed friendliness. It worked. In the months to come, we would meet for coffee in Harvard Square every week. We gossiped. Terri would tell me about the men she went out with, and I would counsel her. We enjoyed each other very much, but af-ter we drew away from each other on the couch that one evening, no further erotic spark passed between us.

It all seems so obvious now. I had conjured Terri forth out of my need. I created her as a romantic foil to accomplish what I could not seem to manage otherwise—I used her to break out of my re-lationship with Marcie. And when that was achieved, the mole-cules rearranged themselves again. The valence changed. I was alone—for the first time since those heartsick months after I re-turned to Ann Arbor.

Alone, and very much on the financial skids. I had paid Richard for the upcoming month, and that had cleaned out my resources. Right away I was down to tuna fish and quarts of cheap beer. Feel-ing very much like one of those literary characters whose fate it is to drop excruciatingly through the last grates of respectability—

Orwell in *Down and Out in Paris and London,* Miller in *Tropic of Cancer,* Hamsun's nameless narrator in *Hunger*—I patched together what passable clothing I had and set out to find a new job.

I looked again to bookstores, my one area of expertise, and after a few frustrating inquiries, I found my luck. Or what, settling now for very little, I regarded as luck. After being told by the store manager of the downtown Barnes & Noble that I was ridiculously overqualified—a consideration I anxiously waved away—I was hired on to work as a clerk in the basement, tending tables of publishers' overstock and superannuated textbooks. The basement manager, a high-strung young woman named "George" (for Georgiana)—I noted the theme of recurrent Georges—gave me the beige jacket I was to wear at all times and made a big to-do of making up a nametag for my lapel. And for the next long months that was my home, that gymnasium-size space lit by crackling fluorescents, with table after table to be arranged, tended, and replenished from the overstock area in back. But as with any other job I'd known, spurts of busyness were more than balanced off by periods of stupefying inertia, punishing hours when not only was there nothing to do, no alphabetizing or vacuuming left, but all of us had to play the game of keeping George happy. For she had made it very clear at the outset that she would not abide any of her crew standing around talking or idling over the books. My job at the Brattle—I saw it all so clearly now—had been paradisal compared to this. But here my fall had landed me—and I scrambled.

My initiative was as low as it ever had been, and my self-esteem was rapidly withering away. I had fantasies in which old classmates from Cranbrook, now successful doctors and brokers, wandered into the basement on their lunch breaks and recognized me. Deadbeat. Hippie burnout. I fancied I saw signs of contempt—or, worse, pity—in the glances of attractive women. After I made my way home at night, I would close myself off in my little room. I sat in the brown canvas sling chair I had bought secondhand, reading novels and rationing my beer. I was not really a beer drinker, but I couldn't afford to buy wine anymore. I cracked open my window and smoked cigarettes.

In all of this I don't think I ever overtly thought of myself as depressed. This was my life, this was how things were. I assumed that somewhere, somehow, better times would come, but I made no move to change anything. I was twenty-seven. I no longer knew what to change.

Every so often, but increasingly, I was afflicted by anxiety. Existential dread, I considered it, though the phrase sounds terribly pretentious now. The very idea of life, of being in a room, of having to fill the day with task and motion—it could seem almost unbearable. Mine was not a suicidal feeling, though. Quite the reverse. I could not stand the thought that I was going to die, that we were all going to die. From there, on the worst nights, it was but a short step to the conviction that death was imminent. I would lie on my back, unable to sleep, feeling my heart racing. I would turn on the all-night classical station, put the radio next to my ear, and try to enter the music. But music was not enough. I was also waiting for the first signs of daylight outside the window. Only then would I relax enough to sink into sleep—two or three hours before my alarm roused me for work.

Where was my family in all of this? I don't believe I gave them the slightest inkling of what I was going through. We had our Sunday telephone conversations, exchanged news. I told them the basic story of my work life, asked about things at home. My brother, Erik, was now ten, playing baseball and soccer. His life, different in every way from what I had known, was leaping forward in clean, straight lines. Did he move through those rooms the way we had, quiet and watchful? I tried to imagine it. My parents also gave me updates on Andra, who was now studying art in Halifax. My father, not a phone talker, confined himself to headlines about his latest projects. And I was always glad—relieved—that everyone else was doing so well. I was not about to spoil the picture. I did not want my parents, my mother especially, to worry that anything was wrong with me or that I was unhappy. Where my father was concerned, I felt mainly shame—shame buttressed by defensiveness, shades still of the old rebellious anger.

"Can you live on what that bookstore pays you? Can't you find something better?"

"I don't need anything better. This gives me plenty—and I can read and write. I'm around books."

"Books . . ."

In terms of our ancient and defining standoff, he had won. He had long ago insisted that my refusals—of more school, of career, of all the markers of normalcy—were childish and doomed.

I flapped the banners of my idealism, my artistic purity. But I could not really reproach him. His own purity was doing just fine. He did what he loved, *and* he enjoyed his Italian suits. I was hoarding my quarters for beer. It was hard to face the implications.

My father did not understand why I had left Ann Arbor again. What was I after? What had happened to building a life, something solid and worthy that could eventually accommodate a family? I had no response for him. But I persisted in my ways, taxing the last of his goodwill and tolerance by setting myself up—again—as a writer. I could not ever let him know how complete my sense of failure was, how I lay awake through the night trying to steady myself into sleep. I could not bear the thought that he would offer help or propose some solution that would be more charity than anything else. I believed—foolishly, I now realize—that he wanted me to succeed at something just so that he would not have to be ashamed of me.

If I lived, as I sometimes imagined, in Baudelaire's "forest of symbols"—where all events could be viewed as possible guides and markers—then some sort of thematic apotheosis arrived that March with the reactor disaster at Three Mile Island. I was in my room, reading, listening to the classical station at low volume, when I caught a shift in the tone of things. Voices, that quickened matter-of-factness particular to emergency. Minutes later I was tuned to an all-news station, caught like millions of others just then, in a nightmare that seemed to just keep intensifying. There was talk of confirmed leaks, toxicity levels, wind patterns at different atmospheric altitudes. Experts called in with statistics and projections. The escaped radiation might easily be carried to the Northeast. "We just don't know." This from the announcers, the scientists, the officials who made themselves available for comment. "We just don't know."

I was never much of a news or disaster hound, but Three Mile Island had me in a state of mortal terror. I had not experienced such raw anxiety. I did not know what to do with myself. I was alone in the house, afraid to go out, not just because I might miss something, but because I might find confirmation of my fears on the faces of others. I lay on my back with my eyes open, trying to breathe deeply. The certainty was slowly growing: This was it. This was what we had all been living toward. It was the perfect ordained conclusion, the end result of all our hubris. Here connected our catastrophic bungling of the twentieth century and my foolish mismanagement of my life. Outer and inner were in accord, coming together, all wires drawn taut by the toxic plumes that were even now sweeping northward on volatile air currents. I tried to keep a grip, to focus on the concrete things around me: the window sash, the brick-and-board arrangement of my shelves. But now, suddenly, everything I turned to looked thin, rickety, no defense at all against these unseen elements.

"We are monitoring weather conditions very closely," said the announcer. Did I hear the slightest tremor in his voice, some held-down private panic trying to slip free?

I wished I had something to drink. I considered a quick run to the liquor store, but I could not imagine being out in the street. Frail as my little room was—the one window now tightly locked, the shade pulled down tight against the afternoon—I burrowed away in it like any animal.

Could this be it? Usually I found some way of imagining the aftermath of a situation—end of the storm, the fever—but here I failed myself. There was just this darkening day and the successive reports of escaping radiation. The feeling was intolerable. I curled up under my Mexican blanket and began to offer up my crude prayers. The place of final appeal: *Dear God, please get us through this, let us understand how we should be living*—

And it helped. I lay there and muttered, and the more I muttered, the better I somehow felt. I did not promise anything; I did not offer to come to religion if only things would work out. Nor did I think when I heard that the danger was over that God had intervened. But praying—if that's what it was—somehow mattered then. And when the next day brought assurances that no larger devastation was in the offing, I felt a wave of cleansing relief pass through me. I turned off all my monitors and for the first time in a long time I let myself sleep.

The one thing that had always sustained and fortified me, even when all else in my life had gone hollow, was reading. In the evil months after my breakup with Jess, it had been poetry, a small handful of novels. I remember with special vividness reading Malcolm Lowry's *Under the Volcano* and Saul Bellow's *Humboldt's Gift,* convinced at certain moments that the prose concealed a secret thread that could guide me up and out, if only I could find it and hold it. Reading was then more than just escape or distraction. It was as if my own self-lacerating misery were giving me something extra, a will to cancel myself in the face of a stronger vision, a more experienced understanding. I could feel—so much as one is actually able to feel such things—an actual expansion of my own perspective on the world. While I read, the radical foreshortening enforced by my various travails dissolved. I took that step past the self that gives the first inkling of maturity. And then—alas—I subsided back. I would close the covers and feel the fear and trembling take over again.

But this time I was much closer to grasping what I needed. Piqued by the title, lured in by a few stray references in the works of other writers, I took up Robert Musil's great unfinished novel of the Habsburg collapse, *The Man Without Qualities*. If I did not have much going on the plus side of the ledger, I did have time. Time and a kind of furious, tight-spring energy. Coming in at night from my dreary day of pacing the basement perimeter, or lying wide awake in my little nest of blanket and pillows, I was ready to give myself to reading.

I have seldom enjoyed such a period of pure absorption in a novel. I can name the occasions since adolescence: reading *Madame Bovary* in the bunkhouse on the cattle ranch in Montana, drawn in as much by the ache of homesickness as by the thrilling precision of Flaubert's sentences; falling like Alice down the rabbit-hole into García Márquez's *Macondo;* into Mann's *The Magic Mountain,* in my last year in college; my isolated exalted bouts with *Anna Karenina, Lost Illusions, Crime and Punishment* . . . And now this, my unforeseen and absolute immersion in Musil—not just the narrative, but, even more, the thought-world of his world-weary protagonist, Ulrich. Something here registered and held me—the melancholic drift of his irony, his yoking of the scientific and the mystical, the pressure behind everything of a mind intent on solving the vast differential equation of subjective existence. At the same time, not to be denied, was Musil's conjuring of a city, Vienna, on the brink, its slow-motion dream poised to shatter into modernity. I read and I transposed, finding there, unexpectedly, my grandparents' Riga, the place I'd reared up for myself from the stories I'd heard all my life.

I was swept away, beyond the customary, into open water. I wanted to find out everything I could about this most enigmatic writer; I wanted to draw in as close as I could to the secret, the source of my intense identification. What I discovered, with a shock, was that there was almost nothing to be found, certainly not in English. I went to the monumental card catalog at Widener Library and gaped in disbelief. There was one study in English—this, along with a few scholarly dissertations, marked the boundary line. Beyond lay the terra incognita.

The step from this discovery to the first tentative flash—that I might myself try to write something—looks very short in the gaze of retrospect, but in truth it represented a major interior shift and was not achieved in a single burst. It was more that I had begun to feel a nagging sense of possibility, one that persisted past all my resistances. I tantalized myself with the idea that if I thought hard enough about the work—the scenes, the observations, the theories—I might come up with something vital. I did not know what, but the idea of trying had lodged itself.

Before I could do anything, though, before I could even get over the initial unworthiness barrier, I needed a prod. I had to feel the actual sentence-making itch. This desire, which I experience, when I do, as an almost visceral hankering to fit sounds and rhythms into semblances of order, had been there, a daily excitement, all through the writing of my ill-fated novella. Then, like some traumatized entity, it had withered away, wedged itself into some obscure inner crevice.

But now it did return, the wanting. I read and reread favorite passages, I thought about the stunning Baroque architecture of Musil's sentences, the spark of their connections and leaps, and I wanted to possess that magic. I did not know to what larger end, how they might serve me, and I had no clear sense about how to proceed.

I started where I felt the most comfortable. I went back and studied the essayists I most admired—Edmund Wilson, Erich Heller, Susan Sontag, Cyril Connolly, Hugh Kenner ... Never mind that they were, in key respects, as different as could be. I paged back through their work, looking for the tone, pondering the dynamics of assertion and explication. I read, and reading, I felt myself slowly revving up for my own attack.

I learned the art of the literary essay from scratch. I emulated and I diverged. I had transcribed pages taped to the walls around my desk. I made free-flowing sketches that resembled nothing so much as the doodles my father spun out at his drafting table—circles and lines, curvaceous figures that rose and fell, decorated by the private codes of my inspiration: "hammer quote," "Nietzsche," "impossibility/mysticism." I don't recall how long I diverted myself in this way before I found—with an authentic-feeling "click"—what I now think of as the line, the drama, of the argument. How many evenings and weekend hours? At some point, though, I began typing. Every thought, every vector of insight, was fed to the page, revealed itself slowly above the platen of my green Olivetti portable, the typewriter my parents had given me when I graduated from Cranbrook. I think of the hours, the pathetic progress I made with my one-handed, two-fingered keyboard style, the pages I typed again and again as some mistake or variant phrasing dictated.

And still I persisted, lowering myself with each exertion deeper into the world of my project. I knew my argument, my sentences—knew them so well that in time they began to feel absolute—ordained—to me. I was so lit up with my venture that I began to experience what has since become a familiar sort of dementia. I mean the conviction that I had better hurry, that someone somewhere had to be tapping these same insights. Never mind that I was a twenty-seven-year-old bookstore clerk putting down his thoughts on an all-but-forgotten Austrian novelist; the world was waiting for the news to break.

In this spirit, agitated and exalted, I finished. My months-long engagement with the spirit of Robert Musil was distilled down into twenty pages. I was so proud. I shuffled and reshuffled those pages, just to be touching the paper. It was as if I could feel the energy of my mind trapped there. I felt no shame, then, about reading and rereading my own words. I liked my opening especially and felt excited about the quotes I had selected. Mesmerized by my own

sound, I saw no way to improve the cadence of my lines or inten-
sify the thrust of my presentation. I even had a title I liked—
"Robert Musil's Atlantis." I had only to decide what to do with the
thing now.

I had for some time kept my eye on a local literary journal, published in large periodical format, a somewhat less formidable
cousin to the *New York Review of Books*. Then it was called the
New Boston Review, and it survives to this day, several distinct in-
carnations later, as the *Boston Review*. I decided to submit. But I
did not want to risk writing the query letter, the odds being too
great that the reply would be discouraging. So I wrote a cover letter—*sweated* over the task—and then packed my pages into a
manila envelope, and with a trepidation I can scarcely resurrect,
dropped it into the mailbox, from which it would have to travel
less than a half mile, geographically speaking, but as far as I was
concerned would move beyond geography, into some vertically defined zone that it dizzied me to contemplate.

This writing and sending of an essay felt like one of the most
impetuous and riskiest things I had ever done. I did not, as I sometimes would in later years, wish to retrieve the envelope, destroy all
traces of my work. But I was in a state of agitation that was new to
me. I was on the line. I drove myself half-crazy with speculation.
They must have it now, I reasoned. The editor might be turning
the pages at this very instant. Should I have included a telephone
number? What if they tried to call? Or—reversing everything—I
imagined an editorial meeting, staffers leaning back with their feet
propped up on the big desk. "Listen to this, guys: 'The career of
Robert Musil excelled in disappointments and bitter ironies.' Who
the *hell* is Robert Musil?"

But the piece was accepted. I got a note from the editor about a
week after I had submitted, the most misleading introduction I
could have gotten to the ways of editors with manuscripts. The

woman claimed to love the piece; she would run it in the next issue with just a very few changes. Nothing on earth could have been simpler or more gratifying. The editorial "we"—as in "we are very pleased to accept"—thrilled me to the marrow. I studied those mainly pro forma sentences until their flat syllabic beat was incised in my mind. I grew ecstatic in the contemplation of what my words would look like translated into columns of print. I turned the pages of an old copy of the journal and imagined I was someone else—who?—coming upon the words of this unknown new writer. Who read the *New Boston Review*? I had no idea. But this was Cambridge, the intellectual nerve center of the country. I could with little exertion picture almost any luminary I chose sitting back in his armchair and slowly smoothing out the first page of my article. Would my name be on the cover? The journal did advertise its featured pieces in bold type. Would Musil merit feature attention? Would I? I was antic with conjecture.

However quickly the editor had responded to the submission, the actual appearance of the issue was another matter altogether. I went to the news kiosk in Harvard Square daily, taking the T the extra distance from my regular stop at Central Square just to experience again the buildup/smack-down effect: the mounting anticipation as I rode up on the escalator and allowed myself premonitory flashes of what the stack of new copies might look like; the impatient agitation with which I rustled through the display stacks, sure that I had simply looked right past the obvious; and then the weighted disappointment with which I dragged myself down the street, knowing I now had at very least a night to get through before I could repeat the process. What intolerable frustration. What an expense of spirit. But what a misguided—and wonderful— sense of mattering attended that very first publication. I can honestly say that nothing in my subsequent writing life, not even the publication of my first book some years later, has come close to matching it. The investment was total. In some key way, the whole of my life was implicated in that expectation. My pacing and fussing, my going so far as to call the journal to ascertain the printing date, my slow circuits through Harvard Square, striding along with the intense absorption of a hired assassin while I waited for the delivery truck to show itself coming up Massachusetts Avenue—it was the notion of some sort of rebirth that drove me. And if rebirth did not exactly follow—transformations are seldom so dramatic—change did. Slow, steady, rejuvenating change, and all of it was somehow connected to the extraordinary lift I felt when I at last rounded the corner of Out-of-Town News and saw the small pile of freshly minted copies of the *New Boston Review,* the headline ROBERT MUSIL'S ATLANTIS prominent above the fold.

CODA

I WAS TWENTY-SEVEN THEN. AS I WRITE THIS, I AM PUSHING WITH what feels like terrible steadiness toward the fifty-year mark. I had never imagined I would think in terms of years and chronologies; I have even flattered myself at various points that I was succeeding, was escaping the game. But no, suddenly that line is there, garishly painted across what has begun to look like an extended but perceptibly narrowing highway.

The image derives quite naturally from a certain peculiarity of circumstance. Coincidentally, or maybe not, when I first undertook to write this portion of my story, I had just taken on a teaching job that had me commuting back and forth to the other side of the state. I became a driver of distances. Twice a week in the fall, once in the winter semester, for the last three and a half years I have been threading my way back and forth over the same ninety-mile stretch. I know every bump and turn, every striation on the asphalt surface.

The teaching is the point, but more and more it has come to seem the pretext, the real meaning having become the drive, the inundation that overtakes me every time I slip past the stop-and-start distraction of the town at either end. As soon as the highway opens up, I take my place in what can at times feel like a dream resumed. Most everything that has to do with dailiness peels away. At seventy-five miles per hour, so I have found, I move into the time zone of my inner life. Everything changes. It is as if the larger accumulation of my experience were available to me in these moments, embodied somehow in the panorama, the steady stream of vista: hills, river valleys, and abruptly looming granite rock faces. I set myself no agenda, I simply drive, straight into the wilds of midlife.

When I published my Robert Musil essay, my whole life changed in a way that felt like part of a larger orchestration, as if somewhere, on high, a subtle but definite nod had been given. A few weeks after that baptism into print, while the ink was, figuratively speaking, still fresh on my fingers from so much endearing, then rapidly tiresome, handling of those pages, I was invited by my old bookstore friend Paul to a May Day party that some of his Marxist study-group comrades were giving. Not wanting to arrive dateless, I called Terri, but Terri was busy. Which turned out to be a providential thing for me, for in my solitary discomfort I took a seat at one end of a long living room couch. At the other end, deep in conversation with a philosophy grad student I'd met before at Paul's, was a pretty young woman with long auburn hair. She turned out to be that grad student's roommate, Lynn, and she would, after a series of opportunistic initiatives on my part, become *my* partner in deep conversation, and then, after many complicated and emotional vicissitudes—and here we see the extraordinary condensing power of the periodic sentence—my girlfriend, my live-in partner of many years, eventually my wife and mother of our two children.

Narratives unfailingly project lives as fates. Which is why so many of us resort to narratives: we want to feel carried in this way.

But as years pass, the narrative keeps changing.

Last Thanksgiving, slightly ahead of the official date, but for various good reasons the optimum time, my sister, brother, and I arranged to celebrate my parents' fiftieth wedding anniversary in Boston. As a commemorative gift, to be presented at the anniversary dinner, we decided to pool resources and have an enormous studio Polaroid taken by photographer Elsa Dorfman. Ourselves, our partners, our children.

We all met at Dorfman's studio in Cambridge. A chaotic knot of people. My brother, Erik, had just flown in from Seattle with his wife, Alison, who was almost seven months pregnant with their first child. My sister, Andra, her husband, Harris, and their two children, Owen and Olivia. Lynn and I with our two, Mara and Liam. There were exclamations, compliments, fingertip regards paid to Alison's protruding stomach, and constant cautions to the kids not to knock anything over.

Understandably, it took Dorfman a great long time to get all of us arranged. We tried this way and that, sweaters on and off, children with and without props. Positioned as ordered at the back, joking and elbowing my brother, who towers over me in a way I will never get used to, I felt a familiar detachment steal in, as if part of me had been vaporized and pushed ever so slightly to one side of things. I had the thought then that in the photographer's eye we were just so many pieces of a jigsaw puzzle and that there was an order, a momentarily "right" combination that would best show us forth. And what *did* she see? I imagined myself on the other side of the room; I slowly took in our small crowd of prosperous-looking adults and their antic but well-groomed children. "We're getting there, stay where you are, we are *very* close . . ." Dorfman was coaching and coaxing, already steadying herself behind the camera, when all at once everyone shifted. Someone said, "Oh—" My son jumped to his feet, breaking ranks. Directly behind the camera, in the open doorway, a sudden, unsteady shape. Dorfman jerked away from her task and turned. There was a man, bearded and matted, teetering, leaning in toward us while holding a flat bottle loosely by the neck. He looked blurry, confused. I heard him slurring something in our direction. Dorfman now moved to the phone by the wall, while Erik, Harris, and I hurried forward, deploying far more bulk and threat than was needed. The poor drunk—obviously a street person—was barely able to stand. When he saw us coming, he shrank back with an exaggerated grimace. The three of us then walked him slowly to the elevator. "Let's get you out of here before the cops come," I said. The man paused only to tuck the bottle into the waistband of his pants; he offered no re- sistance. When the elevator door opened, he crushed himself into the far corner and regarded us with a sudden frank curiosity. We stood that way for a long moment. Then the door closed. Erik, Harris, and I looked at each other and shrugged.

The disruption must have been just what was needed. We gath- ered back into our spots, and in five minutes Dorfman had taken two Polaroids. "That was *weird*." She said it several times. The kids seemed strangely chastened—they had never seen a display quite like this before.

"What will he do?" asked Olivia, who is six, my son's age.

"He'll be okay," my sister assured her. "He won't come back." And then we gathered around the table to look.

There it was, convincingly eccentric, credible, the assembled puzzle: family. The youngest kids, Liam and Olivia, were starkly impish. Owen and Mara, meanwhile, were trying on their poses of fidgety discomfort. Behind them the phalanx of adults, arranged to showcase Alison's belly. Erik, hovering in back of her, had, as someone put it, the look of being "caught in the headlights." And over in the corner, a flare of reflected light on one of his lenses making him look just the slightest bit alien, I found the old famil- iar: the bemused onlooker, the late-blooming family man.

I drive, I write. Sometimes then the sluices open and I feel ac- counted for. Not in immediacy, not in bodily presence—there I cannot seem to coincide with myself—but in terms of the bigger sweep. Midlife: the constant collision of the then and the now, the sense of loss that grows and grows. How I struggled to keep a grip on it. And how long it took me to get it, the hard paradox: that it was not in any specific way the times—Maine, Ann Arbor, Cambridge—that I wanted back, nor was it, much as I had loved them, the people. What I wanted from the past was, more than anything, the sense of future it had contained, the feeling I'd had of things in the works, unfolding. My old suspicion—that I was being watched over, nudged toward something—had slowly worn away over the years, had been replaced by the daily plentitude of work and domesticity. But now, suddenly, slipping across the landscape like a ghost, I felt bereft, stripped of something as primary as happiness itself.

The hollow sensation was insupportable, and it led, in relieving increments, to the page. Small bursts of writing: sketches from my own life, the part of my life when my life was all I had. Images would surface: Mike in his paint closet, arranging his brushes, Howard waiting for me as I came up the path to his house, Jess flinging an old green tennis ball to Woodman's dog, Johann. These things, I felt it, connected. And very gradually, day by day, through that long first season of driving, I came to understand that something was being offered to me, extended, and that accepting it would have everything to do with writing, the solitary motion of it, as well as the sense-making demons it releases into the blood.

We gather, eleven of us, including three of my parents' oldest friends who have flown in for the occasion, at a small restaurant near Kenmore Square. The kids are all at home with sitters; this is to be a calm, celebratory event. Which it will turn out to be. I have the Elsa Dorfman portrait—signed, framed—wrapped and put aside inconspicuously by my end of the table. The food is excellent, as is the wine. We are all elegantly dressed and festive and as relaxed as it is possible to be on such a sentimentally formal occasion. Perched at one end of the long table, some distance from my mother and father, who sit halfway down on either side, I try to bring everything into the right emotional focus. The whole family, fifty years of marriage—this is a big night. And there is so much— the recurrent litany of these middle years—to be grateful for.

I study my parents covertly, first one, then the other, and I marvel. Almost jealously. They are both in their seventies, but they look good. All that history, that time, sits lightly on them. My mother looks shyly mischievous as she talks to her old friend August. My father gestures using his glass—I can tell without hearing a word that he's talking architecture. Everything looks so normal and natural. Where is the grave weight of it all? Where is any trace of the burdening pressure of time and loss I've been feeling since I started on this project? I look up and down, taking in the faces. I feel it so strongly, the sense of resolution and arrival, the deep momentum that has only briefly stalled around this fancy table. We've all pushed through so much for so long, and now we're here, pleased to still be going on, resolved to keep going just this way for as long as we can. How does all this connect with all that—I mean those years of flexing and fighting and coming up against each other? Was that all just *on the way* or was that *it*? There is my father, smiling, benign, leaning in close to his friend Solveiga, confiding something. She is smiling, too. My mother deftly checks her lipstick with a tiny pocket mirror. I look at Lynn, who tells me with the merest nod that everything is going fine. I am, as always on these formal occasions, very far away, but I trust her.

After dinner, in the lounge, we offer toasts to fifty years of marriage. August rambles slightly as he explains how it had been his idea, half a century ago, when they were still in Germany, to bring his best friend together with this pretty young woman who happened to be an old family friend. He characterizes my father as a bit of a ladies' man, which I can see pleases my father. My mother, of course, denies all imputations of interest on her part. My sister laughs, then my brother. We have been speaking English all evening, of course, but now the older generation lapses into the mother tongue. Quips fly back and forth in Latvian. This is when I know my parents have relaxed, when things have become real—the rest of the world is suddenly excluded. Lynn is used to the switch, but I see Alison give Erik a look; he bends to her ear and translates. Finally, Ruta, August's wife, coaxes August slowly back to his seat. Whereupon—clink of the glasses—the photograph is presented and solemnly unwrapped. There is more clinking as everyone gets up and crowds toward the light.

"Oh boy," says my father. "Look what we started here, Duda."

"That's for sure," mutters my sister sotto voce.

I lean in over Lynn's shoulder, enjoying the experience now, checking the reactions, happy that we've created this little stir, but also—peering down again at the photo itself—startled by what has happened since the other day. Those faces, those immobilized expressions—I had them so clearly a moment ago. How quickly it happens. All it takes is a simple tilt of the head. I bend in closer and I can almost see it happen, the metamorphosis. Present into past, now into then. Even as I stand here, our little group is rounding the corner—away, into another time.

ACKNOWLEDGMENTS

My special thanks to those who read and commented on this work as it progressed: Tom Sleigh, Askold Melnyczuk, Dr. David Tread-way, Helen Pratt, Ray Roberts, James and Anne Kelly, and my wife, Lynn Focht. I owe much to the archival memory of my mother, Sylvia Birkerts.